Animated Mischief

ALSO BY BRIAN N. DUCHANEY
AND FROM MCFARLAND

*The Spark of Fear: Technology, Society
and the Horror Film* (2015)

Animated Mischief

Essays on Subversiveness in Cartoons Since 1987

Edited by BRIAN N. DUCHANEY
and DAVID S. SILVERMAN

McFarland & Company, Inc., Publishers
Jefferson, North Carolina

This book has undergone peer review.

LIBRARY OF CONGRESS CATALOGUING-IN-PUBLICATION DATA

Names: Duchaney, Brian N., 1977– editor. | Silverman, David S., 1969– editor.
Title: Animated mischief : essays on subversiveness in cartoons since 1987 /
edited by Brian N. Duchaney and David S. Silverman.
Description: Jefferson, North Carolina : McFarland & Company, Inc., Publishers, 2023 |
Includes bibliographical references and index.
Identifiers: LCCN 2023015994 | ISBN 9781476663975 (paperback : acid free paper) ∞
ISBN 9781476648705 (ebook)
Subjects: LCSH: Animated films—United States—History and criticism. |
Animated television programs—United States—History and criticism.
Classification: LCC NC1766.U5 A4755 2023 | DDC 791.43/34—dc23/eng/20230501
LC record available at https://lccn.loc.gov/2023015994

BRITISH LIBRARY CATALOGUING DATA ARE AVAILABLE

ISBN (print) 978-1-4766-6397-5
ISBN (ebook) 978-1-4766-4870-5

Front cover image © Ollyy/vvoe/Shutterstock

Printed in the United States of America

*McFarland & Company, Inc., Publishers
Box 611, Jefferson, North Carolina 28640
www.mcfarlandpub.com*

This book is for Mom, who let me indulge in sugary cereals
and cartoons while she slept in on Saturday mornings, and Dad,
who only pulled me away from the TV for yard work occasionally.

Also, to my son Owen, who may not be old enough to know the joy
of Saturday morning cartoons but will live to see them as corporations
work to sell me on my nostalgia (so that I will pass my memories on
to you. But we'll get the last laugh; they didn't need to sell me
what I already own in the form of obsolete DVDs).
—BND

* * *

I'd like to dedicate this text to animation fans, both young and old
alike. "They" told you were wasting your time watching "cartoons,"
as if the cartoons in question were some kind of disposable
commodity not worthy of study. "They" were wrong.

I'd also like to dedicate this to my wife, Olga, and my
daughter, Stevie, both of whom share my love of
animation. Thank you for always being there.
—DSS

Table of Contents

Introduction

BRIAN N. DUCHANEY *and*
DAVID S. SILVERMAN

From the earliest cave drawings, humans have been representing the essence of humanity by giving a conceptualized idea a tangible element. In other words, early artists were trying to capture the concept of human culture in a form that can be revisited. Luckily, some of these drawings can be found as part of large reliefs or friezes that have been enshrined in museums as artifacts. In the case of the cave dwellers, who left their imprint on walls rather than paper or canvas, the idea was to leave a legacy for future generations while simultaneously capturing the particulars of society's existence at the time. This was true of the great painters of the world, who wished to share their vision of humanity by recording it in ink, oil, watercolor, and acrylic for future generations, the likes of which include Rembrandt, Michelangelo, Degas, and Botticelli. These painters gave us images of the ideas of their generation.

These renderings varied widely. From Caravaggio's *Medusa* to Monet's series of waterlilies, artists have sought to represent both the horror and beauty of the human experience as they relate to societal understanding and, more important, its culture. Thus, as society turned away from secularism and embraced humanism, it is noteworthy that the Renaissance's artistic output of epochal biblical scenes and Greek and Roman myths eventually gave way to the Romanticism of Delacroix's *Liberty Leading the People* and then the Neo-Impressionism of Seurat's *A Sunday Afternoon on the Island of La Grande Jatte* (Fr. *Un dimanche aprés-midi à l'Île de la Grande Jatte*). As a result, art began to eschew didacticism and began to reflect an interpretation of the world through its ideas and cultures. Much like the earliest humans, artists once again began to capture societal viewpoints as a graphic representation of thought.

Then, in 1962, Andy Warhol defined both a cultural movement and his artistic legacy when, fed up with the standoffish culture of the art

1

world, he debuted his first painting of a can of Campbell's Tomato Soup. At first controversial, Warhol's *Campbell's Soup Cans* have since become an iconic symbol of his legacy and the reach of a Pop Art movement led by Warhol. The pioneers of Pop Art—including the likes of Roy Lichtenstein and Jasper Johns—launched a scathing attack on the art world and its condemnation of mass culture, thereby subverting the assumptions of artistic culture to deliver a message with mass appeal to consumers.

Though the roots of the word imply a revolution (the word comes from the Latin *subvertere*, meaning "to overthrow") subversion in the popular sense implies a rejection of cultural norms. More directly, subversion is a rejection of the Establishment and the status quo, but subverting popular or mainstream identity needn't be a bad thing. For instance, after World War II, as "a master narrative in which a closely knit, classless, village-oriented, white America grappled with dramatic challenges at home and abroad"[1] and the national consciousness turned to the threat of another conflict, another sect of America was busy moving on with their lives, enjoying the domestic bliss ushered in by the promise of the American Dream. For many, the start of the Cold War was a thriving time of cultural change spurred on by new opportunities. It was a time when institutional barriers began to fall, and individualism started to show up in the form of rebellion. Maybe that's where American popular culture finally started to divide once and for all.

Pioneered by Walt Disney in 1955 with the opening of Disneyland, the nostalgic endurance of Main Street U.S.A. in the post-war years persisted through the media landscape, mostly through live-action sitcoms that sought to commodify pre-war American values. These shows were an escape from the continuous cycle of world politics and events that dominated the cultural consciousness and the news cycle. Live-action sitcoms were a refuge, where the problems were minor and the brief intrusion of reality obscuring the American dream was neatly resolved by the end of the episode. In contrast, the post-war animations of Warner Bros. carried on with what Michael Barrier calls "comedy in vigorous conflicts and hazardous existences."[2] Instead of following the lead of live action, Warner Bros. animation opted instead to amplify the emotional rollercoaster of emotions following the war years.

When Warner Bros. ramped up production of *Looney Tunes*, the studio once again relied on a two-character format while employing punched-up vaudeville stage acts that playfully poked fun at American culture through sight gags and cultural references. Instead of conflict, Looney Tunes was performance art of the highest caliber, Greek theater where "Bugs [Bunny] ... emerged as something approaching a true *eiron*—the 'canny and restrained' stock figure in ancient Greek comedy who, in

Max Eastman's words, 'always had something more in mind than he was telling you.'"[3] The Golden Age of Looney Tunes culminated in the cartoons of Chuck Jones, whose characters were compulsive but "full-blown personalities"[4] with "depth and complexity,"[5] echoing the incessant pursuit seen in William Hanna and Joseph Barbera's *Tom and Jerry* cartoons of the 1940s.

When compared side by side, the partnership of Hanna-Barbera and the continuous progression of Looney Tunes can be seen as a *de facto* psychological study of American society. In his oft-cited assessment of Chuck Jones's legacy in the American canon, M. Thomas Inge compared Jones with the American humorist Mark Twain, not just for his ability to channel a multitude of influences into his work, but to realize that Jones's work highlight a "playful self-referentiality in which characters frequently acknowledge to the audience that they are simply cartoon characters, one-note relationships between the characters ... and consistency in the personalities of characters who carry a single act or response to an extreme."[6]

Hanna-Barbera carried this movement forward with the syndicated *The Huckleberry Hound Show*, which debuted on September 29, 1958. Not only did the program introduce the now famous title character, but it also gave the world two other future H-B stars, Yogi Bear and Boo Boo. The program aired in (near) prime-time in many markets and found an audience among adults—and especially college students—for its satire and the title character's penchant for "breaking the fourth wall." Yogi Bear rummaged around the "mythical" Jellystone Park looking for "pic-a-nic baskets" much like the real bears of Yellowstone Park. He was named after the famed baseball player Yogi Berra (and shared the latter's use of malapropisms), and was voiced to sound like Art Carney's Ed Norton from *The Honeymooners*. Together, Yogi Bear and Boo Boo explored—and skewered—various aspects of life in the latter part of conformity-seeking Eisenhower years. The same counter-culture audience later discovered and embraced a similar subversive vibe found in Jay Ward's *The Adventures of Rocky and Bullwinkle and Friends*, which debuted on the ABC Network afternoon schedule on November 19, 1959, and focused on the title characters and their struggles against Cold War foes Boris Badenov[7] and Natasha Fatale. While children could laugh at the comic hijinks of "moose and squirrel," the adults found humor in the parodied East-West conflict and the frequent use of high-brow puns. One notable example featured a story arc in which our heroes searched for a jewel-encrusted boat that featured the original owner's name—Omar Kyam—on the bottom: literally, the "Ruby Yacht" of Omar Kyam.[8]

Debuting on Friday, September 30, 1960, on ABC, Hanna-Barbera modeled *The Flintstones* heavily on the popular CBS sitcom *The Honeymooners*. As has been pointed out by many, Fred and Wilma Flintstone were drawn to resemble Ralph and Alice Kramden, and a cursory examination of the characters' surface reveals some interesting connections. Fred and Ralph have similar backgrounds: both have blue collar jobs (Fred is a construction worker; Ralph is a bus driver); both devise "get rich quick" schemes that backfire; and both, while loud and boisterous, make empty threats to their wives, who ultimately control their respective relationships. However, what is different is that *The Flintstones* engineered a different view of society through innovation. Though the Flintstones had many of the same luxuries as their audience, they provided comic relief by presenting the inconveniences of modern technology as they lived with it—literally. Among the many amenities the show presented were: an elephant shower; a pig garbage disposal; a bird "Polorock" camera (which chisels images); an octopus dishwasher; and a dragon toaster. Before expensive CGI or lackluster puppetry, *The Flintstones* was able to give audiences a new view of society by moving beyond the real and into a realm of possibility, all the while embracing its heightened awareness of popular culture (even parodying the Beatles' arrival in the U.S. in an episode about "bug music"). *The Flintstones* evolved the sitcom by including what adult audiences remembered from their childhoods, by appropriating "features of other forms such as the use of slapstick and parody as well as anthropomorphism, traditionally used in theatrical animation but unlike anything seen in live-action sitcom."[9]

The Flintstones was also able to present an image of family and society that went beyond the familiar consciousness of American viewers. According to M. Keith Booker, *The Flintstones* is "a continuous sense of estrangement that allows the show's viewers to see their own society, which they might otherwise simply take for granted as the natural way for a society to be, in new ways, reminding them of how unusual and relatively new their affluent, high-tech way of life really is."[10]

The success of *The Flintstones* was followed by *The Jetsons*. Though it pales in comparison to *The Flintstones*, *The Jetsons* delivered in the same method of social experiment that provided *The Flintstones* with its comedic and commercial success. In this future world, the aspects of modernity are revitalized in that futuristic notions of contemporary American society are explored. For instance, George works one and a half hours a day pushing a button at Spacely Space Sprockets, meals come in pill form, and Rosey the robot maid assists with parenting. In this world, Hanna-Barbera envisioned a simplified American Dream, perhaps even sickeningly so, where the sole sources of conflict arrive from work and family problems. *The Jetsons* as a sitcom developed the idea of farce by presenting a world in which misunderstandings are the norm. Here, the family was the center of the show, whereas *The Flintstones* presents the world under a microscope.

The Flintstones, on the surface, may have appeared to be the "modern stone age family," however, they represented the late realization of Herbert Hoover's campaign promise of "a chicken in every pot and a car in every garage." Though Hoover served as President some thirty years before *The Flintstones* first aired,[11] his promise of modern American domesticity was on display throughout the 1950s in sitcoms such as *Leave it to Beaver* and *Ozzie and Harriet*, and ultimately, through *The Flintstones*. On the other hand, *The Jetsons* offered a challenging version of a society in flux, where George's anxieties center on his home life and a dystopian state of affairs where his choices are removed. Unlike Fred and his Water Buffaloes (a play on the Elks Lodge), George had no social club. Worse, he had few contemporaries and was often outsmarted by his talking dog. George Jetson was the anti–Fred Flintstone. Where Fred was boisterous and assertive, George was a whipping boy: to his boss, his wife, even his robot housekeeper.

These incarnations of the American family should not be simply assessed as comedies. Both *The Flintstones* and *The Jetsons* exhibited what mainstream America viewed as acceptable; otherwise, their novel approach to parody and sardonic views of typical, suburban life in the United States in the early 1960s would have faded like many other shows that have failed to land an audience. What was (and still is) unique about both shows is that they exhibited a particular appearance of the American family against a cultural backdrop, a defining feature of animation that is the fundamental basis for many popular animated series to this day. And yet, even today, modern audiences still tend to overlook the impact these shows had on other cartoons and cartoonists (especially in the case of *The Flintstones*, which has been embraced by viewers long after its original prime-time run, spawning decades of spin-offs, reboots, and live action films, as well as a slew of instantly recognized with commercial products—notably *Flintstones* vitamins, and two breakfast cereals).

After *The Flintstones* left the network prime time line up in 1966, nearly all television animation in the United States was still found on either the Saturday morning network lineups, or as syndicated afternoon filler for local stations with little exception and led to less adult-themed animation in general for the next twenty years.[12] *The Flintstones'* departure coincided with a growing grassroots and political movement to clear the airwaves of sex and violence in all televised content in an effort to improve American broadcasting in general (and animation in particular). This resulted in a voluntary move by the major networks to either tone down or remove altogether any violence in animated domestic programming that appeared throughout the 1970s and introduced a decade of network production that brought educators into the fold (in the form of academic consultants). By the dawn of the Reagan era, however, the deregulation of (children's) television led to pure capitalism as toy companies rolled out their own animation studios, turning Saturday mornings and weekday afternoons into a series of thirty-minute commercials, which in turn led to a new round of grassroots activism and, ultimately, the Children's Television Act of 1990.

Now, some sixty years plus after the debut of *The Flintstones* (and with some minor adjustments), the "modern" animated family often portrays domestic struggles as innovative assessments of family. And, like the families of sitcoms such as *Leave It to Beaver, Father Knows Best*, and *Ozzie and Harriet*, little has changed, due to the fact that the American Dream is largely upheld as a standard through indicative stereotypes. Today, many cartoons stay close to the model of success that established the American Dream as a model for achievement. Family struggles and the hierarchy of success and order still play out in shows like *The Simpsons, Family Guy, The Fairly OddParents, The Proud Family, F Is for Family*, and *Bob's Burgers*.

Likewise, family is the central focus of Seth MacFarlane's *American Dad!* and Dino Stamatopoulos' *Moral Orel*, where both creators— using similar composition, writing style, and characterization—subvert the moralism of Art & Ruth Clokey and Dick Sutcliffe's *Davey and Goliath*, a show whose moral underpinnings espouse Christian teachings and a respect for authority. However, unlike their predecessor, what sets *American Dad!* and *Moral Orel* apart from other domestically situated animated comedies isn't the social unrest or the problems of family; in fact, they're noticeably the driving forces behind each of these shows. In microcosms of blissful suburbs, the location of middle-class achievement, MacFarlane's heroic Stan Smith and Stamatopolous' Orel Puppington are both characters trapped in a world where social change isn't something to be negotiated—instead, it becomes a nemesis.

This text is a reflection of the legacy of animation as both an expression of childhood and as a way to undo all of the expectations that society promised for the future. Subversion, in this sense, is meant to underscore the false hopes and promises of previous generations, the belief that hard work and determination will pay off. The American Dream is not within the realm of possibility for many, and that's okay. But, when the system is failing so many, animation finds a voice with which to fight back, and has led to a resurgence in animation over the past thirty-five years. Separated into three parts, this book brings together different ways of exploring taste, culture, and expression through animation:

"Part I: Historical Constructs and the Rise of Subversiveness" features essays that outline how historical changes in animation and society gave rise to an outsider-ness that found a home in animation. In "Saturday Morning Trojan Mouse: The Origin of the Creator-Driven Television Cartoon," Lev Cantoral and Tyler Solon Williams explore Ralph Bakshi's *The New Adventures of Mighty Mouse* that appeared on CBS beginning in 1987. Next, Jared Bahir Browsh examines the commercialization of animated characters in "Capitalization in a Half Shell: Multimedia, Cross-Demographic Marketing of Animated and Comic Content from Mickey to Michelangelo." Finally, Jane Batkin examines the animated landscape of the last decade of the twentieth century in "'Someone's coming! Act natural': Visions of Animated Childhood in 1990s America."

"Part II: Rethinking American Culture Through Social Challenges" examines animation further, with essays on the practical use of animation as a voice for the underserved. In "*Rocko's Modern Life* and the Pains of Early Adulting," Adrián García explores how a show originally produced for Nickelodeon attracted and retained a sizeable "grown-up" audience. Next, Chandrama Basu explores the seedier side of a certain ogre in "*Shrek* and the Art of Subversion." Then, David Perlmutter looks at how sugar, spice, and Chemical X combine to create perfect little girls with a mission in "'Once again, the day is saved': How the Subversive Feminism of *The Powerpuff Girls* Permanently Changed Television Animation," while Sasha Dilan Krugman discusses why "We Need to Talk about *The Lego Movie!*"

"Part III: Modern America and the Transformation of Social Order" presents essays examining the ways animation has reshaped society through the acceptance of outsider status and embracing otherness. For example, Dan Abitz explores the fluid nature of gender in "'This is me now!' Gene's Gender Play in *Bob's Burgers*," while Danielle Hart explores the adaptation of an existing media into fanworks and Non/Disney videos in "Giving Cinderella a Girlfriend." Marcus Mallard's "'Who Are You? Who Am I!?' The Raunchy Identity Moratorium in Netflix's *Big Mouth*" explores how gender identity and developmental theories are exhibited in early adolescence through an exploration of the show's use of frank language about sexuality. Finally, coeditor David S. Silverman (re-)examines MTV's *Daria*, which, stripped of most of the pop music once featured on the show, leaves us with the very universal (and still relevant) feminist message of self-discovery in "*Daria*: Still Standing on Our Necks, Then and Now."

From feature-length films to self-produced YouTube videos, from shows focusing on targeted demographics to creator-driven projects that explore the creative process, the essays in this text reflect a shared love of animation and its ability to reflect upon and comment on society in a manner that no other art form can. Throughout this book, we will explore how animation is used to explore major cultural shifts while allowing a platform for audiences to explore our changing cultural awareness and, if necessary, to challenge the assumptions of the status quo. Animation and subversion go hand in hand in that they allow the audience to safely explore the changing, warped reality of society that goes beyond the limitations of live action, removed from the potential drawbacks and criticisms of the real world.

As society progresses, the next generation is always waiting to undermine the assumptions of their predecessors. In animation, this has played out in numerous versions, from Peter Griffin's domestic rivalry with a giant chicken, Homer Simpson's repeated strangling of Bart, Elmer Fudd's perpetual undoing by Bugs. For every Wile E. Coyote purchase of ACME brand bird seed or rocket skates, the Road Runner will find a way to outsmart him. For every haunted amusement park run by a creepy guy with a projector, Scooby and Shaggy and the Gang will get to the bottom of the case. This is because animation is about finding balance and order in society. Despite their differences in theme, style, and content, they all seek to do the same thing: define what America truly is. As a culture, we do outgrow our previous forms of entertainment, but we never seem to outgrow our childish inner selves.

NOTES

1. Roland Marchand, "Visions of Classlessness, Quests for Dominion: American Popular Culture, 1945–1960," *Reshaping America: Society and Institutions, 1945–1940*, 15, quoted in LeRoy Ashby, *With Amusement for All: A History of American Popular Culture Since 1830* (Lexington, KY: The University of Kentucky Press, 2006), 279.

2. Michael Barrier, *Hollywood Cartoons: American Animation in Its Golden Age* (Oxford University Press, 1999), 476.

3. *Ibid.*, 471.

4. *Ibid.*, 483.

5. *Ibid.*

6. M. Thomas Inge, "Mark Twain, Chuck Jones, and the Art of Imitation," *Studies in American Humor* no 10 (2003): 11–17.

7. A pun on 16th-century Russian tsar Boris Godonuv.

8. *The Rubáiyát* of Omar Khayyám is the title that Edward FitzGerald gave his 1859 translation from Persian to English. One of many jokes that Ward and company aimed at the "adults" in the room.

9. Nichola Dobson. *Historical Dictionary of Animation and Cartoon* (Rowman & Littlefield, 2020), 78.

10. M. Keith Booker. *Drawn to Television: Prime Time Animation from the Flintstones to Family Guy* (Praeger, 2006), 3.

11. Hoover served as the nation's 31st President from 1929 to 1933.

12. One notable exception was the syndicated *Wait Till Your Father Gets Home* (1972–74), which was the last attempt at a prime-time animated program until *The Simpsons* debuted in 1989.

PART I

Historical Constructs
and the Rise of Subversiveness

Saturday Morning Trojan Mouse

The Origin of the Creator-Driven Television Cartoon

Lev Cantoral *and* Tyler Solon Williams

In the fall of 1987, a cadre of rebellious animators set loose an unlikely revolutionary onto American Saturday morning television airwaves: the plucky, inoffensive hero Mighty Mouse. Years before *The Simpsons* and *The Ren & Stimpy Show* reintroduced American adults to smart television cartoons, Ralph Bakshi and John Kricfalusi recast the operatic super mouse as the hapless figurehead of a series of surreal animated misadventures that aesthetically challenged the naïve norms of the Saturday morning cartoon from within. *Mighty Mouse: The New Adventures* was a "Trojan mouse," a seemingly conventional kids' cartoon actually produced with ambitious cinematic techniques that reimagined the art and craft of the television cartoon as a space for unconventional freedom of expression. While little-remembered today, this pivotal television series should be recognized for making possible the production model of the creator-driven television cartoon that would go on to dominate cable television animation in the 1990s and beyond.

While *Mighty Mouse: The New Adventures* (1987–88) appeared to be a commercial star vehicle for its marquee character, the subversive plan of the artists behind the reboot was in fact to fundamentally change the television cartoon by marrying it with aesthetics influenced by the golden age of cinema animation. The new cartoon looked back four decades to the cinema cartoon shorts of the 1940s to recover vital animation production practices that television cartoon studios had jettisoned in the 1960s. Terrytoons' earnest original *Mighty Mouse* series (1942–1961) was the seed, but the new show sought to recapture the mischievous spirit of Warner Bros.' madcap *Looney Tunes* (1930–1969). While some in early years hailed the new medium of television as "the eighth art,"[1] many critics and commentators in subsequent decades saw it as a "vast wasteland."[2] Admittedly, these critics had a point: between 1966 and 1986, the era of the dominance of the Saturday morning cartoon, broadcast television cartoons suffered from an intractable creative inertia stemming from commercial motivations, activist demands, overseas production outsourcing, indiscriminating viewers, and creative complacency at studios.[3]

The despair gripping the Hollywood animation industry in the mid-1980s, however, made it ripe for artistic change. In defiance of pervasive low expectations about the television cartoon, aging countercultural animator/filmmaker Ralph Bakshi (*Fritz the Cat*, 1972) sought to reinvent the media form by teaming up with young radical animator John Kricfalusi (the now-disgraced creator of *The Ren & Stimpy Show*). On *Mighty Mouse: The New Adventures*, director Bakshi stepped back to become producer while Kricfalusi stepped forward into the lead director role. The two would creatively lead what network CBS apparently thought would be a clever but conventional kids show. Instead, Bakshi and Kricfalusi treated the mandate to deliver the show as motivation to realize their dream of founding a revolutionary new kind of animation studio. They sought to transform the milquetoast, dialogue-heavy narratives of Filmation and Hanna-Barbera into a vibrant, gag-driven anarchy reminiscent of golden age cartoon shorts.

The creatives hired onto the production staff of the studio were mostly young artists. Some were frustrated by the creative limits imposed while working at large television cartoon studios; the rest were fresh out of art school.[4] In establishing the workplace culture of his studio, Bakshi eschewed Hollywood professionalism in favor of a countercultural do-it-yourself ethos. John Kricfalusi's creativity dramatically emboldened the aesthetics of the production. His mercurial temperament alienated some artists who worked with him, though, and his legacy has since been marred by inexcusable social transgressions.[5] Nevertheless, many animators subsequently carried the risk-taking spirit of this production forward in their careers. Their raw creative talent would earn some leading roles at other Hollywood television and cinema animation studios, where their subsequent works would recreate what animation was and could be.

Each of the four sections of this chapter reveals an important truth about Mighty Mouse's *New Adventures*. First, producer Ralph Bakshi's and director John Kricfalusi's cartoon reintroduced a creative philosophy into commercial television animation. Second, Mighty Mouse has a long history as a character, from his earnest beginnings to this later subversive outing, and an improbably large influence. Third, this principal producer and director rescued neglected golden age cinema animation techniques from oblivion, and transformed the television cartoon by integrating these into a now-contemporary production process. Fourth, the show's artistry was innovative but ultimately burdened it with creative costs that a children's cartoon could not uphold.

The aesthetic space explored by *Mighty Mouse: The New Adventures* enabled television cartoons to evolve into not just a mediated means of idiosyncratic creativity but also a commercial phenomenon. Two shows in particular are recognized for making possible the model of the creator-driven television cartoon of the 1990s, a period many call the "animation renaissance."[6] *The Simpsons* (1989–present) was an influential programming innovation for the cable-like broadcast network Fox. It would soon transform the television cartoon through sophisticated adult scriptwriting and voice acting. *The Ren & Stimpy Show* (1991–1996), one of cable network Nickelodeon's most influential original animated series, harnessed stunning visual invention. But arguably, the underrated *Mighty Mouse* served as an earlier precedent for these two shows, breaking the mold of the Saturday morning cartoon by pushing the commercial form past its aesthetic limits.[7] In the paradigm shift that followed in the 1990s, television cartoon making opened up to a new generation of artists that would explore new frontiers of television in many unique cartoons of their own creation.

A Philosophy of Creativity

"Here he comes, that Mighty Mouse—coming to vanquish the foe, with a mighty blow! Don't be afraid any more, 'cause things won't be like they've been before!" So declares the spirited opening theme of *Mighty Mouse: The New Adventures*. The cartoon had an improbable genesis in April 1987, when producer Ralph Bakshi sold CBS an imaginative superhero kids' show. His collaboration with supervising director John Kricfalusi would shake the foundations of how cartoons were made for television. While not a creator-driven television cartoon itself, the crew radically reimagined its long-established lead character. Mighty Mouse's *New Adventures* was a collective production run by its many talented young creatives: "[P]roduction involved the creative skills and input of the entire … production team."[8]

"Don't Touch That Dial" is considered by many to be the pinnacle of *Mighty Mouse: The New Adventures*.[9] This late second-season episode of about 11 minutes directly states the crew's artistic philosophy, both lexically in its script and visually in its animation. Throughout this episode, a pudgy boy of six or seven years sits in front of a massive family television set to watch cartoons, presumably on a Saturday morning. A procession of cartoon parodies unfolds on the screen, each laced with intertextual in-jokes. The first parody lampoons the quaint heroism of Mighty Mouse's own original cartoons. When the boy loses interest and changes the channel, our protagonist is suddenly thrown into the next cartoon parody, sometimes barely surviving the farce-to-farce combat. A ridiculously kitschy crossover of *The Jetsons* and *The Flintstones* is followed by an annoyingly pro-social Scooby-Doo. The evolving comic style of each parody grossly exaggerates the caricature already inherent to the source cartoon. When the boy quickly flips channels multiple times, Mighty Mouse, tormented by the boy's fickleness, breaks the fourth wall to speak to us: "Now I know why they call television a medium: because nothing on it is rare or well done!"

The production crew's defiant artistic ideals come to light when vapid commercialism becomes a life-or-death matter for our hero. Mighty next pals around with an overly goofy Rocky and Bullwinkle, when a threateningly serious non-parody breaks down the door. Four vaguely technological young men, a cross between *The Real Ghostbusters* and sci-fi Japanese anime, attempt to stop the fun. When Mighty Mouse turns their ray-gun weapon back on them, the serious are attacked by their own seriousness—in this double-negative, the poseur-aggressors transmogrify into hyper-silly clowns. Mighty easily banishes them "back to Whimsytown."

When the boy viewer is still unmoved by the feat, Mighty loses his temper, preventing another channel flip by flying straight towards us, breaking out of the television screen and confronting the boy. "I'm *bored*," the helpless boy mutters. Stepping onto a metaphorical soapbox, Mighty actually agrees: "Look what you're watching—hour upon hour of electronic pablum. Imitation is the sincerest form of … television!" In a flash of inspiration, the boy realizes that he could instead play outside. Before scampering off, Mighty reminds him, "If you must watch a television show, be sure to watch the all-new adventures of *Mighty Mouse!*" With tragic irony, Mighty now wraps up his lecture only to us: "But enough of this lying and hypocrisy. Time for what television's *really* about!" A common network-style live action transition to "these messages" is transposed into the episode, cheekily pointing out that the commercialism of network television takes precedence over artistic integrity.

Here, Mighty Mouse reminds both the kid and the viewer that we need not accept what was passing for Saturday morning cartoons. That complacent, risk-averse genre in fact reflected the state of broadcast television more broadly at the time—it was dominated by what networks deemed the "least objectionable programming."[10] Broadcast executives had been largely unwilling to take chances on original concepts for almost two decades, instead unfailingly insisting on bankable familiar characters as "insurance policies."[11] The head writer of *The New Adventures*, Tom

Minton, recalled producer Ralph Bakshi's opposing philosophy: "A ... cartoon is only good if it's a reaction to something else."[12] Essentially speaking for the whole crew involved in the effort, Minton added: "And *Mighty Mouse* was a reaction against a lot of mediocrity."[13]

Ralph Bakshi went to great lengths to protect his artists' creative agency from unwanted meddling by CBS. While he would pretend to entertain network personnel's attempts to give notes to the crew about things CBS wished to have changed, he consistently thwarted such behavior, allegedly burning the notes instead.[14] "I have fought very, very hard to keep animation personal, and to keep animation under the control of artists," Bakshi said later. "My whole belief was that producers don't do anything."[15] Like Leon Schlesinger at Warner Bros., as a producer, Bakshi took a completely hands-off approach to his artists; as long as they were productive, he gave them nearly free rein. But Schlesinger's motivation was making money. Bakshi's primary motivation was different: "to me, it's always about the art."[16] Remarkably, in an era of interchangeable television cartoons, Bakshi even approached the task of making a humble children's TV cartoon with the same stubborn allegiance to artistic integrity he brought to his legendary, very adult feature films.

Recognizing the young John Kricfalusi as a rebellious animation director like himself, Ralph Bakshi entrusted him with the responsibility to make the day-to-day production decisions for the nonconformist new show. "I was desperate to get a project for John to headline," Bakshi said. "He was in every way as explosive as I was.... I wanted to be a mentor."[17] Bakshi presided over the story meetings, where plotlines were hatched, and he lightly supervised Kricfalusi's direction. As senior director, Kricfalusi used the ambitious production techniques Bakshi had used since the 1950s to play around with the animation. "Kricfalusi was ... determined not to allow the economics of limited animation to prevent him from making strong visual statements," animation historian Harvey Deneroff has written. "In an interview.... Kricfalusi explained, 'We just wanted to prove to people that it is possible to make a real cartoon, and keep it on a cheap budget.'"[18] The radical animation techniques and rebellious attitude that would garner "John K." fame and notoriety as the creator and head director of *The Ren & Stimpy Show* in 1991 took shape in nascent form here at Bakshi's studio in 1987.[19]

Mighty Mouse was a cartoon made by a team of artists wresting creative control over television cartoon production back from the clutches of media and commerce by sheer force of will. Bakshi's radical approach to making animation implicitly established the experimental style of the studio and its cartoon, although it may be debatable whether there was one unifying creative vision. We generally accept the recognized term "creator-driven" in this chapter. But arguably *Mighty Mouse* is a "creative-driven" cartoon, that is, one authored by the collective sensibilities of the many people who worked in concert to bring it to the television screen.

During its brief life of thirteen months from 1987 and 1988, *The New Adventures* broadcast this newly creative philosophy out like a siren call to anyone that would listen: a television cartoon series can take risks and still get on the air. Each episode opens with a mini fanfare, crediting its authorship by "Bakshi Animation."[20] The unconventional series the studio produced admittedly suffers from variable quality, aesthetic heterogeneity, and lack of narrative credibility. Nonetheless, as a uniquely multifarious effort it remains funny, offbeat, and generally insane. This adult animation posing as a kids' cartoon struggled to find a wide audience, but its cancellation increased its visibility. Following in *Mighty Mouse*'s footsteps, young artists would take a creative leap of faith into the wide-open medium of cable television.

Mighty History

Mighty Mouse debuted as a character in America in 1942, shortly after the United States' entry into World War II. Then a topical cross between Superman and Mickey Mouse, the "Super Mouse" (as he was initially named) was a creation of Paul Terry's New York City-area Terrytoons studio, which pitted him against powerful evildoers in epic melodramas. Always arriving just in the nick of time near the end of the cartoon, the tiny mouse bested even the most redoubtable villains through outsize displays of physical force. During that fearful time of war, the plucky hero routinely rescued his meek and imperiled rodent brethren, singing his way into the hearts of audiences with his rousing theme song, "HEEERE I come to save the DAAAY!"

Initially a minor player in cinema, on television Mighty Mouse seemed to be in the right place at the right time. Mighty's cute, friendly cartoon face seemed universally recognized, and helped invite television sets into the homes of families not just across the U.S., but also, increasingly, globally. In his heyday in the early years of television, Mighty Mouse became so popular around the world that the United Nations International Children's Emergency Fund (UNICEF) named him an official ambassador in 1961 and 1962.[21] Over several decades, the earnest heroism of his early cinema shorts would give way to a sly subversion.[22] He seemed to conquer even overexposure. "Mighty Mouse is such a strong character that he survived weak stories and animation to capture the hearts of decades of fans."[23]

During the postwar boom, CBS purchased Paul Terry's studio and cartoon library outright in 1955, using Terry's most memorable character as the basis for a new show, *Mighty Mouse Playhouse* (1955–1966). Composed entirely of previously produced cartoons, this successful and long-running show was the first all-cartoon series to air regularly on Saturday mornings[24]—giving the brave rodent the ignoble honor of inaugurating the major U.S. broadcast networks' Saturday morning animated block for children. Through his regular broadcasts over the next decade, he would move mountains. Mighty Mouse helped inspire the birth of the Japanese animation industry,[25] and then played a role in the creation of the American superhero television cartoon.[26]

Ralph Bakshi, in his first job in animation as a young man, directed other cartoons at Terrytoons between 1956 and 1966, a rare historical juncture of the cinema cartoon's latter years and the early years of the television cartoon. Bakshi then created one of the earliest superhero television cartoons in early 1966; CBS paired his goofy characters with their star in the hour-long *Mighty Mouse and the Mighty Heroes* (1966–1967). But Bakshi had bigger dreams. After leaving Terrytoons, he went on to form his own animation studio, Bakshi Productions, and produced *Fritz the Cat* (1972). Building upon his earlier experience (and moving as far away from kids cartoons as conceivably possible), Bakshi's feature film was suffused with sex, drugs, rock 'n' roll, and cats. This boundary-pushing feature film, a vehicle for countercultural social critique, bringing an entirely new kind of intimately adult animation into the world. While becoming one of the most financially successful independent films ever, Bakshi's film woke audiences and critics up to the power of animation to refashion human experience.[27]

Since the mid–60s, the Saturday morning cartoon format had been developing as an innovative programming trend expressly directed at children viewers. Each broadcast season brought forth new and old characters to star in, increasingly, bracing straight adventure television cartoons. The 1970s saw the deepening of the Saturday morning ritual into a childhood institution, but the television cartoon program form itself was slumping into a kind of glutted routine. Advertisers were pumping money into strikingly flashy commercials for the kid-focused programming block, but American networks and studios were generally unwilling or unable to take creative risks to innovate in programming. The decade's aesthetic ennui was reflected in a litany of retreads and novelties featured on Saturday morning schedules, a bland mix which congressional regulators in 1978 dubbed "kidvid."

John Kricfalusi got his start in animation production in 1979 at the television cartoon factory Filmation. In another surprising twist, the young Kricfalusi worked on Mighty's first original television adaptation,

The New Adventures of Mighty Mouse and Heckle & Jeckle (1979–1980). This mildly diverting program set Mighty's heroics in modern contexts, but as the show dialed down his violent retributions and operatic melodrama, our hero lost some of his most distinctive traits. It was no sweet gig for restive John K., who resented the compulsory artistic conformity and declared the resulting show "horrible beyond belief."[28] The nadir of Saturday morning cartoons may have passed in the late '70s, though. By the early '80s, producers and networks began to alter established norms, incrementally producing memorable new kids' cartoons.[29]

In late 1986, at a professional low, Ralph Bakshi was struggling to find another project to interest film studios. His last feature film in 1983 had been unsuccessful,[30] and he looked back towards television with a new hope. John Kricfalusi, itching for opportunities to develop his artistic chops, caught the attention of the elder iconoclast, who shared his penchant for rebellious freedom of expression. *Pee-wee's Playhouse* (1986–1990) had recently been making waves on CBS with its off-the-wall take on television. A motley crew of creatives there came together to smash together a mind-bending confection of live-action slapstick comedy, puppetry, video technology, classic cinema cartoons, and rock and pop music.

In early 1987, Bakshi formed a development team with Kricfalusi and a handful of other experienced artists to prepare pitch concepts for the three national broadcast networks, ABC, NBC, and CBS.[31] That April, Bakshi pitched the group's numerous original characters and show concepts, but the risk-averse broadcast networks were unwilling to try anything new. During the final, desperate meeting with CBS, out of other options, Bakshi tried pitching marquee cartoon star Mighty Mouse. CBS's head of children's programming loved the idea and purportedly bought the series on the spot.[32]

Neither Bakshi nor Kricfalusi ever intended to make a safe superhero cartoon starring the squeaky-clean super mouse. In a plan at once ambitious and foolhardy, the producer and director decided to make their television cartoon by adopting an elaborate production model resembling that of Leon Schlesinger's Warner Bros. cinema cartoon studio in the 1940s. The specific artistic techniques of this model, then arcane, were not dissimilar from what Bakshi had learned early in his career. But, these complex animation processes had been abandoned by early television cartoon studios for good reason: they were thought to be too expensive and time-consuming. The producer and director had little money or time—the first scheduled air date for the new show was only five months away, in mid–September of 1987—yet they accepted the long odds and soon set to work.[33] The two needed to quickly pull off the seemingly impossible task of reengineering the television cartoon from scratch.

Animation Craft and Art

While its star made the show superficially resemble many other conventional 1980s cartoon vehicles for a "pre-sold" character, Mighty Mouse's good boy charm provided cover for the covert operation to scale up this venturesome production. Kricfalusi and Bakshi expressly rejected the mode of production established for television animation. Instead, they recovered dusty but sturdy cinema techniques to structure their studio's production. Specifically, the studio adopted four animation production techniques that had been fundamental to golden age cinema animation but were unheard-of in Saturday morning television cartoons:

1. Dividing the crew into distinct units, each led by a different director;
2. Elevating storyboard drawings in the writing process over typed scripts;
3. Composing character pose layouts in-house;
4. And reviving a cartoony design aesthetic throughout the production process.

These four techniques would become central to the sea change set to remap the world of television animation. Their adoption here allowed animators and artists much greater creative expression than any other television cartoon production.

As reflected in the episode "Don't Touch that Dial," the staff largely saw the Saturday morning cartoons around them as un-cartoony, self-serious action-adventure series. At the time, creative control in television cartoon productions had long ago been taken away from fun-loving directors and animators and given over to business-minded producers and network executives, who insisted above all else that cartoons have broad commercial appeal. Many television writers were journeymen less familiar with writing for animation, and their scripts emulated the simple-minded realism baked into most concurrent television cartoons. Inherently, trying to make a visually funny cartoon from typed scripts is challenging, because a script emphasizes narrative and dialogue over comic gags. "Nobody had tried to make a funny cartoon on Saturday morning for … almost 20 years," recalled *Mighty Mouse* story artist Jim Reardon.[34]

The first golden age cinema technique that John Kricfalusi and Ralph Bakshi brought into their television production was the unit production structure. In earlier cinema animation, a unit structure was the foundation for artistic control within the animation production system, especially at Warner Bros.' famed "Termite Terrace" studio. By the 1980s, the oversight responsibilities of the television animation director were subdivided between different, non-overlapping departments, a management structure that deprived any one individual from claiming an original, innovative vision for an episode or series. Explaining the situation he encountered at Filmation and Hanna-Barbera, Kricfalusi said:

> There was no such thing as a "director." [In the unit system of the 1930s and 1940s,] each unit [was] headed by a director who would follow the cartoon from script to final edit. Everyone had a creative stake in the outcome of the films.[35]

When John Kricfalusi took the reins of *Mighty Mouse* as the supervising animation director, the restoration of the unit structure granted him greater creative control by restoring the role's authority.[36] The crew was divided into four "units," each a handful of artists led by one director, all working in parallel.[37] A unit created its own episodes independently, handling every creative step through the layout phase, after which episodes were sent overseas to be animated.[38] John K. led one of the four units, and as head director supervised the other three units to varying degrees. In this system, artists in each unit create the cartoon together through close collaboration, their efforts fusing together into an aesthetic whole. Not yet as controlling as he would later become, Kricfalusi gave his artists far greater autonomy than a typical animation studio of the time. Instead of tightly controlling the tasks given to artists, he often kept an open mind about what kind of cartoon episodes artists in the crew would create. In the second season, Kricfalusi left to pursue another another series; his role was assumed by Kent Butterworth.[39] In many ways, the show belonged nearly as much to the crew of creatives as to the director. In fact, "Don't Touch that Dial," was produced after John K.'s departure.

The second cinema animation technique the studio adopted was a storyboard-oriented approach to writing. This was the defining creative process of the show, in which the artists in each unit constructed a story through illustration rather than text. Television's traditional script-driven model is based in lexical words. In contrast, a storyboard tells the story visually through a sequence of drawings, resembling a comic strip. The idea is that, "since animation is a pictorial art, the story might as well be worked out in visual form by sketching a series of panels—a storyboard."[40] The storyboard's purpose is to communicate the episode's story by presenting each narrative beat as a drawing, with directions demonstrating the on-screen action and camera movement, visualizing the moments of the story in sequence.

A storyboard-oriented process is naturally suited to animation because it empowers artists with creative agency to visually tell the screen story. Productions emphasizing storyboards foreground visual humor and gags over formal narrative cause-and-effect logic. This motivates artists to make drawings comic enough to make other artists laugh.[41] The network attempted to assert control by requiring that episode scripts be typed and approved beforehand. But the crew chose to treat the script merely as a rough template or jumping-off point, allowing the storyboard to serve as the formative authority of the episode's narrative.

For its writing staff, the studio chose to only hire visual artists— no traditional scriptwriters were allowed. Head writer Tom Minton and a small team of artist-writers began the process by typing loose scripts that left plenty of creative flexibility for subsequent visual adaptation: "This mindset worked against the network's edict that the final picture must reflect the writer's script verbatim."[42] To compensate for the limitations of the network's script-based process, Kricfalusi insisted that each unit "plus" its scripts, or spice them up by adding visual gags during the storyboard process.[43] By the time the episodes were finished, the visual animation was often at odds with the voice actors' performance of the script.

While the script-oriented process had been the norm for decades, this classic-era model of board-driven animation production would subsequently inspire a whole new kind of television cartoon. It appears that *The Ren & Stimpy Show* was the first television cartoon to be written by storyboard in perhaps 25 years.[44] *Ren & Stimpy* hired many artists from *Mighty Mouse*. *SpongeBob SquarePants* (1999–present), long among the most popular television cartoons in the world, has historically been a storyboard-driven show, and has hired many *Ren & Stimpy* artists. Script-driven cartoons are quite similar to live action television shows; both are linear, verbal, and more aural than visual. Storyboard-driven cartoons are naturally associational, visual, and kinetic. *Mighty Mouse* pushed against its scripts, towards visual freedom.

The third cinema technique prioritized in the new television production was in-house character layout. Layout is the foundation of animation, the process of carefully refining the rough, preliminary storyboard sketches into the detailed renderings that will ultimately appear on the television screen. At other studios, layouts were composed by carefully designing poses according to the studio's house style, as reflected on character design model sheets. The finalized layout drawings, called "key poses," represent visual extremes, the points that define characters' movement. These are the exact drawings that will be inked and painted onto celluloid to become the transparent "cel" panels, each of which is one frame of the final cartoon's animation.

John Kricfalusi and Ralph Bakshi both aspired to make "character animation" for television. The problem was that cinema-style character animation had rarely been achieved, or even attempted, in the majority of television cartoon production. TV cartoons rely on aural voice acting and sound effects, rather than fluid animation, to carry the weight of the narrative. Typically known simply as "animation," Walt Disney established character animation as the standard in cinema in the 1930s. The storyboard and layout artist alike become "actors with a pencil," as Warner Bros. animation director Chuck Jones often said. In the character animation of cinema, the artist develops each character visually, staging them by drawing specific poses of their body to express their intentions, thoughts, and emotions. By comparison, dialogue is secondary. Animating character movement is the process of actually drawing the poses "in-between" the key frames, those showing the character in movement. Television cartoons had always minimized character movement; this is the reason they are commonly called "limited animation." By the 1980s, animating movement was actually more of a technical process than a creative one: most North American and European television cartoon studios had been outsourcing the process of animating movement to studios overseas in Asia for decades.

Kricfalusi believed that reintegrating layout was essential to reclaiming the directorial vision he sought for *Mighty Mouse: The New Adventures*. At other studios, layout was likewise considered technical work, not creative work; it was commonly an afterthought in the production process. In-house artists would only adapt scripts into storyboards, before leaving the rest of the process to animators overseas. In the most limited of animated productions, layout was little more than a process of tracing stock character models onto stock backgrounds, with little thought given to narrative or performative specificity.[45] Yet character animation cannot be achieved without deliberately composed layout poses, because careful attention to the original artists' storyboard drawings is needed to prevent their artistry from being lost in translation. To better approximate the evocative animation of golden age cinema shorts, Kricfalusi emphasized strong, expressive, funny pose drawings. Thad Komorowski, author of the *Ren & Stimpy* history *Sick Little Monkeys*, writes that the director "strove to make the acting and actions as precise as possible in the preproduction stage while also instilling life into the work. Ergo, something special might actually survive in the overseas pipeline."[46]

The fourth cinematic technique John Kricfalusi and Ralph Bakshi brought to their *Mighty Mouse* was an emphasis on boldly cartoony designs and animation. Modeled after the Warner Bros. cartoons of old, *The New Adventures* sought to revive a wildly caricatured production design aesthetic across its many visual elements. Wacky designs for characters, props, and backgrounds were expected, befitting the show's warped cartoon world. While all cartoons are inherently caricatured to some degree, conventional 1980s cartoons maintained a measured realism in character design and rationalist, formal assumptions of architectural construction in background design. By contrast, this cartoon stylized its aesthetics beyond measure: "Don't Touch that Dial" illustrates how the show further caricatured the already caricatured Saturday morning cartoon aesthetics of familiar shows, sometimes to the point of unrecognizability.

In nearly every earlier television cartoon, the visual appearance and movement of the characters was standardized. Character design model sheets given to artists prescribed uniform ways animators were to draw the typical body poses and facial expressions of the core characters; aberrations were often not allowed. In diametrical opposition to the norm that characters have a customary appearance, John K. not only disapproved of model sheets—he insisted that his artists reinterpret characters differently in every shot.[47] Kricfalusi's penchant for wildly "off model," laugh-out-loud drawings was central to the unbridled visual invention of the cartoon. This comic exaggeration was likewise emphasized in the show's painted background designs. Contemporary 1980s television productions emphasized lines meeting at right angles and the preservation of traditional perspective. Instead, *Mighty Mouse*'s "wonky" design sensibility exaggerated the inherent non-naturalistic flatness of the cartoon image.[48] The show's retro-modernist styling repopularized UPA's and Warner Bros.' "cartoon modern" designs of the 1950s; many subsequent 1990s creator-driven productions would likewise borrow from this aesthetic tradition.

Cartoony drawings are caricatured. Cartoony animation typically exaggerates movement according to a bouncy, "squash and stretch" aesthetic; that is, it doesn't attempt to mimic the realism of photographic live action film. The realist cartoons that dominated Saturday morning schedules lacked both exaggeration and stretchiness—raising the question of whether these were even "cartoons." In opposition, the staff of artists at Bakshi's studio let loose creatively, pushing their cartoon towards aesthetic anarchy. On the budget of a Saturday morning production, though, the crew could not come close to capturing the precise, fluid artistry of classic cinema character animation. Instead, in search of comedy, they embraced difference, strangeness, and the unimaginable.

Bakshi and Kricfalusi actively encouraged every artist to bring their own unique style into their work for the show. Surprisingly, the act of creation was more important to all involved than the ultimate product. On a typical day in the studio, it appears likely that, as storyboard artist Bob Camp recalled of Kricfalusi's next cartoon, "everyone [was] just doing whatever the hell they wanted."[49] Evidently, Bakshi and Kricfalusi encouraged this behavior, which another studio might have seen as goofing off. Bakshi told the artists: "The process of making is everything. If the picture turns out good—great. If it turns out bad ... great—you've learned something."[50] The resulting episodes often unfold in bizarrely unexpected ways, to the degree that the narratives frequently lose cohesion and credibility. Mighty Mouse continually mutates in appearance from shot to shot. But the producer and director accepted this radical multiplicity. For Bakshi, "it had more to do with who we are as human beings than ... the mouse."[51]

Creative Benefits and Costs

Instead of following the taken-for-granted pretensions of earlier Saturday morning cartoons, *Mighty Mouse: The New Adventures* threw quality control to the wind, presenting to the world something sloppy, audacious, and uncategorizable. John Kricfalusi said that Ralph Bakshi worked a miracle in getting CBS to air the thing.[52] Through aesthetic provocation, the cartoon sought to prove to other artists, industry-types, and viewers that the television cartoon had much broader potential than the patronizing commercial format it had been restricted to. Incredibly, the world listened to the message of this unlikely herald. The show was gradually recognized for establishing an array of new precedents about how animation could be made differently for television. Two groundbreaking series that began within three years of *The New Adventures'* cancellation cemented the new creator-driven paradigm in the public imagination: *The Simpsons*, and *The Ren & Stimpy Show*. Both series took different lessons from *Mighty Mouse*; together, these three cartoons resoundingly transformed television animation from a stale commercial product into a hybrid showcase for rambunctious creative voices.

In his climactic rant ending "Don't Touch that Dial," Mighty Mouse uses his own Saturday morning cartoon to denounce the Saturday morning cartoon form itself. The mouse served as a figurehead giving a defiant voice to artists opposed to the norm of overplayed, uninspired cartoons. *The New Adventures* planted potent seeds of cultural rebellion in its subversive animation, which would take root in future series. But, as the title of the episode implies, the irony of "Don't Touch That Dial" is that, grievances aired, Mighty immediately returns to form as a corporate shill and dutifully promotes his own cartoon. He sarcastically concludes that television is about commerce—implying instead that it should be about art.

This episode aired in October 1988, in the wake of a controversy over the show's content that had begun brewing over the summer: a conservative watchdog group accused the show of making a drug reference to cocaine.[53] While CBS defended the show at first, the brouhaha strained the already tenuous relationship between network and studio, and the show was soon canceled.[54] While its demise was tragic, the controversy surrounding it actually increased the show's visibility. *Mighty Mouse: The New Adventures* became recognized as something of a martyr that died defending artistic freedom. The notoriety served to "[bring television] animation into the mainstream of popular culture."[55] The cartoon's modest success and controversial end preceded the creation of two far more well-known original shows.

The Simpsons claimed a lexical, script-driven identity and lineage different from the visual, storyboard-driven *Mighty Mouse*. Pursuing comedy through subverting cultural meanings, *The Simpsons* is given well-deserved credit for investing in talented writers and making them the creative engine of the series. While it boldly asserted creative agency, arguably, *The Simpsons* is not a "creator-driven" television cartoon.[56] Initially, even this fundamentally different show looked to *Mighty Mouse* for guidance, by initially hiring Kent Butterworth, its supervising second season animation director. Butterworth's hyper-cartoony sensibility did not gel with the *Simpsons* crew, who were seeking a more subtle aesthetic for their "sitcom that happens to be animated." "*The Simpsons* is a writer's show, it's not an animator's show," Butterworth commented after departing.[57] *The Simpsons* reinvented the media format of the television cartoon not through the animation unit but through the writer's room.

The Ren & Stimpy Show was technically one of the first three contemporary creator-driven cartoons; it shared a programming block with cable channel Nickelodeon's other original series, Jim Jinkins' *Doug* (1991–1999) and Gábor Csupó and Arlene Klasky's *Rugrats* (1991–2004). Unlike its more child-directed peers, John K.'s *Ren & Stimpy* also aired on MTV for that cable network's hip 18–34-year-old demographic. This newer show, a direct descendant of *Mighty Mouse: The New Adventures*, is recognized for fearlessly asserting the eccentric vision of its creator, pursuing comedy through visually subverting preconceived notions about television and cartoons. Kricfalusi negotiated an unprecedentedly open-ended production arrangement with Nickelodeon. From one perspective, he then let his imagination run wild at his studio Spumco. From another perspective, he went mad with power. While a landmark series, *Ren & Stimpy* is arguably a cautionary tale. Kricfalusi became possessive about his creation, and many of his artists found it impossible to meet his idiosyncratic, manipulative demands in their work.[58] *Mighty Mouse's* noteriety presaged *Ren & Stimpy's* controversy, "which in a way helped bring animation into the mainstream of popular culture." Aesthetically revolutionary, *Ren & Stimpy* reveals how boundless cable television can be for animation, in contrast to the familiar strictures of broadcast television's least offensive programming. Yet, Kricfalusi's reckless, self-aggrandizing leadership would force him out of his own series in its second season and threaten the ability of networks to trust subsequent television cartoon creators enough to grant them full control.

Artists should be given opportunity to make art for their own reasons, as authentic expression of their unique personal vision, Ralph Bakshi has said.[59] Instead of focusing on his audience, like most other Hollywood animation producers in the 1970s and 1980s, he made animation that spoke to him personally. Bakshi took creative risks no one else had been willing or dreamed to take. He handed this torch to John Kricfalusi who, buoyed by the talents of many other artists, attempted to carry it farther forward.

Such artistic ambition can carry great risks. John Kricfalusi's once endearing penchant for subversion would cross over into inflammatory perversion at the expense of aesthetic substance.[60] His legacy has recently become irredeemably tainted by disturbing revelations about sexual misconduct.[61] We recognize the objections of those who believe that Kricfalusi's transgressions should marginalize him in discussions of animation history.[62] Even *Ren & Stimpy* historian Thad Komorowski distanced himself, writing on social media that "the continued reverence of John K. is modern animation's greatest shame."[63]

Still, it is arguably impossible to conceive what animation might be like today had these two boundary-pushing artists not infused their rebel spirit into animation in the 1970s, '80s, and '90s. Before the storm, referring to John K.'s studio, Jerry Beck wrote: "[L]ove it or hate it, ... there's no question Spumco changed the face of television animation—and still influences series, students and independent animators today."[64] By the 1990s, the center of gravity in the television animation industry finally shifted from the conservatism of the Saturday morning cartoon era to the progressivism of the creative-led animation renaissance. The 1980s, which saw broadcast television cartoons as commercial products to be bought and sold, quickly evolved in the 1990s into a range of wildly diverse cable television cartoons, making cable a subversive space for the exploration of personal and social experiences outside the mainstream.[65]

Fomenting an Animation Revolution

Mighty Mouse: The New Adventures acted as a Trojan mouse that imploded the kid-focused Saturday morning cartoon from within. Ralph Bakshi and John Kricfalusi delivered to CBS not a commercial product so much as an experimental artistic statement. By the 1980s, even cinema animation was at risk of forgetting the groundbreaking techniques pioneered in its own medium in the 1940s. This unlikely production revealed television to be a new frontier for animation, which could finally welcome its capacity for "caricaturial comment and critique."[66] Mighty Mouse's *New Adventures* rejected the conceits and formulas of even the greatest earlier television cartoons.[67] During the height of the postmodern pop culture of the '80s, this Saturday morning cartoon pushed past the pastiche of Saturday morning cartoons to enter into a contemporary parodic territory of self-reflexivity that would soon become *de rigeur* in the '90s.

When *The New Adventures* hit the airwaves, the animation world reached an aesthetic crossroads. The radicalized mouse's subversive flair reshaped how people interpreted television animation, a sea change after which even the recent past seemed like a distant memory.[68] The show expressed a new philosophy of animation in its profoundly pointed differences from other television cartoons. While *Mighty Mouse* is not strictly a creator-driven cartoon, adhering to the tired formula of the Saturday morning cartoon would subsequently no longer feel safe or tenable. In reinventing the art form, "*Mighty Mouse: The New Adventures* ... laid the groundwork for a renaissance in television animation."[69]

Mighty Mouse: The New Adventures, *The Simpsons*, and *The Ren & Stimpy Show* are three television cartoons whose influence established the creator-driven model. These shows remade television animation by taking their crafts seriously and taking creative risks in search of new perspectives. *Mighty Mouse* and *Ren & Stimpy* were the first television cartoons since the early 1960s to demonstrate the entertainment value of the storyboard-driven approach. The storyboard-driven production model would redefine television cartoon production for decades to come.

In these compelling early series, cartoon creatives braved the intense and longstanding stigma against "kiddie" cartoons, daring to invite adults back to watching cartoons on television. Before *The New Adventures*, it seemed no network would buy any kind of original animated series. But, within five years of its 1987 premiere, multiple broadcast and cable television networks realized the power of animation to personalize their programming to target niche audiences, and animation became increasingly central to both the content and marketing of television programming.

The real credit for *Mighty Mouse* should truthfully be given to the crew as a whole, in all its diversity. A crucial silver lining in the controversy is that this scrappy cartoon kick-started the careers of many talented young animators. Of the promising artists who found their sea legs working in *The New Adventures*' countercultural studio environment, a handful went on to become industry leaders still today reshaping Holly-wood animation.[70] As he thought back on the accomplishments of his crew of artists, Ralph Bakshi later said, "Those ... were *kids*, out of school. On schedule—on budget—[*they*] changed the industry. And everyone's been copying them since then."[71]

Mighty Mouse's dark horse *New Adventures* is, we suggest, the oper-ative origin point of the television animation renaissance. After this wild Saturday morning cartoon met its end in late 1988, America woke up in the early 1990s to discover that cartoons were suddenly a cutting edge of popular culture.[72] Before *Who Framed Roger Rabbit?* (1988), former mat-inee idol Mighty Mouse first re-embraced subversive animation as a cul-tural space apart from commercial imperatives. If Mighty Mouse's 1950's *Playhouse* began the ruin of television animation into a Saturday morning wasteland, it may be fitting that his 1980's *New Adventures* began trans-forming it into a lush cultural wonderland.

NOTES

1. Robert Lewis Shayon, ed., *The Eighth Art: Twenty Three Views of Television Today* (New York: Holt, Rinehart and Winston, 1962).

2. In his (in)famous 1961 anti-television polemic, FCC commissioner Newton Minow lamented that, on television, "[y]ou will see a procession of ... violence, and car-toons." In 1985, *The New York Times* described "Saturday morning" as "one big 'cartoon ghetto.'" Newton Minow, "Television and the Public Interest." (Speech to the National Association of Broadcasters convention, May 9, 1961.) https://www.youtube.com/watch?v=FDddNnP4sQE; Salmans, "Cartoon Ghetto."

3. Jerry Beck, "Saturday morning Blues," in Beck, *Animation Art*, 246. The claims about activists, outsourcing, and viewers are Beck's; those about commerce and complacency are ours.

4. Thill, "*Mighty Mouse.*" The artists who had already worked in the animation industry included Ken Boyer, Eddie Fitzgerald, Jim Gomez, Bob Jaques, Vicky Jenson, Tom Minton, Lynne Naylor, Jim Smith, and Bruce Timm. The artists recently out of art school included Ed Bell, Mike Kazaleh, Rich Moore, Jeff Pidgeon, Jim Reardon, and Andrew Stanton. The grad-uates largely studied animation at the peerless California College of the Arts ("CalArts").

5. We discuss this scandal in the subsequent section "Creative Benefits and Costs."

6. Jerry Beck, "1990–2000: Renaissance," in Beck, *Animation Art*, 302.

7. Eagle, *Breaking the Mold*. The title of Jeffrey Eagle's 2010 documentary about the show speaks to this historical role the show played.

8. Simensky, "Cartoon in the 1990's," 273–4.

9. "The series' towering moment belongs to 'Don't Touch That Dial,' which drops Mighty Mouse into a series of dead-on send-ups of the cartoon wasteland surrounding the show, then tells viewers to stop wasting so much time watching television." Keith Phipps, "*Mighty Mouse: The New Adventures, The Complete Series,*" *The A.V. Club*, January 13, 2010, https://www.avclub.com/mighty-mouse-the-new-adventures-the-complete-series-1798164099. "Don't Touch that Dial" was written by Jim Reardon and Tom Minton, and directed by Kent Butterworth.

10. Todd Gitlin. *Inside Prime Time* (New York: Pantheon, 1983).

11. Grossman, *Saturday Morning TV*, 367.

12. Tom Minton, *Breaking the Mold*, 26:46.

13. *Ibid.*, 26:54.

14. *Ibid.*, 28:58.

15. Ralph Bakshi, question and answer session, Dragon Con, Atlanta, GA, September 2, 2011, 23:54, https://www.youtube.com/watch?v=ue2EkHnOwV4.

16. *Ibid.*, 27:21.

17. Gibson and McDonnell, *Unfiltered*, 210.

18. Deneroff, "TV Wakes Up," 273.

19. "We experimented every step of the way," John K. said later. Thill, *"Mighty Mouse."*

20. Komorowski, *Sick Little Monkeys*, 13–17. Officially, the studio was called Bakshi-Hyde Ventures.

21. Grossman, *Saturday Morning TV*, 364.

22. Stand-up comedian Andy Kaufman's very odd early bit of lip-syncing to the original Mighty Mouse theme song garnered him enough word of mouth to be featured on the very first episode of *Saturday Night Live*, on October 11, 1975.

23. Cawley and Korkis, "Mighty Mouse," 138.

24. *Ibid.*, 135.

25. Frederik L. Schodt, "Designing a World." *Mechademia* 8 (2013): 236. Osamu Tezuka credited Mighty Mouse as a central influence on his character *Astro Boy*, the first popular television cartoon in Japan.

26. Mitchell E. Shapiro, *Television Network Weekend Programming, 1959–1990* (Jefferson, NC: McFarland & Company, 1992), 39, 131. Mighty may have been the only cartoon superhero on television during his early tenure. *Mighty Mouse Playhouse* typically aired on CBS on Saturdays at 10:00 or 10:30 am. Upon its retirement, it was approximately replaced by the first straight television superhero cartoon, Filmation's *The New Adventures of Superman* (1966–1970), which began airing on CBS at 11:00.

27. Harvey Deneroff, "Ralph Bakshi & Fritz the Cat," in Beck, *Animation Art*, 244.

28. John Kricfalusi, "John K. Talks Ren & Stimpy, Mighty Mouse, Ralph Bakshi," interview by Cliff Broadway, *TheOneRing*, August 1, 2012, https://www.youtube.com/watch?v=FDddNnP4sQE.

29. The following 80's kids' cartoons were more innovative than the majority of conventional series: Hanna-Barbera's *The Smurfs* (1981–1989), Filmation's *He-Man and the Masters of the Universe* (1983–1985), Jim Henson/Marvel's *Muppet Babies* (1984–1991), and Disney's *Adventures of the Gummi Bears* (1985–1991). More contemporary new cartoons were in production, but had not yet begun airing, including Disney's *DuckTales* (1987–1990) and Fred Wolf's *Teenage Mutant Ninja Turtles* (1987–1996).

30. *Fire and Ice* (1983), a darkly animated epic fantasy adventure.

31. Gibson and McDonnell, *Unfiltered*, 210–211. The artists Bakshi trusted to create new cartoon concepts from the ground up were Eddie Fitzgerald, John Kricfalusi, Tom Minton, Lynne Naylor, and Jim Reardon.

32. Bakshi, Robinson interview. Judy Price, who led CBS' Saturday morning cartoon block in 1987, greenlit the show.

33. Komorowski, *Sick Little Monkeys*, 11.

34. Jim Reardon, *Breaking the Mold*, 4:45.

35. Thill, *"Mighty Mouse."*

36. Komorowski, *Sick Little Monkeys*, 13.

37. Gibson and McDonnell, *Unfiltered*, 211. Schlesinger's studio at Warner Bros. had also divided its artists into four units.

38. Cuckoo's Nest Studio in Taiwan handled the complex task of animating the cartoon.

39. Komorowski, *Sick Little Monkeys*, 21–22. John K. produced and directed *The New Adventures of Beany and Cecil* (1988), a short-lived series based on characters created by Bob Clampett, the Warner Bros. animator who most influenced him.

40. Beckerman, *Animation*, 110.

41. Simensky, "Cartoon in the 1990's," 274. Director Tom Sito made this point about the process.

42. Komorowski, *Sick Little Monkeys*, 11.

43. *Ibid.*, 10.

44. John K.'s suggestions about developing *Ren & Stimpy* to Vanessa Coffey, the first vice president of animation production at Nickelodeon, imply that he was conceiving the concept of writing by storyboard anew. John K. suggested to Vanessa Coffey, the first vice president of animation production at Nickelodeon: "Why don't we make cartoons the real way, like back in the days when they didn't use scripts?" Elsewhere, he finished this thought. "I had ... explained ... to her ... that old cartoons were not 'written,' they were drawn on storyboards. She agreed to this system. At last!" Jerry Beck, "Ren & Stimpy," in *Not Just Cartoons: Nicktoons!*, ed. Jerry Beck (New York: Melcher Media, 2007), 12; John Kricfalusi, "Artists Finally Win Some Respect and Credit," *John K. Stuff* (blog), October 19, 2009, http://johnkstuff.blogspot.com/2009/10/artists-finally-win-some-respect-and.html.

45. Sam Simon, "Sam Simon," interview by Karen Herman, April 13, 2013, Television Academy Foundation, 11:36, https://interviews.televisionacademy.com/interviews/sam-simon. Future *Simpsons* co-developer Simon worked at Filmation in 1979, and described the studio's writing process as constructing stories by filling around 40% of the episode with earlier stock footage.

46. Komorowski, *Sick Little Monkeys*, 5.

47. John Kricfalusi, "'How Can I Get Life In My Drawings?'—Tell A Story," *John K. Stuff* (blog), February 13, 2010, https://johnkstuff.blogspot.com/2010/02/how-can-i-get-life-in-my-drawings-tell.html.

48. John Kricfalusi, "Origins of Wonky," *John K. Stuff* (blog), September 21, 2008, http://johnkstuff.blogspot.com/2008/09/origins-of-wonky.html.

49. Komorowski, *Sick Little Monkeys*, 37. Bob Camp recalled this about working on Kricfalusi's *Beany and Cecil*, but it appears likely the studio culture during *The New Adventures* was similar.

50. Bakshi, *Breaking the Mold*, 27:03.

51. *Ibid.*, 28:43.

52. John Kricfalusi, *Breaking the Mold*, 28:28.

53. Craig Wolff, "Mighty Mouse Flying High On Flowers?" *The New York Times*. July 26, 1988, https://www.nytimes.com/1988/07/26/nyregion/mighty-mouse-flying-high-on-flowers.html.

54. Gibson and McDonnell, *Unfiltered*, 216–217.

55. Deneroff, "TV Wakes Up," 273.

56. Our editor Brian Duchaney helpfully reminded us that *The Simpsons* was developed by a group of people—producer James L. Brooks, writer Sam Simon, and artist/creator Matt Groening—despite the typical implication that Matt Groening was the central creative force of the show. Brooks assiduously shielded the show's script writers from network meddling, much as Bakshi insulated his artist writers.

57. Miller, "Fine Tooning," 65.

58. Komorowski, *Sick Little Monkeys*, 110–111, 152.

59. "I wasn't after a box office... I was after what I wanted to make." Ralph Bakshi, question and answer session, Comic-Con, Dallas, TX, October 20, 2012, 10:34, https://www.youtube.com/watch?v=K8B1Ex_1T6k.

60. Of all of Kricfalusi's works, his *Ren &Stimpy: Adult Party Cartoon* (2003; Spumco/MTV Networks) is a controversial and short-lived television cartoon that is among the farthest beyond the pale.

61. "Lange, "Disturbing Secret." A 2020 documentary wades into this controversy, interviewing Kricfalusi and a once-underage victim, Robyn Byrd. However, some have critiqued how the film appears to accept John K.'s characterization of these events. Thad Komorowski, *"Happy Happy Joy Joy: The Ren & Stimpy Story* (Review)," Forces of Geek, August 3, 2020, directed by Ron Cicero and Kimo Easterwood, produced by Ladies & Gentlemen, Inc. https://www.forcesofgeek.com/2020/08/happy-happy-joy-joy-the-ren-stimpy-story-review.html.

62. We respect the views of anyone who might criticize our decision to discuss John

Kricfalusi so prominently here. The legacy of John K. and *Ren & Stimpy* is very open for debate. We publish this chapter in a spirit of dialogue, and hope that it may contribute to broader discussions, such as about how to tell the histories of sexually abusive artists.

63. Thad Komorowski, "Continued reverence of John K.," Facebook, March 29, 2018, https://www.facebook.com/thadwell.

64. Beck, Review.

65. Early '90s' shows that advanced the artistic ambition of television animation in similarly radical ways include: *Tiny Toon Adventures* (1990–92), *Æon Flux* (1991–1995), *Batman: The Animated Series* (1992–95), *Beavis and Butt-Head* (1993–1997), and *Rocko's Modern Life* (1993–1996). As different as they may seem, *Tiny Toons* and *Batman* were both creatively helmed by *Mighty Mouse* alumni artists, who here too innovatively reinterpreted existing source material.

66. Wells, *Animation and America*, 12. In this book structured as a history of animation in the United States, Paul Wells develops an insightfully theoretical account of the nature of animation as metamorphosis.

67. *Mighty Mouse* directly lampoons Hanna-Barbera's foundational *Flintstones* and *Jetsons* cartoons in this episode.

68. Some may find it provocative of us to claim that the revolution of the creator-driven television cartoon solely began with this one, nearly forgotten Saturday morning cartoon. It is true that many factors led to the revival and reinvention of animation, including important feature films. But in understanding the history of television animation, we believe it is necessary to reckon with this cartoon's pivotal role.

69. Deneroff, "Ralph Bakshi & Fritz the Cat," 245.

70. At the risk of elevating some of these artists over others with considerable accomplishments, several are widely recognized for their large and ongoing influence on the animation industry: Vicky Jenson, Rich Moore, Jim Reardon, Andrew Stanton, and Bruce Timm. As a viewer of animation, you may wish to look up these animators and reflect on what their creative work has meant in your own life.

71. Bakshi, *Breaking the Mold*, 27:26.

72. Schoemer, "Twisted Humor." By 1992, ecstatic reviews were appearing in places like *The New York Times*. Journalist Karen Schoemer commented about an ostensible kids' cartoon that because of its "twisted humor," *Ren & Stimpy* "gains a cult."

Capitalization in a Half-Shell

*Multimedia, Cross-Demographic Marketing
of Animated and Comic Content
from Mickey to Michelangelo*

JARED BAHIR BROWSH

Nine decades after Mickey's whistle in *Steamboat Willie* signaled the beginning of the Golden Age of Animation, cartoons and their characters continue to hold a significant place in popular culture. The popularity of one mouse has led to a multi-billion dollar industry, but the establishment of the animation industry did not occur in a vacuum, and other media including literature, music, and especially comics were hugely influential in the development of the genre.

Later media like radio, television, and video games also have clearly influenced animation's growth and expansion throughout the 20th and early 21st centuries. The malleability, adaptability, and immortality of animated characters make them unique products in this capitalist society. Unlike live-action stars, who are bound by space, time, and their own self-image, animated characters have the flexibility to appear across various media, cultures, and geographic borders. As a result, multimedia considerations are commonplace in animation as characters are developed and marketed within this revenue-driven environment.[1]

This chapter examines major animated characters of the twentieth century to better understand how multimedia marketing strategies have evolved, using animation, comics, and popular culture phenomena to identify approaches by media companies that utilize different media to reach audiences across demographics featuring the same characters or properties. The later portions of this chapter examine franchises that transformed the development and marketing of animation as case studies before cable, the Internet, and the rapid growth of general audience animation since the early 1990s changed the media environment forever. *The Simpsons* is one of the most popular current examples of this strategy utilizing animation, adult humor and satire, merchandising, comics, and content across other media (like video games, film, and theme parks) to support a multibillion-dollar empire.[2]

The relationship between comics, both books and strips, and cartoons begins in the silent era of film when the animation industry was just beginning to establish itself as a profitable genre in the emerging media of motion pictures. Animation originally gained popularity through its exhibition during vaudeville shows. The spectacle of moving drawings was ideal interstitial material as vaudeville actors changed wardrobes and sets during a show. Like vaudeville skits, most of these animated shorts had only a few minutes to tell a story, so early animated films adopted many characteristics that made vaudeville shows popular.[3] While there were many positive attributes that these early cartoons adopted from vaudeville shows (such as music, slapstick comedy, and even dancing), animation during the Golden Age also embraced some of the derogatory features of vaudeville—most notably the blackface minstrelsy that strongly reinforced negative stereotypes of African Americans. Many of the visual and behavioral characteristics of early popular characters are strongly linked to African American stereotypes.[4]

Advancements in animation and motion picture technology presented opportunities for the industry to expand beyond one shot films with funny animals dancing to produce series with storylines that helped establish cartoons stars. The most popular animated star of the silent era, Felix the Cat, was an instant hit after debuting in the 1919 film *Feline Follies*. Felix's black fur and exaggerated white eyes clearly signify the influence of vaudeville blackface minstrelsy through which animation had originated. In fact, Sullivan modeled Felix after the pickaninny characters that appeared in literature and advertisements through the nineteenth and early twentieth century.[5] Animators like Felix's Pat Sullivan and Otto Messmer used African American–inspired characters' disobedience, rebellion, and lack of understanding about "normal" (aka white) social conventions as a source of comedic fodder for the audience, reinforcing dominant white ideologies. By the end of most films, characters like Felix were often punished for sinful behaviors; this most often was depicted through drinking, which was not only a vice but also illegal due to Prohibition. As with vaudevillian blackface minstrelsy, this cycle of rebellion and punishment as a source of entertainment recalls a similar cycle maintained by the oppression of African Americans reinforcing white supremacy and the social order.[6]

The cost of animation discouraged risk, so producers recognized what was popular among audiences and often imitated it. Due to Felix's quick rise to fame, racist blackface minstrelsy was imitated throughout the Golden Age of Animation from the late 1920s through World War II.[7] Several animators, like Walt Disney, Hugh Harmon, and Rudolf Ising successfully emulated this design, creating popular (yet derivative) characters for their studios. This history of imitation also led to animators to seek already established characters from other media to adapt. Comic strips were a natural source of inspiration for animators, since the drawn character already had a backstory and a loyal audience that could be attracted to theaters by seeing their favorite strip put into motion. Early adaptations of *Krazy Kat* and *Mutt and Jeff* actually predate Felix's debut, but animation was still developing in the mid–1910s, and these films merely copied the comic strips while adding slight motion to the drawings. Krazy Kat reappeared in 1925, redesigned by Bill Nolan to look and act more like Felix. Unlike the first series featuring Krazy Kat, Nolan created his own storylines for the feline rather than adapting George Herriman's stories from the comic. Krazy Kat cartoons were seen irregularly in theaters through 1940, with animators changing the design several times to reflect popular characters at the time. For example, in the 1930s, Kat was altered to look more like Mickey Mouse after the Disney creation exploded in popularity. The Krazy Kat cartoons not only exhibited the rampant imitation taking place throughout the insular animation industry, but also serve as an early example of the problems that arose related to artistic agency in cross-media adaptations of popular characters, which continues to be an issue in contemporary animation and media.[8]

Even after Mickey Mouse carried animation into its Golden Age, comics continued to have a strong connection with animation. Disney, like many animators, had gotten his start drawing comic strips and political cartoons for newspapers, but visually animation moved away from comics as producers created conventions and characteristics that helped make animation unique. This included sound, which helped animation truly take off in the 1930s. However, even with these technological advancements, comics and animation continued their close relationship. Sullivan and Messmer recognized the value of creating a multimedia presence for their character, and in 1923, Felix began to star in a comic strip, allowing audiences to keep up with the adventures of the feline in between new releases of his short films. Felix also began appearing in merchandise produced by German toy company Schoenhut, enabling children to connect with the character in a more tangible form. As animation and other media institutions quickly learned, the production of merchandise not only allowed audiences to form more intimate relationships with their favorite characters, but also presented more ancillary revenue sources for their content and characters beyond films and other media representations of these stars, increasing the value of the characters.[9]

Throughout the Golden Age of Animation, and beyond, Disney built his empire by maintaining complete control over his properties—including multimedia marketing of his characters. Much like Felix, Mickey and the other popular Disney characters began to appear in comic strips, books, watches, toys, and other merchandise soon after debuting on screen. Less than a year after *Steamboat Willie* premiered, at the urging of King Syndicates, Disney and his animator Ub Iwerks began working on a comic strip featuring the mouse. Many of the early Mickey Mouse strips adapted film storylines into comic form, but as the series went on, and Iwerks gave up control to Win Smith, then Floyd Gottfredson, who went on to draw the comic strip through the 1970s, original stories began to be featured in the comic.[10] At the same time, Mickey Mouse dolls and other merchandise appeared in stores, expanding upon the multimedia strategy utilized by Felix in previous years. Like Felix, early Mickey Mouse cartoons targeted general audiences, but the production of dolls and toys featuring the rodent were evidence of his appeal to younger audiences.[11]

Throughout the 1930s and early 1940s, numerous popular characters debuted through emerging animation studios; Donald Duck and Goofy from Disney; Porky Pig, Daffy Duck, and Bugs Bunny from Warner; Max Fleischer's Betty Boop; Walter Lantz's Woody Woodpecker; and William Hanna and Joseph Barbera's *Tom & Jerry* from MGM, among others. In addition, other comic adaptations, like Fleischer's adaptations of *Popeye* and *Superman*, also proved popular as animation grew in popularity before World War II. All of these characters developed a multimedia presence through merchandising, publication, and even recordings of film scripts and their scores. In 1940, Disney agreed to license his characters to Dell Comics, increasing the media presence of Mickey and his pals, and starting one of the longest running series in comic book history.[12]

In spite of the Great Depression, the animation industry was relatively prosperous leading up to World War II; however, America's entrance into the war changed the animation market both domestically and internationally. Animation studios that relied more on American audiences and had the backing of a larger studio, like Warner Bros., were not hit as hard by the closing of the European market as Disney, who had established an international presence in Europe and Asia before war broke out throughout the continents.[13] For example, *Snow White and the Seven Dwarfs* made over 60 percent of the revenues from the film's original run from markets outside of North America.[14] The animators' strike also decimated the independent studio's staff, forcing Disney to find other revenue sources. This included introducing Disney content to new markets, like the Global South through Franklin D. Roosevelt's Good Neighbor Policy, and producing government films and propaganda. This adaptability of animated and comic characters to serve various purposes, while conforming to various markets and needs of diverse audiences, made these and many future characters extremely valuable to the companies that controlled their rights. This also proved vital as the media environment faced major changes as a result of new technologies, government policy, and the continuous changes in audience tastes over time.[15]

One of the most well-regarded animated series of the Golden Age actually premiered less than three months before Japan's attack on Pearl Harbor, and was based on the character that introduced what many regard as the Golden Age of Comics, *Superman*. Jerry Siegel and Joe Shuster debuted their iconic superhero in 1938, and the first Fleischer adaptation of Clark Kent's adventures appeared in theaters on September 26, 1941.[16]

Audiences were drawn to the patriotic themes and high quality of the films featuring the superhero, and the series quickly became a hit, earning Fleischer Studios an Oscar nomination for the first film, *Superman*. Financial troubles and interpersonal conflict between the brothers, Max and Dave, forced them to give up the studio to Paramount, who renamed it Famous, quickly changing directions for the series from a comic adaptation to more propagandist series due to the United States' entry into World War II. Famous ended the series after 17 films, citing waning interest, but the high budget connected to the quality of the cartoons also motivated them to focus their energy on the *Little Lulu* series adapted from the comic created by Marge.[17]

The *Superman* radio serial provided an aural avenue to enjoy the superhero, similar to other comic-based serials like *Blondie*, bringing Superman into the home like the soundtracks, recordings, and toys did for other cartoon and comic characters. Superman did not return to theatrical shorts, but did inspire several imitations and parodies, most notably *Mighty Mouse*, which deconstructed the action/adventure genre at the time, and utilized his diminutive size to emphasize his role of the underdog, similar to the way Disney (Mickey), MGM (Jerry Mouse), and later, Warner (Speedy Gonzales) did with their rodent characters.[18]

Transitioning to Television

Unsurprisingly, Disney was the first animator to consider the role of television in the media landscape, ending his relationship with United Artists when they asked for the television rights to his cartoons in 1935, leading to an agreement with RKO to distribute his pictures, allowing him to maintain the television rights for his growing stable of content.[19] He was also the first studio head to truly profit from the medium when he agreed to produce content for ABC in exchange for financing Disney-land, which was also the name of the first series he produced for the network in 1954. Along with broadcasting old shorts featuring characters like Mickey Mouse, who only appeared sparingly in new films after 1940, *Disneyland* (which later became *The Wonderful World of Disney*), also previewed upcoming movies, theme park attractions, and featured original content made just for television.[20] Other animators imitated this strategy, most notably Walter Lantz, who adapted his most popular character for television, creating *The Woody Woodpecker Show*.[21]

Finding revenue outside of theaters became more integral after the *United States v. Paramount* decision in 1948 banned studios from owning theaters, preventing these companies from selling films, and short films, in blocks to theaters, decreasing the market for cartoon shorts that played in between features that theaters were forced to exhibit. At the same time, the nascent television environment began to create new opportunities for animators. During the late 1940s and 1950s, MGM reissued the popular *Tom and Jerry* films to try to reduce budget deficits. These re-released films earned almost as much as new films, allowing MGM to cut back production of new animation. MGM completely shut down their animation studio in 1958, but the success of old *Tom and Jerry* shorts provided evidence that there was a market for animated shorts, particularly among young audiences.[22] The new medium offered opportunities to profit from these characters that could previously be seen only in theaters or through printed materials like books and comics. Also, unlike movie theaters, the television resided in the home, increasing the audience exposure to these films beyond when exhibitors decided to play them in theaters. This enabled motion picture visual content to enter the living room repetitively and without an admission fee, something radio, comics, theaters, or toys could not provide.

Throughout the 1950s, most of the animation studios continued to produce shorts, even as the market shrank. William Hanna and Joseph Barbera, however, saw television as an ideal market for new animation, not just retreads, of their theatrically-released films. Animated shorts had appeared on television earlier as a part of live action shows like *Howdy Doody*, but NBC was concerned whether a half hour animated program could attract a consistent audience, so they provided Hanna and Barbera with extremely limited funding for a new series. Even after MGM cut their budget, the duo typically received about $50,000 to produce each short for theaters, but NBC was only willing to commit $2,800 per episode for their new show. As a result, Hanna-Barbera had to figure out how to produce a quality show while significantly cutting corners in their process.[23] To stay within budget, Hanna-Barbera decided to focus on entertaining dialogue, jokes, and slapstick humor while using limited animation techniques. This reduced the drawings needed for their cartoons from 60 per foot of film to two. These techniques included drawing characters with collars so they only had to animate scenes from the neck up, frequent long close-ups on the characters, and drawing broad scenes and realistic backgrounds that could distract from the limited movement and could be used repeatedly across their shows.[24]

Even with these limitations, Hanna-Barbera helped establish an animation market where a television program could be the center of the franchise. Adaptations from other media continued to play a large role in animation, but by the late 1950s, the characters and content created specifically for television became the origin of such franchises. Shows like *The Flintstones* and *Top Cat* (essentially reworked from *The Honeymooners* and *Sgt Bilko*, respectively) were the source material for adaptations and merchandising, establishing television as a viable medium to introduce new animated characters, while also continuing its role as a place to feature or reintroduce characters from comics, literature, and film. Hanna-Barbera had worked with NBC to develop their first program, *The Ruff and Reddy Show*, which featured Hanna-Barbera animation wrapped around old Columbia Pictures animated shorts. The cartoons were introduced by a live-action host against the wishes of the animation studio, since NBC did not think a show that was completely animated could work.[25]

Partially due to conflicts experienced with NBC, Hanna-Barbera helped popularize the use of syndication to distribute animated content on television, a strategy that became increasingly important in television animation in the 1970s and 1980s. *The Ruff and Reddy Show* struggled its first year partially due to the fact it was scheduled against more established children's programs on the other networks, but its audience grew by 1958, providing evidence that television animation could work, motivating them to pursue other projects.[26] The series clearly targeted children and Hanna-Barbera wanted to attract a more general audience, so they created *The Huckleberry Hound Show* and *The Quick Draw McGraw Show*, selling both directly into syndication, realizing that without the network, they had more freedom to produce the content they wanted.

Eventually, Hanna-Barbera produced *The Flintstones* and *The Jetsons* through ABC, but they experienced interference by the network, particularly on *The Flintstones*, which they felt diminished the quality of the show over time. After the landmark program's second season, ABC wanted to increase merchandising opportunities, so they convinced the studio to introduce a pregnancy storyline and a child, and the show developed a much younger tone—even dropping sponsor Winston Cigarettes. Ratings dropped, but the transition did enable them to move *The Flintstones* to Saturday morning fairly easily after the series initial six season run.[27] The funding for these syndicated programs came from sponsors like Kellogg's, but as their series grew in popularity, they were able to supplement production costs through merchandising.[28] In fact, both *The Magilla Gorilla Show* and *The Peter Potamus Show* were both sponsored by Ideal Toys, combining the source of these two revenue streams.[29]

The growth of the television animation market spearheaded by Hanna-Barbera helped pull most animated content out of the theater, aside from the occasional select shorts and feature films produced by Disney. Also, between the fact that children bought most of the merchandise and the establishment of Saturday morning as a haven for children's animation, Hanna-Barbera began targeting younger audiences almost exclusively as networks showed little interest in prime time animation. Hanna-Barbera was much less discerning than Disney about how their characters were used, so products featuring Hanna-Barbera characters of variable quality inundated the market, increasing the presence of the dozens of characters they introduced throughout their peak from the 1960s through the 1980s. Over this time, some of Hanna-Barbera's most popular shows were adaptations of comic series, including the *Fantastic Four, Josie and the Pussycats, and Super Friends* (featuring members of the Justice League of America), *Popeye,* and *The Smurfs.*[30]

Other studios, like Warner and Filmation, also contributed to the expansion of Saturday morning, making it the ideal place for advertisers to target children with toys, cereals, and other merchandise, many of which had licenses with the cartoons during which they advertised. By the late 1960s, Action for Children's Television (ACT) began lobbying to limit or eliminate all advertising during children's programming and animation after witnessing the host of the Boston version of *Romper Room* advertising toys during the program. ACT felt that advertisers were taking advantage of children due to their perceived inability to tell the difference between the program and the commercials.[31]

These battles between the networks, studios, advertisers, and parents' groups like ACT continued through the 1970s and the early 1980s, before Ronald Reagan and FCC chair Mark Fowler began deregulating the media while animation producers found ways to work around the restrictions. One of these included barter syndication that exchanged airtime for the broadcasting rights to the show, allowing the program producers to solicit their own advertising and create their own content without network interference. It also introduced an era of toy-based shows that appeared throughout the 1980s.[32] Toy-inspired animated shows were not a completely new concept, as *Hot Wheels* ran on Saturday morning between 1969 and 1971, but complaints from both parents' groups and other toy manufacturers helped push it off the air, since they saw the show as a program-length advertisement for Mattel's line of miniature cars.[33] The lack of regulations surrounding syndication created an environment where several toy-lines were either inspired by or were produced in conjunction with the development of the television program. Rather than just licensing the rights to toys connected to the show, the studios, toy manufacturers, and other media entities worked together to make sure the storylines matched up with the merchandise, and often, but not always, the other media properties.[34]

Multimedia Marketing Across Demographics

As the menu of streaming platforms and digital media grows, there is an increasing number of channels to distribute content both old and new. Popular franchises and properties are being revitalized, providing audiences with more access than ever before to media featuring their favorite characters. Nostalgia and emotional connection to this content has led owners of this media to attempt to attract consumers across various age demographics. Some, like Hanna-Barbera/Warner Bros. Discovery's *The Powerpuff Girls* or Disney's *Phineas and Ferb,* attempt to attract their original audiences in reboots with new content while others, like the upcoming *Jellystone!* aim to attract new audiences based on familiarity with their characters. This cross-demographic marketing is taken further when considering that several of the Hanna-Barbera (now Warner Bros. Discovery) characters featured in *Jellystone!* starred in adult comics through their corporate sibling, DC comics. As audiences are fragmented through increasingly available content, the desire to reach larger audiences across demographics and different media to expand their market reach will only increase in the future.[35]

Similar to animators like Disney and Warner, toy companies recognized comics as another tool to disseminate their characters and content. The multimedia presence of many of these characters not only increased their visibility, but it created opportunities to target different audiences and demographics through the same franchises. Although some of the Dell Comics series based on the Warner Bros. cartoon characters had less mature themes than the animated films from which they were adapted, one of the first franchises to target different demographics with a comic and animated television content was *Peanuts.* Charles Schulz's comic strip had a much more mature, existential tone from its debut through its peak during the 1960s than the animated advertisements during *The Ford Show* that led to the first *Peanuts* special, the award-winning *A Charlie Brown Christmas,* both of which were clearly less mature or complex than the source material.

The popularity of the Christmas special, and subsequent productions featuring the *Peanuts* gang, led Schulz to adjust the comic strip to create stories that were more appropriate for the young audience that expected the characters to act the same as their animated counterparts, exemplifying how audience considerations from one medium can influence content in other media connected to a franchise. The fact that the Christmas special is now considered a holiday classic and the jazz song "Linus and Lucy" continues to be in rotation during the Christmas season has guaranteed the gang's visibility more than five decades.[36]

Hanna-Barbera and DC Comics notably utilized this ability in the development and production of the several iterations of the popular *Super Friends* franchise, which aired on Saturday morning from 1973 to 1986. Due to concerns about violence, and the younger Saturday morning audience, Hanna-Barbera toned down the content from the source material—comics featuring Superman, Batman, Wonder Woman, and the other Justice League superheroes. The animation studio also created three new characters specifically for the animated series, Wendy, Marvin, and Wonder Dog, none of which had any powers (although Marvin did wear a costume and tried to fly once). Wonder Dog spoke in a manner similar to Scooby-Doo, a fact no one questions throughout his appearance in early versions of the series.[37] The three characters were utilized to both connect to the younger audience and to introduce pro-social or educational messages.[38] When the series was rebooted in 1977, the Wonder Twins and their pet monkey Gleek, the first Justice League superheroes to debut through the animated series, replaced Wendy, Marvin, and Wonder Dog. The Wonder Twins were later introduced to the DC Comic Universe through the *Super Friends* comic before transitioning to other comic series, like *Extreme Justice*.[39]

The presence of these characters in an animated program helped familiarize a younger audience to the DC characters, not only opening up more merchandising opportunities by attracting a younger market, but also leading this animation audience to become consumers of the comics featuring these characters. Hanna-Barbera and Marvel also employed a similar strategy in the production of the less popular *Fantastic Four*, which ran from 1967 to 1970. As this series grew in popularity, DC developed a comic based on the cartoon to further profit from the property and introduce this younger audience to comics through these characters and the cartoon series, which had simpler plots than the original comic series.[40] DC would loosely link the *Super Friends'* universe with the continuity of the comics featuring the same characters, but the focus on the younger audience and connections with the TV series limited these opportunities. One of the lasting legacies of the television series was the introduction of the Hall of Justice, which DC officially introduced into their Justice League comics in 2007.[41]

Hanna-Barbera eventually became a subsidiary of Warner after the Turner-Time Warner merger in 1996.[42] Under Turner and then Warner, older Hanna-Barbera animated programs like *The Flintstones* and *Top Cat* appeared on Cartoon Network beginning with the cable channel's debut in 1992. The ownership of these properties also led to new programs and other media featuring these characters. This included two shorts produced by John Kricfalusi of *Ren & Stimpy* fame that took a more mature approach to the Yogi Bear franchise. The most enduring media to emerge from this approach were two series that deconstructed Hanna-Barbera animation from the 1960s and 1970s, *Space Ghost Coast to Coast* and *Sealab 2021*. These series helped inspire and launch the programming block *Adult Swim*, which was later recognized as a network by Nielsen similar to *Nick at Nite*, due to the fact it courted an older audience than its daytime companion.[43]

Toys Take Control

As the *Super Friends* entered syndication after ABC cancelled the series in 1983, the franchise had to compete with popular toy-inspired series that were growing in popularity. *The Masters of the Universe* debuted as a toy line in 1981, and throughout its development and release, Mattel wanted to ensure that it had a multimedia presence. The toy line and its backstories were developed in conjunction with television animator Filmation to ensure the future television show matched the line. The original toys also included mini-comics revealing the origin story for the characters, and by November 1982, Marvel began production on a limited comic series based on the characters. After the toy line proved to be popular, Mattel and Filmation pitched the television show to ABC, which rejected the idea based on concerns that the show was a half hour advertisement for a toy line.[44] Mattel and Filmation continued developing the series, instead selling it directly into syndication in 1983, setting up a model for the other toy-inspired programs that succeeded it throughout the 1980s. *He-Man and the Masters of the Universe* became one of the iconic programs of 1980s animation, and a future cult classic, but the comics never came close to the success of the animated series. The limited series produced by DC from 1982 to 1983 was met with lukewarm reception, even after DC tried to merge the *Masters of the Universe* with *Superman* through the *DC Comics Presents* series. *He-Man* left the comic world until 1986 when Marvel picked up the series under its Star imprint, targeting younger comic readers. During this time, Mattel produced a *He-Man* video game through their Intellivision division, utilizing the emerging home game market as another avenue to promote their character while giving the player some control and agency of the popular character, increasing their connection with the franchise. The animated series had actually ended production in 1985, after 65 episodes, the minimum episodes required for second-run syndication, but reruns still appeared in various markets before the USA Network purchased syndication rights in 1988. The Marvel Star comic featured many of the newer characters and vehicles that debuted in the toy line after the series' cancellation and in 1987 adapted the live-action movie, *Masters of the Universe* starring Dolph Lundgren into a one-shot double length issue. After the fourteen-issue Marvel run ended in 1988, *He-Man* disappeared from American comics until 2002, hoping to capitalize on the growing nostalgia among the audience of the original productions. The production and marketing model for *He-Man* was emulated numerous times by other toy companies and media producers.[45]

As *He-Man* was growing in popularity, providing Mattel with another hit toy, Hasbro began working with Marvel, Sunbow Productions, and Toei Animation to employ a multimedia strategy to revitalize one of their most famous action figures, G.I. Joe. The three-prong strategy to promote G.I. Joe included toys, comics, and an animated series. In 1982, Hasbro relaunched the G.I. Joe line of toys under the name *G.I. Joe: A Real American Hero* at the same time Marvel premiered a comic series of the same name. Like the *Star Wars* line that revolutionized the action figure industry, the new G.I. Joe figures were 3.75 inch, making them cheaper to purchase and easier to collect. This also enabled users to reenact storylines from the show through the use of larger and more expensive vehicles and playsets.[46] In 1983, the first *G.I. Joe* five-part animated mini-series debuted in syndication and was followed by another mini-series in 1984. The success of both mini-series led to the development of a full series that debuted in 1985.

As with *He-Man*, *G.I. Joe* introduced vehicles, characters, and locations which were emulated in toy form. Marvel, Sunbow, Hasbro, and Toei produced 55 episodes during this season, bringing the total episode count to 65 including the 10 mini-series episodes, producing enough episodes to join *He-Man* in the second-run syndication market. Unlike *He-Man*, however, the comic series proved to be a big success, leading to a twelve-year run, one of the longest for a comic series connected to a toy line. A characteristic that made the comic so popular was the fact that it diverged from the animated series, taking a more serious, realistic tone, focusing on the complicated pasts of the Joes and their enemy, Cobra.[47] Similar to the way the *Super Friends* targeted a younger audience while the comics featuring the Justice League and its members were meant for older teens and adults, *G.I. Joe* was able to tap into multiple demographics by attracting children and pre-teens with the cartoon and older comic readers with the more mature storylines in the Marvel series. Hasbro used the commercials for the Marvel comic as a way to also advertise the toy line, working around regulations that limited commercial content for toys connected to the animated series to a few seconds and required these commercials to feature actual children playing with the toys, a restriction that did not apply to comics.[48]

The 1987 film *G.I. Joe: The Movie* had a darker tone than the series; similar to the comic, but was released straight to video after *Transformers: The Movie* bombed at the box office. The film was included in the *G.I. Joe: A Real American Hero* syndication package as a five-part mini-series. DiC developed another G.I. Joe series that continued where the Sunbow/Marvel series left off, but proved less popular and was cancelled after 44 episodes. Unlike Mattel, Hasbro did not have an electronic games division, but G.I. Joe still made his video game debut in 1983 in *G.I. Joe: Cobra Strike* for the Atari 2600, which had the same title as the first mini-series that introduced the animated characters. In spite of this, *G.I. Joe: A Real American Hero* remained in the public eye through 1994, when the comic series ended and Hasbro decided to revamp the toy line.[49]

Numerous companies and production studios copied this strategy. Hasbro, Sunbow, Marvel, and Toei teamed up again to produce *Transformers*, which adapted several Japanese productions and toy lines for the American market, and achieved similar success to *G.I. Joe*.[50]

As with *G.I. Joe* Marvel produced a comic, which was originally conceived as a four-part limited series, but the run was soon expanded after the mini-series proved popular, resulting in 80 published issues between 1984 and 1991. Unlike *G.I. Joe* where the comic book is considered by many as the source of the canon, the *Transformers* comic was less dark and was more similar to the TV series that targeted a child audience.[51] Hasbro also adapted their *My Little Pony* line of toys into a syndicated set of special—and then a series starting in 1984—to try to capitalize on the young girl audience the same way their other series targeted boy toy consumers.[52] Hasbro, however, did not partner with Marvel or any other comic producer to create a companion comic book for the series, assuming (incorrectly) that young girls did not read comics.[53]

Hanna-Barbera, with their experience in cartoon production and licensing, also hoped to employ the multi-prong franchise marketing strategy. Like Marvel would later do with *Transformers*, Hanna-Barbera tapped an international toy property, bringing a toy-inspired series to Saturday morning and network television. The animation studio partnered with NBC and Peyo to adapt *The Smurfs* from the Belgian comic book after the toy line based on the characters was an instant hit in North America in the late 1970s. The Emmy Award-winning series not only premiered in 1981, preceding *He-Man* by two years but also was in production for much longer, partially due to the support and regular scheduling by NBC. *The Smurfs* ran for nine seasons and 256 episodes, not including seven specials, eventually ending in 1989 after NBC tried to reboot the show. The network cancelled the series to make room for a weekend version of *Today*, and live-action programming for pre-teens that included *Saved by the Bell*.[54] *The Smurfs* was able to avoid the same scrutiny that was faced *He-Man* and *G.I. Joe* as a fantasy-comedy show featuring small blue humanlike creatures. Unlike *He-Man* and *G.I. Joe*, *The Smurfs'* production was overseen by NBC and featured dialogic and light slapstick humor, instead of the violent syndicated action/adventure that had less interference from censors and the networks. Also, unlike the Mattel and Hasbro productions, it did not blatantly target either girls or boys, avoiding gender-based criticism of shows like *G.I. Joe*.[55]

As these toy-based series changed the television animation landscape, a comic from an independent publisher premiered in 1984 that would not only help the comic industry transition into a new era, but also inspired one of the most profitable popular culture phenomena of the late 1980s and 1990s. The producers and marketers for the franchise recognized the mistakes of the predecessors, maximizing success over a relatively short period of time. In 1983, Kevin Eastman, Peter Laird, and other artists formed Mirage Studios and the next year they debuted *Teenage Mutant Ninja Turtles* at a convention in their home state of New Hampshire. The black-and-white issue was an instant hit in the comic community, inspiring several imitations throughout the 1980s. *Teenage Mutant Ninja Turtles* was originally a single-issue parody of Marvel's *The New Mutants* and *Daredevil*, DC's *Ronin* and *Cerebus*, but its initial success led Eastman and Laird to continue the series.[56] Mark Freedman, who helped Hanna-Barbera properties like *The Flintstones* and *The Jetsons* build their merchandising empires, represented the publisher and approached the toy-marker Playmates about producing action figures based on the characters in the comic. Freedman hoped to tap into the cult following of the comic and the popularity of action figures like Kenner's *Superman* and *Star Wars* lines. After Mattel and Hasbro's success with their recent toy line-inspired series, Playmates required a deal to develop an animated mini-series before they agreed to produce the toys, since they were concerned that the cult audience was not big enough to warrant a toy line.[57]

After the five-part miniseries premiered in 1987, Playmates released the first set of toys in 1988. Like Hanna-Barbera's *Super Friends*, the

Teenage Mutant Ninja Turtles animated series took a much lighter tone than its comic counterpart, partially due to Mirage not having any input into the cartoon.[58] The series focused on humor and pizza, rather than the more mature themes of its source material, even replacing the human foot soldiers with robots in the animated series to avoid portraying human deaths. The cartoon, and the toy line, became huge mainstream hits, selling over $1 billion in merchandise by 1992. CBS picked up the previously syndicated series to help revitalize its Saturday morning lineup, before expanding broadcasts to weekday afternoons due to the overwhelming popularity of the anthropomorphic turtles. By 1989, two popular video games, an arcade game and a home console game for the Nintendo Entertainment System (NES), were also released. The NES game was more closely related to the comic, featuring artwork produced by Eastman and Laird while the arcade game was based on the animated series. By 1994, the *Teenage Mutant Ninja Turtles* inspired 19 different video games across various platforms.[59]

As CBS prepared to bring the *Turtles* to Saturday morning, an independent film featuring the origin story of the superheroes was released on March 30, 1990. Produced on a budget of $13.5 million by Golden Harvest, a Hong Kong–based production company, the film struggled to find a distributor of the movie after *Masters of the Universe* bombed in 1987. New Line Cinema, which at the time was a small film distributor of B movies, agreed to take on the responsibility halfway through production. The popularity of the toys, television, and comic helped *Teenage Mutant Ninja Turtles* become one of the highest grossing independent films of all time earning over $200 million at the box office. Two sequels followed the hit film, in 1991 and 1993, the second of which partially based off the popular arcade game, *Teenage Mutant Ninja Turtles: Turtles in Time*. No film adaptation featuring the superheroes achieved the same box office success of the first film, including the CGI *TMNT* (2007), until *Teenage Mutant Ninja Turtles* in 2014.[60]

Even though earlier franchises successfully utilized a multi-prong, multimedia, and intra-demographic marketing strategy before the *Teenage Mutant Ninja Turtles*, no franchise had found so much success in so many media at the same time. However, by the mid–1990s there was some evidence of overexposure as future iterations of the *Turtles* declined in popularity, including a live-action series on FOX, *Ninja Turtles: The Next Mutation* (1997) was adapted from the feature films and was produced by Saban Entertainment, who developed *Mighty Morphin Power Rangers* for the same network in 1993. In 2003, 4Kids Entertainment, who brought the extremely popular *Pokémon* series to America a year after the video game was released, began production of a new series in conjunction with Mirage Studios. With the publisher's involvement, *Teenage Mutant Ninja Turtles* was darker, edgier, and closer to the source material than the original series. This helped revitalize the franchise leading to a Nickelodeon series with the same name in 2012 after the children's network acquired the rights to the property. The previously mentioned Michael Bay produced film was released two years later, with a sequel *Teenage Mutant Ninja Turtles: Out of the Shadows in 2016*.[61] In 2018, Nickelodeon debuted *The Rise of the Teenage Mutant Ninja Turtles,* a lighter series with visuals inspired by anime. The Turtles also continued their connections with comics with the crossover *Batman vs. Teenage Mutant Ninja Turtles* co-produced by Warner Bros., DC Entertainment, and Nickelodeon in 2019. Kevin Eastman and Peter Laird also returned to the comic series in 2020 with the release of *Teenage Mutant Ninja Turtles: The Last Ronin* mini-series. The series has been adapted into a video game with rumors that a live-action series based on the new comic is being developed possibly for the streaming platform Paramount+.[62]

Pixelated Cartoons

While the 1980s television environment evolved, another media was also gaining traction amongst children and families. Video arcades exploded in popularity as games improved in terms of their visual quality, depth, and the player's ability to control the on-screen action. Technological advances enabled the production of smaller consoles that brought many popular games, like *Pong, Space Invaders*, and *Pac-Man* from arcades into the home. Video game developers and animation producers recognized this new source for material. At the same time, as many toy-based shows entered the animation market, Hanna-Barbera tried to profit off of the video game trend, developing *Pac-Man* in 1982 while their sister company, Ruby-Spears, debuted *Saturday Supercade* featuring segments starring video game characters like *Frogger, Donkey Kong*, and *Q*Bert*, in 1983. Although animation producers had limited success with video game-based programs through the 1980s, this trend helped introduce another medium to promote franchises and characters with animated characters like *Tom and Jerry*, the *Pink Panther*, and *Popeye* found their way into video games.[63] In fact, toy-based programs like *He-Man and the Masters of the Universe* and *Transformers* were some of the first shows to be adapted for straight-to-console video games, which also presented opportunities for cross-product promotion by toy companies since Mattel, who produced the *He-Man* toys and TV series, also manufactured video games and the Intellivision console.[64]

The multi-pronged marketing strategy that included animation was profitable for numerous works adapted from comics, films, television series, and even toys but adaptations involving video games continued to find limited success outside their pixelated environment. *Pac-Man* and *Saturday Supercade* struggled to find a consistent audience, partially due to the limited source material that often involved the title or "star" character chasing a single villain across a flat or side-scrolling 2D world. When Nintendo's success in the home console market helped popularize their flagship character, Mario, Nintendo joined with DiC and Saban Productions to produce a cartoon based on the plumber and another popular Nintendo property, *Zelda*. Even after *The Super Mario Super Show* only achieved moderate success in syndication, Lightmotive decided to discuss a film adaptation with Nintendo, leading to the production of *Super Mario Brothers*, which was co-produced with Walt Disney's Hollywood Pictures. The film was a historic flop, leading to even further hesitation from the film industry about adapting non-violent video games. Action series like *Street Fighter* and *Resident Evil* did have moderate box office success, the latter leading to a six-film series.[65]

When Sega Genesis debuted in America in 1989, the console struggled to compete with NES even though it featured better graphics and more responsive game play than its main competitor. NES continued to hold the rights to most of the popular arcade series, and Sega sales slumped even as they contracted celebrities like John Madden and Michael Jackson to help improve sales at the urging of former Atari Electronics Division President Steve Katz. Katz was quickly replaced by former Mattel executive Tom Kalinske as CEO of Sega of America due to low sales of the console outside of Japan. Kalinske urged Sega to cut the cost on their system while developing a flagship series and character. This manifested itself when *Sonic the Hedgehog* made his American debut in 1990, combining attributes from superhero media and past animated characters. Sonic's super speed and his mission to save the forest, rather than a single princess, separated him from Mario, while his identity as a rodent mirrored strategies employed by the producers of Mickey Mouse, Mighty Mouse, and Speedy Gonzales to use the typically diminutive nature of a rodent to present Sonic as an underdog fighting a larger enemy. *Sonic the Hedgehog* was hugely popular and the success of the game and its sequels helped Sega eventually surpass both Nintendo consoles, NES and the 16-bit Super Nintendo, in total sales by 1992, with Sonic becoming Sega's official mascot.[66]

Sonic's popularity and mainstream success led DiC, which developed the Mario animated series, and Sega to produce two series in 1993: *The Adventures of Sonic the Hedgehog* and *Sonic the Hedgehog*. The first series was sold directly into syndication, appearing on weekday afternoons in most major markets. DiC produced 65 episodes, enabling them to sell it into second-run syndication after the first season. *The Adventures of Sonic the Hedgehog* was lighter than its companion series, featuring relatively witty dialogue, slapstick humor, and very little character development, partially due to the lack of narrative background in its source material. *Sonic the Hedgehog*, which appeared on ABC Saturday morning for two seasons, was edgier and more violent than the syndicated version. The series only lasted for 26 episodes, but it did inspire a video game, *Sonic Spinball,* and a series produced by Archie Comics.[67]

In November 1992, Archie published a four-part mini-series based on the video game franchise, and after it achieved moderate success for the publisher named after its most popular creation, a full series debuted in May 1993. The series was originally based on the video game, creating an origin for the speedy hedgehog, but later drew storylines from other sources including the animated series, creating more significant backstories for Sonic, Tails, and the other characters from the video game and animated series. This was something the Mario properties struggled to do convincingly in the various productions starring the plumber and his brother, Luigi. The *Sonic the Hedgehog* comic series would not only become the biggest series for the company not associated with their namesake, but it is the longest running series based on a video game franchise in comic history.[68] No Sonic animated series matched the popularity or longevity of the comic, including *Sonic Underground* connected with the 3D video game *Sonic Adventure,* but the Japanese import *Sonic X* did achieve some success in the American market.

The anime spawned another Sonic comic series of the same name, which, like its predecessor, began as a limited series but was expanded to forty issues due to demand, eventually leading to the current *Sonic Universe* comic series. The spin-off computer animated series, *Sonic Boom* aired on Cartoon Network after debuting in the fall of 2014. Just days after the premiere of the *Sonic Boom* series, Nintendo released separate games for Wii U and 3DS that actually served as prequels to the series, creating a multimedia storyline for Sonic and his friends. *Sonic Boom* lasted two seasons while Sega released a sequel to the 3DS game in 2016. Sonic has also achieved success in the mobile game market, with the 2013 game *Sonic Dash* downloaded over 100 million times on various mobile devices.[69] In February 2020, the feature film *Sonic the Hedgehog* premiered, earning over $300 million at the box office, making it the highest grossing film based on a video game passing another film based on a cross-media franchise, *Detective Pikachu,* with a sequel released in 2022 that made over $400 million at the box office.

Multimedia marketing strategies are now required when developing or revitalizing franchises. Various forms of animation and its cousin, comics, continue to be a major part of this strategy due to malleability, popularity, and character immortality seen in both the genre and medium. Although media companies have utilized multimedia strategies for nearly a century, franchises are being developed and acquired based on their ability to be adapted across a variety of platforms. Disney in particular has utilized this strategy in their acquisitions of Pixar, Marvel and the *Star Wars* franchise, incorporating them into their various networks and properties. The conglomerate also has the advantage of featuring these productions in the popular Disney theme parks, a medium few other media companies can fully utilize, although there is some concern over Disney's influence on these brands by passionate fan bases (as movies like *The Avengers* have shown). However, there are clear advantages to having a parent company with the resources to disseminate content across all available media, even if it does bring up questions of the negative effects of conglomeration and issues of control between a conglomerate and its many subsidiaries.

Conglomeration, profit maximization, and multimedia considerations continue to transform how content is developed and disseminated, presenting both new possibilities and limitations to the creation of media across various platforms. This strategy will only increase as streaming platforms like Disney+ and Warner Bros. Discovery's Max offer increasing opportunities to disseminate older series and films alongside new content through a medium directly controlled by these corporations.

Notes

1. Jason Brennan, "What the Mickey Mouse Club says about Capitalism" *Fortune,* June 19, 2014 http://fortune.com/2014/06/19/what-the-mickey-mouse-club-says-about-capitalism/.

2. Madeline Berg, "'The Simpsons' Signs Renewal Deal For The Record Books," *Forbes,* November 4, 2016, https://www.forbes.com/sites/maddieberg/2016/11/04/the-simpsons-signs-renewal-deal-for-the-record-books/#612cdf9c1b21.

3. Leonard Maltin, *Of Mice and Magic: A History of American Animated Cartoons* (New York: Penguin, 1987), 1–3.

4. Michael Barrier, *Hollywood Cartoons: American Animation in its Golden Age* (New York: Oxford University Press: 1999), 155; Nicholas Sammond, *Birth of an Industry: Blackface Minstrelsy and the Rise of American Animation.* Durham: Duke University Press, 2015.

5. Nicholas Sammond, "Who Dat Say Who Dat?" in *Funny Pictures: Animation and Comedy in the Hollywood Studio Era,* edited by Daniel Ira Goldmark and Charles Kell (Berkeley: University of California Press, 2011), 142.

6. *Ibid.,* 142–143.

7. Barrier, *Hollywood Cartoons,* 29.

8. Jochen Ecke, "Spatializing the Movie Screen: How Mainstream Cinema is Catching up on the Formal Potentialities of the Comic Book Page" in *Comics as the Nexus of Cultures: Essays on the Interplay of Media, Disciplines, and International Perspectives,* edited by Mark Berninger, Jochen Ecke, and Gideon Habercorn (Jefferson, NC: McFarland, 2010), 13.

9. Edward L. Palmer and Shalom M. Fisch, "The Beginnings of *Sesame Street* Research,"

"G" is for growing: Thirty years of research on children and Sesame Street edited by Shalom M. Fisch and Rosemarie T. Truglio (Mahwah, NJ: Lawrence Erlbaum Associates, 2001), 19.

10. "85 Years Ago Today, Mickey Mouse's Career Turned a Page," *D23*, https://d23.com/first-mickey-mouse-comic-strip/.

11. Jim Korkis, *The Book of Mouse: A Celebration of Walt Disney's Mickey Mouse,* New York: Theme Park Press, 2013.

12. Bradford W. Wright, *Comic Book Nation: The Transformation of Youth Culture in America* (Baltimore: Johns Hopkins University Press, 2001), 18.

13. Barrier, *Hollywood Cartoons,* 284–285.

14. Neal Gabler. *Walt Disney: The Triumph of the American Imagination.* (New York: Random House, 2007), 276–27.

15. Dale Adams. "Saludos Amigos: Hollywood and FDR's Good Neighbor Policy." *Quarterly Review of Film & Video* 24, no. 3 (2005): 289–290.

16. Maltin, *Of Mice and Magic,* 120–122.

17. *Ibid.,* 132. Famous/Paramount later created Little Audrey to avoid paying Marge royalties for adapting her creation.

18. Delfin Carbonell Basset, "Speedy Gonzales' Relationship with the Hispanic Community," *The Huffington Post* October 10, 2013, http://www.huffingtonpost.com/2013/10/03/speedy-gonzales-hispanic_n_4039787.html.

19. Keith Gluck, "The Genesis of Disney Television," *The Walt Disney Family Museum,* July 23, 2014, https://www.waltdisney.org/blog/genesis-disney-television.

20. Alison Alexander and James Owers, "The Economics of Children's Television," in *The Children's Television Community,* edited by J. Alison Bryant (Mahwah, NJ: Lawrence Erlbaum, 2007), 62–63.

21. Brennan, "What the Mickey Mouse Club says about Capitalism."

22. Jason Mittell, "The Great Saturday morning Exile," *Primetime Animation: Television Animation and American Culture,* edited by Carol A. Stabile and Mark Harrison (New York: Routledge, 2003).

23. Leonard Maltin. "Interview with Joseph Barbera," *Archive of American Television.* Studio City, CA. February 26, 1997 accessed April 29, 2014 from www.emmytvlegends.org/interviews/people/joseph-barbera.

24. Maltin, *Of Mice and Magic,* 305–306.

25. Hal Erickson, *Television Cartoon Shows, An Illustrated Encyclopedia* 1949–1993 (Jefferson, NC: McFarland, 1995), 423–424.

26. *Ibid.*

27. Jerry Beck, *The Flintstones: The Official Guide to the Cartoon Series* (New York: Running Press, 2011), 11.

28. Joseph Barbera, *My Life in 'Toons: From Flatbush to Bedrock in Under a Century.* (Nashville, TN: Turner Publishing, 1994), 71–75.

29. Erickson, *Television Cartoon Shows,* 522–523.

30. Maltin. "Interview with Joseph Barbera."

31. Mittel, "The Great Saturday morning Exile," 45–46.

32. Donna Mitroff and Rebecca Herr Stephenson, "The Television Tug-of-War: A Brief History of Children's Television Programming in the United States," in *The Children's Television Community,* edited by J. Alison Bryant (Mahwah, NJ: Lawrence Erlbaum, 2007), 15–23.

33. Erickson, *Television Cartoon Shows,* 255...The mediocre storylines did not help.

34. Alexander and Owers, "The Economics of Children's Television," 62–63.

35. Sonia Rao, "From Peacock to HBO Max, Here's What Every Major Streaming Service Can Offer You" *The Washington Post,* July 15, 2020, https://www.washingtonpost.com/arts-entertainment/2020/07/15/peacock-nbc-hbo-max-streaming-service-guide/.

36. Sarah Boxer, The Exemplary Narcissism of Snoopy, *The Atlantic,* November, 2015, http://www.theatlantic.com/magazine/archive/2015/11/the-exemplary-narcissism-of-snoopy/407827/.

37. Erickson, *Television Cartoon Shows,* 486–487.

38. Timothy Burke and Kevin Burke, *Saturday Morning Fever: Growing Up with Cartoon Culture* (New York: St. Martin's, 1999), 103.

39. Scott Beatty, "Extreme Justice", in *The DC Comics Encyclopedia*, edited by Alastair Dougall (New York: Dorling Kindersley, 2008), 117.

40. Erickson, *Television Cartoon Shows*, 486–487.

41. Anthony Couto, "Meanwhile... A History of the Justice League's Hall of Justice," *Comic Book.*

42. Mark Landler, "Turner to Merge into Time Warner, a $7.5 Billion Deal, *The New York Times,* September 23, 1995, from http://www.nytimes.com/1995/09/23/us/turner-to-merge-into-time-warner-a-7.5-billion-deal.html?pagewanted=all.

43. Bryan Menegus, "The History of Adult Swim's Rise to Greatness" *Sploid,* April 11, 2016. http://sploid.gizmodo.com/an-oral-history-of-adult-swim-1770248730.

44. Alexander and Owers.

45. Erickson.

46. Karen J. Hall, "A Soldier's Body: GI Joe, Hasbro's Great American Hero, and the Symptoms of Empire, *Journal of Popular Culture* 38, no. 1 (2004): 34–54, here 37.

47. Christopher Norlund, "Imagining Terrorists Before Sept. 11: Marvel's *GI Joe* Comic Books, 1982–1994, *ImageTexT,* vol. 3, no. 1 (2006).

48. Rob Lammie, "The History of G.I. Joe: A Real American Hero, *Mental Floss,* July 4, 2015, http://mentalfloss.com/article/62636/history-gi-joe-real-american-hero.

49. Joe Latchem, "Going Retro," *Home Media Magazine,* July 20, 2009, http://www.homemediamagazine.com/tv-dvd/going%E2%80%89retro-16390.

50. Cathleen Schein, "From Lassie to Pee-Wee," *The New York Times,* October 30, 1988, http://www.nytimes.com/1988/10/30/magazine/from-lassie-to-pee-wee.html?scp=7&sq=The%20Real%20Ghostbusters&st=cse&pagewanted=2.

51. Alex Kurtzman, "The History of Transformers on TV," *IGN,* June 27, 2011, http://www.ign.com/articles/2011/06/27/the-history-of-transformers-on-tv.

52. B. Carol Eaton and Joseph R. Dominick, "Product-Related Programming and Children's TV: A Product Analysis," *Journalism and Mass Communication Quarterly* 68, nos. 1–2 (1991): 67–75, here 70–71.

53. Wright, *Comic Book Nation,* 57.

54. Erickson, *Television Cartoon Shows,* 457–460.

55. Katia Perea, "Power Girls Before Girl Power: 1980's Toy-Based Girl Cartoons," *Refractory: A Journal of Entertainment Media,* vol. 22 (2013).

56. Wright, *Comic Book Nation,* 279.

57. Rob Lammie, "The Complete History of the Teenage Mutant Ninja Turtles," *Mental Floss,* June 27, 2015, http://mentalfloss.com/article/30862/complete-history-teenage-mutant-ninja-turtles.

58. Janice C. Simpson, "Show Business: Lean, Green and on the Screen." *Time,* April 2, 1990 http://content.time.com/time/magazine/article/0,9171,969727-2,00.html#ixzz0h91fn Brj.

59. Rob Lammie, "The Complete History of the Teenage Mutant Ninja Turtles."

60. Nancy Carlsson-Paige and Diane Levin, "The Subversion of Healthy Development and Play: Teacher's Reactions to Teenage Mutant Ninja Turtles," *Day Care and Early Education,* vol. 19, no. 2 (1991): 14–20, here 15.

61. Rob Lammie, "The Complete History of the Teenage Mutant Ninja Turtles."

62. Seth McDonald, "UPDATE: A New Teenage Mutant Ninja Turtles Series NOT In Development At CBS All Access," *LRM Online,* June 24, 2020, https://lrmonline.com/news/a-new-teenage-mutant-ninja-turtles-series-is-in-development-at-cbs-all-acess/.

63. Hector Postigo, "Video Game Appropriation through Modifications," *Convergence: The International Journal of Research into New Media Technologies,* 14, no. 1 (2008): 64.

64. Martin Goodman, "Dr. Toon: When Reagan Met Optimus Prime," *Animation World Network,* October 12, 2010, http://www.awn.com/animationworld/dr-toon-when-reagan-met-optimus-prime.

65. Nathan Rabin, "Pixelated Case File #139: *Super Mario Brothers*," *A.V. Club,* June 10, 2009, http://www.avclub.com/article/pixelated-case-file-139-isuper-mario-bros-i-29032.

66. Steven L. Kent. *The Ultimate History of Video Games: The Story Behind the Craze that Touched our Lives and Changed the World*. (Roseville, California: Prima Publishing, 2001), 424–431.

67. Erickson, *Television Cartoon Shows*, 461–462.

68. "Sonic the Hedgehog enter Book of World Records." *Archie Comics*. July 7, 2007. https://web.archive.org/web/20080912135723/http://archie-blogs.archiecomics.com:80/sonic/2008/07/from_the_cuinness_book_of_worl.html.

69. Marc Petronille and William Audureau, *The History of Sonic the Hedgehog* (Richmond Hill, ON, CA: Udon Entertainment, 2013), 178–179.

"Someone's coming! Act natural"

Visions of Animated Childhood in 1990s America

JANE BATKIN

The 1990s represented more than the closure of one century and the dawn of the next; America reflected on its successes and catastrophes at this time while simultaneously embracing the new. Within this final decade, seen by many as one that would naturally contrast with the hedonistic eighties as a time of conservatism, fracture lines occurred that led to identity being seen as something difficult to sustain, specifically, generational identity.[1] The cultural glue of the shared television experience was also giving way with the rise of cable. Network channels catered to individual tastes and became increasingly niche in the '90s as a new wave of cartoons launched their assault on the public, from dysfunctional teens Beavis and Butt-Head, the violent slapstick of the neighborhood "dorks" Ed, Edd, and Eddy, and Parker and Stone's troubled *South Park* child, eight-year-old narcissist Eric Cartman, who demanded: "respect my authoritah!" The animated child, during this era, emerged as a weapon of mass destruction on television, and as a representation of the anxieties of a nation battling with fractures in its own identity. The result was a rich tapestry of animated subversion, situated within suburbia, and, crucially, emanating from the specific viewpoint of the '90s child.

Childhood has always been a contested site, it morphs and transitions according to external events that impact upon it; Eric Claparède claimed that the mind of the child gives an impression of "appalling chaos"[2] while Jean Piaget believed that child logic was infinitely complex and something that was very much worth studying.[3] In the 1990s, childhood became both a space for innocence and vulnerability as well as a politically-charged weapon as the United States careered towards a new century. The animated television child reflected those fractures within politics, culture and society and became a figure of mischief, subverting establishment, family and suburbia, while simultaneously trying to find how to fit into its world. This chapter will explore the animated network child during this period, analyzing how Beavis, Butt-Head, the South Park boys, and the three Eds became representations of their time.

The 1990s, intended as a decade of austerity after one of money and power, became a time of technological change, of innovation, yet also of riots, war, the Storm of the Century and the Oklahoma City bombing. O.J. Simpson was acquitted of first-degree murder, President Clinton was impeached over a sex scandal and, in 1999, two teenagers murdered a teacher and twelve of their classmates at Columbine High School. Against this backdrop, through the fragmented cable networks of the time, the animated child found its voice and communicated vitally—through violence, satire and subversion—to the United States and the world.

Reflections of Childhood

Within the final decade of the twentieth century, there were cries about the loss of innocence as children began to grow up with access to a brand new digital world, particularly as accessibility quickly meant access to the *adult* world.[4] Neil Postman theorized about the disappearance of the child, at the time, through its "adultification,"[5] and childhood itself was perceived as becoming skewed as the new century dawned and technology veered onto the super-fast digital highway. How could children be protected with the rise of the Internet and the diversification offered by cable and network television? Schroeber suggests that American television reflected, and continues to reflect and refract, "images of childhood through the lens of adult fears and concerns as well as desires."[6] This was not solely a '90s phenomenon; such images of the child reflect back to the 1950s, with Carol Stabile theorizing that the McCarthy Era, in particular, heralded the "purging" of various culture industries. This meant that there was little progressivism in thinking about the American family and how it might be evolving.[7] U.S. television in the 1950s was dominated by patriarchal moral values, displayed in shows such as *Father Knows Best, Leave it to Beaver,* and *The Adventures of Ozzie and Harriet.*

Such warm-hearted but conservative sitcoms continued into the 1980s with *Family Ties* and *The Cosby Show,* indicating that the traditional family was the preferred trope to reflect American society. It was not until the late 1980s when shows like *Roseanne* and *Married ... with Children* emerged that the traditional view of the family began to be challenged, with what Michael Tueth calls "visions of dysfunctional family life," to subvert the original view.[8] While the children in *Father Knows*

Best appeared to be well-behaved and submissive, Tueth considers them to be confused about much of their parents' decision-making abilities. *Roseanne* revealed more complex issues of working-class family life, such as unemployment, alcohol and drug abuse, and unplanned pregnancies. The sitcom live action kids of the late '80s onwards began to vocalize their anxieties, misbehave and generally challenge authority, and the animated TV child would take this behavior to another level in the 1990s. The question of the image of childhood, however, firstly needs addressing, particularly the image of the American child as a metaphor for freedom and the pioneering spirit, in order for us to understand what happened in the final decade of the twentieth century, and why.

Jean Piaget originally carried out studies about children at L'Institut Rousseau in France in the early 1920s, where he observed its behavior and its self-absorption. He reflected that the child's mind seemed to operate on two different levels, or "looms": the lower level was made up of the wants and desires of the child, while the upper level was developed by the social environment that the child experienced over time.[9] Child logic, Piaget observed, was hugely complex. It involved collective monologues by the child who didn't care who its audience was, or indeed even if anyone was listening, and the point at which the child observed the world and found its place in the universe. Piaget realized that, at this point, the child assigned itself "a place as a thing among things" and made the transition from "chaos to cosmos."[10] The child begins to understand right from wrong, just as it understands how to place blame on others; it is an image of innocence and, conversely, a creature that is fully capable of reckless, mischievous behavior.

In *The American Child: A Cultural Studies Reader*, Caroline Levander and Carol Singley write that "the American nation, since its inception, has been identified with and imagined as a child."[11] They posit that the child is a construct as well as a biological fact, encoding an ever-evolving, complex logic of a group, that the child is not only born but made. The American child represents the pioneering spirit of the U.S and how it has been imagined and dissected for centuries; the image of the child, the authors argue, has been "seized upon" and promoted "as a force of resistance as well as innocent vulnerability."[12] In a sense, the child reflects the United States and its spirit of adventure; it embodies the "American Dream" and is viewed as the hope, as well as the spirit, of its nation. The contradictory view of the child as resisting as well as innocent makes sense here. The American child has grown up in literature and on screen, as a symbol of the complex individual and its struggles to survive.

Adding to this argument, Gillian Brown suggests that child's play is a sacred space within modern life. She reflects on psychologist William

James' Harvard lectures of 1892, entitled *Talks to Teachers*, in which he advised that "Living things ... moving things or things that savor of danger or of blood, that have a dramatic quality—these are the objects that are natively interesting to children, to the exclusion of almost anything else."[13] Brown quotes a boy's poem from a magazine in 1859, on how boys use humor to form friendships: "each has its private joke and cracks it regardless how the other takes it." Children's play in American culture, the author argues, is a hallmark about the principle of pleasure, over any other consequence, perhaps because boys at play were viewed as savages in the nineteenth century.

Brown also discusses the "strange and wild absorptions of boys"[14] at play and links this to American novelists such as Mark Twain, who captured childhood as a precarious, dangerous and essential time of one's life, particularly within *The Adventures of Tom Sawyer*. While children at play have been celebrated and analyzed globally (for example, Charles Dickens' writings on boyhood and the struggle for individuality), the American child has always been viewed as a different, individual creature because of the notions of liberty and pioneering spirit of the U.S. that tie themselves to any representations of its childhood. In the UK, Dickens' boys are victims of class, of poverty and grime and suffering; their goal was largely one of survival. In the U.S., boyhood in particular is celebrated as something that always prevails, because of its spirit of independence and adventure. The child is viewed as a relic at the heart of American society and its representation within film and television has been prolific, entertaining, and enlightening throughout the twentieth century.

Growing up in the last century for the American child meant an "immersion in the sights and sounds supplied by television," suggest George Comstock and Erica Sharrer.[15] The media universe became increasingly fragmented in the late '80s and into the '90s in particular; prior to this, the period between the 1950s to the 1980s represents a classic era of network television, with programs intent on creating as little offense as possible. The acronym LOP (least offense possible) was synonymous with the time and critics claimed that this led to "bland content."[16] Television remained inherently conservative in its offerings, but Michael Curtin and Jane Shattoc suggest that this lasted only until the Nixon administration, when he promoted the idea of cable in order to reduce the power that the major networks had on informing and shaping public opinion (and therefore protecting his image).[17] The growth of cable television was slow. By 1980, only 20 percent of households had cable. Ten years later, this number grew to 56 percent; children typically would spend three hours a day watching television and cable meaning that viewing became "discontinuous, often interrupted and frequently nonexclusive."[18] Identity is the key to child development, and in determining which social group to align one-self with, and what becomes important to children in their lives. Acoff uses Bugs Bunny as an example of how children relate to the same char-acter at different ages and understand the various jokes according to each stage of their childhood and adolescence. Using cognitive filters, children will enjoy Bugs' pie in the face humor at a very young age, progressing to understanding and appreciating Bugs' sarcasm and puns as teenagers.[19] How a young audience relates to and identifies with television charac-ters reflects back to their own development and cognitive skills; therefore, understanding the child viewer is crucial in harnessing the type of pro-grams that networks thought children wanted to watch and, ultimately, in platforming the type of child characters that children either identified with or were amused by.

The 1990s: Restraint, Division, and TV

By the 1990s, the U.S economy had been damaged by the decade of excess that preceded it. The national debt had increased, and '80s policies that were ineffective had trickled into the next decade. By 1999, half of U.S income was earned by just the top fifth of its population.[20] When Bill Clinton replaced Bush in 1992, he declared "To renew America we must be bold."[21] However, many viewed the 1990s as a decade in need of restraint. Indeed, many in the press coined phrases such as "The Sober Nineties" and "The Practical Decade" as early as 1993. Colin Harrison suggests that these "labels" were insights into what the American people expected the 1990s to become: "[I]t was as if Americans needed urgently to fix the meaning of the present before they could live in it."[22]

Anxieties over the closing decade of the century blended with a sort of crisis of memory, Harrison observes, with the past rapidly disappear-ing. The 1990s experienced a transitionary period between the past and the future, which was natural given the significance of its time, but this was tangibly caught up with an over-analysis of the present and specifically what was happening politically, socially and within the home. During the transition between one century and the next, the nation became self-reflective, over-anxious and paranoid.

During this period, a number of events occurred that sparked fear and anger; in 1992, media provided this spark through a video showing the beating of Rodney King by police, ultimately igniting a race riot in Los Angeles. In 1993, it was discovered that David Koresh was leading a com-mune in Waco, where allegedly children were being abused and women were being forced into sexual acts. After an FBI standoff, an attack was led on the commune, and the ensuing fire led to the deaths of 81 members, including women and children.[23] In 1995, America experienced what at the time was its worst domestic terrorist attack, the bombing of Alfred P. Murrah Federal Building in Oklahoma City. That same year saw O.J. Simpson going on trial for murder. The Clinton years ended with the president's impeachment over sexual misconduct in 1998, and in the final year of the century, Dylan Harris and Eric Klebold walked into Columbine High School and murdered a teacher and twelve of their peers. The 1990s, at its onset, was intended to be a decade of sensibilities that followed the hedonistic '80s (much as the Depression-ridden 1930s followed the decadent 1920s), and it was over-analyzed by media and theorists. Instead, America found itself living through a decade of war, terrorism, the most infamous murder trial since the Manson family, cult deaths of innocent children, and a horrific school shooting. The cries about the adultification of children in the face of the new digital age seemed a little defunct, considering the shocking violence towards children that had occurred.

The discussions about the crisis of childhood were beginning to peak around this time, and would continue into the twenty-first century. Michael Grimm, writing in 1994, asserted that children were living in a violent world and that violence surrounded them on a daily basis, more than ever before.[24] Michael Wyness, meanwhile, argued that the crisis at the turn of the century seemed to revolve around the idea that "children no longer know or accept their place,"[25] but he suggested candidly that the crisis about childhood was more a crisis in how society understood it. He argued that children had simply learned to become less reliant on adults and were more able to take care of themselves and to become decision-makers. He focused on the playground as being an important part of child development, that it was here that children began to embrace their growing independence and that in this environment there was a severing of ties with adults. Wyness suggested that, in the playground in particular, children "police their own."[26] We will return to this observation shortly, when we discuss child interaction in animation.

Childhood becomes a construct that mirrors the social and political anxieties of its time. For example, in the 1950s the "birth" of the teenager created generational divides and in the 1960s parents were concerned that they couldn't understand their own children, at a time of civil riots and war. The disparity between the notion of the wholesome, traditional family and the nuclear family continued into the decades that followed. The 1990s are key to this debate, not only through the decade's deaths of cult kids and school kids but also through the fractures within the family unit itself, due to the expansion of cable and network television.

Anxieties felt about the new century seemed to pervade into all of

American life, filtering into the home through the power of television and its burgeoning network channels. Identity of the individual became a concern about generational identities amid a fragmenting society. As television fractured into diverse, niche programs, the question of generation became significant, particularly with the animation renaissance that occurred in the 1990s. Creators such as Matt Groening, Mike Judge, Trey Parker and Matt Stone, and Danny Antonucci had emerged from the first generation of those growing up watching the Saturday morning cartoon shows of the 1950s and '60s. Harrison believes that this explains their attitude towards television animation, that it was "part of the cultural landscape" and was important, rather than being merely viewed as "low" art.[27] With cable networks came a revolution; the usurping of traditional programming meant that the field was wide open for new innovation, rather than mimicry of the same old safe formulas. The central audience base had fragmented and what was "niche" was suddenly embraced.

The 1990s signaled an opportunity for a new direction, particularly for animation, to pervade diverse audience bases and to subvert the safe representations of the previous decades. As Tueth puts it: in the 1990s, animation combined the normative with more deviant threads of family lives through its subversive discourse: "when animation invaded television ... the discourse of television comedy was finally free to perform a more subversive function."[28] What began with *Roseanne* and *Married ... with Children* in the late 1980s found itself defined by the animated family of *The Simpsons* (Matt Groening) in 1989. The family, society, and establishment came under further attack as the 1990s progressed through ground-breaking shows such as *Beavis and Butt-Head*, *South Park*, and *Ed, Edd n Eddy*—which revealed—through subversion and mischief, the divisions and anxieties of society. Here, crucially, animation had found a new voice.

Television animation is rarely "normal." It has an ability to take on what David Perlmutter calls the "major issues of the day" and to address them through unique ways. He goes on to discuss the importance of Fox, Nickelodeon, and Cartoon Network in reshaping television animation and enabling it to show "a new attitude" in the '90s which resulted in unexpected diversity.[29] Animation is able to address issues that live action is not, through its artificiality and its history of slapstick comedy. Established as the "not-real," animation has been viewed by broadcast channels as perhaps a safer mode of address for children who have grown up watching *Looney Tunes*, but it is a medium that is of course fully capable of delivering more than slapstick (as *Looney Tunes* has revealed time and time again). Through subversion, animation is able to tackle dysfunction, difference, politics and culture and, above all, the struggle of the individual. The anxiety about the decade and what it represented filtered onto the screen in fascinating ways through playful subversion within the animated series. The medium is also viewed as one that celebrates violence and anarchy, and has been marginalized because of its tendency to go to extremes and beyond, as well as being seen as the not-real because of its artificiality. While its depictions of violence and anarchy are not solely confined to the 1990s, the closing decade of the twentieth century saw a startling change in television animation, in particular, through the representation of the animated child.

The Animated Child: Subversion and Mischief

Despite concerns about the loss of innocence in the 1990s, through advances in media and the adultification of the child, the era quickly became a playground for the animated child to engage its audience, attack the establishment and appeal to a growing collective consciousness. With emerging network channels grappling for innovative prime time series, one show that proved to be astonishingly popular within the United States as well as global audiences was *The Simpsons*. While much has been written about this series, I want to briefly touch on its representation of boyhood, through Bart, as part of my discussion. The series commands around six million viewers for every new episode, and, since 1989, has established itself as a prime time show that has not only revealed the exploits of a nuclear family, but just how adventurous boyhood can be. In line with the ideas documented in this chapter about the American child as pioneer and as an idea of freedom, the 1990s animated child began to exploit its world and its audiences.

Bart was a figurehead of this time, intent on the manipulation of others using his wit and quickly revealing that his identity was one of "subversive deviousness."[30] Occasionally, Bart is caught in his own trap of rule-breaking mischief, such as in the episode "Marge Gets a Job" (1992), in which Grandpa Simpson asks Bart if he had ever read *The Boy Who Cried Wolf*; Bart's reply is flippant: "I glanced at it. Boy cries wolf, has a few laughs…. I forget how it ends." In this episode, he uses the homework excuse so many times that when he is actually mauled by a wolf, no one takes any notice, and he learns a lesson, of sorts, due to the physical harm he endures. Yet, Bart still retains his status of immortal boyhood. Likewise, in "Bart of Darkness" (1994), the premiere episode of the sixth season focuses on childhood particularly closely; Bart breaks his leg in a clear parody and homage of Hitchcock's *Rear Window* (1954). Springfield endures a heatwave similar to the stifling summer of the original film, and Bart represents James Stewart's broken-legged character who finds himself watching his neighbors through a telescope. After his high dive goes horribly wrong in the family pool and Bart is confined to his room with a plaster-cast, he believes he has witnessed Ned Flanders murdering his wife. When he sends Lisa to investigate (just as Grace Kelly did in Hitchcock's film), he realizes the danger he has put her in and is powerless to stop events from escalating. Child cruelty is prevalent in the episode, through Bart's accident and the relentless teasing he receives from Nelson, who expresses a complete lack of concern that Bart is really hurt, to Bart's subsequent isolation. Martin is also relentlessly bullied at his own swimming pool when his swimming trunks are stolen. James Stewart is parodied when Bart sees himself being spied on by Stewart who calls out: "Grace, c'mere. There's a sinister-looking kid I want you to see."[31]

The Simpsons situates childhood at the intersection of freedom and morality, but much more loosely than a live action sitcom can. The animated child cares little for learning lessons; the thing to be learned is that life is for the taking and the establishment can always be tricked. The child's spirit of freedom and penchant for anarchy and sadism remains at the core of its identity throughout the 1990s. But it is the cruelty of children towards each other, and the lack of empathy they have for each other, that really capture childhood in the '90s here. Bart's own boredom and desire for danger lead Lisa into (what Bart believes to be) a life-or-death situation and the scene where Lisa is carrying the axe up to the attic and is chased by Flanders is convincingly creepy.

Ezell discusses animated television in detail, and in particular its capacity for subversion. He coins the phrase "The Great American Joke" to describe the ironic traits of humor in the U.S. and how this gives a nod to politics and culture:

> American humor possesses a critical, often ironic, strain that highlights the incongruity between the rhetoric that promises equality, wealth and prosperity in American culture and the failure of America to fulfill those promises.[32]

The debate about animation in this context, he argues, centers on its ability to deliberately subvert any dominant ideologies about capitalism and Christianity. Animation became an important motif in the 1990s, finding a way of attacking the establishment in a "playful" manner that enabled it to situate itself in the prime-time marketplace, and specifically used the child as a conduit of this.

The success of *The Simpsons* has ensured that this form of satirical, subversive sitcom was mimicked, both on cable and broadcast networks, explains Tueth. Animation naturally offered more opportunities for physical comedy, quick-fire barbed dialogue and inventive plot twists[33]; where the situation comedy veered towards the subversion of the family unit in the late '80s and continued on this course into the '90s with shows like *Roseanne* and *Married with Children,* the animated sitcom was a veritable bed of anarchy in comparison and the adults became far less present as the animated child journeyed through the decade, finding its voice, its social group, and some sort of belonging.

Beavis and Butt-Head represent two dysfunctional animated teens who have absolutely no adult supervision; they are high school students who spend the majority of their time sitting on a sofa delivering insulting social commentaries on MTV and life in the '90s. They do not empathize with each other or anyone else; they skip school, obsess about money-making schemes, make jokes about sex and music videos. The absence of any parental figures became a recurring theme in '90s animated sitcoms.

In the episode "Our Founding Losers," the duo remove the American flag from their school's flagpole, and Coach Buzzcut demands that they write a report about the founding fathers as punishment. When he asks them what they can tell him about the topic, Butt-Head remarks "once we tried to found Beavis' father but we never did because his mom's a slut." (Their attitude towards each other's parents is later mirrored in *South Park.*) Tueth suggests that a mixture of shock and reassurance characterizes the new animated comedies to emerge in this era, that "in its display of familial dysfunction and other breakdowns in the social order, animated domestic comedy speaks to viewers who feel marginalized from the dominant culture."[34] It is the absence of parental figures, and the derogatory way in which reference is made to each other's, that characterizes the animated child here.

Returning to Wyness, it seems that children took to policing their own, in the playground, and were learning to exist independently at the turn of the century, because of what he calls an abdication of responsibility within the family unit that seemed to be occurring at the time. Rather than calling this a crisis of childhood, Wyness prefers to view this as a crisis in how childhood was perceived by others; the innocence and vulnerability typically associated with the child and the adolescent didn't seem to match the figure that emerged in the '90s and beyond. Wyness argues that children in fact are "competent social actors"[35] who are capable of managing themselves and of adapting to change, although this is contestable: the animated TV child and adolescent is caught between self-sufficiency and dysfunctionality, and I would suggest that the confusion in representations is a mirror of the time; the decade looked into the past and into the future and struggled with its present, and the animated child, in particular, was represented as being confused by events and parental behavior as the century headed towards its conclusion.

Beavis and Butt-Head certainly waver between money-making schemes, the destruction of property and of each other; in the episode "Blood Drive," Beavis and Butt-Head believe they can make money from donating to a blood bank and that they will be given knives to cut themselves with and a drink beforehand. The bank supervisor asks them if they are 18 and when they say "no" he extracts their blood anyway, with the comment "beggars can't be choosers." Later in the episode one says to the other: "I feel like killing myself" and then amends it to "I feel like killing you," which simply makes them both chuckle.

The friends became a staple of 1990s MTV, with Dave Itzkoff calling them "cultural totems of the Generation X era."[36] Mike Judge, creator of the teen icons, commented "it's always a shock when something comes out and it feels so relevant."[37] The characters of Beavis and Butt-Head debuted in Judge's short *Frog Baseball* in 1992, representing what Freeman calls a satire of the worst of youth culture, but Judge was tapping into the MTV generation, the children and teenagers who absorbed pop culture on a daily basis, feeling frustrated with what they saw. Sommerlad wrote that the pair embodied "a particularly sleazy cultural moment" that was the Clinton administration. Generation X tuned in to see "their own disaffection and fecklessness" represented and skewed through subversion, claims Sommerlad, and the duo were more accurate mirror images of adolescents of the time than the Colgate-smiling teens from *Dawson's Creek* or *Saved by the Bell*.[38] The show's enduring moments of controversy—for example, Beavis's obsession with pyromania and his constant exclamations of "Fire!" were blamed for the death of a toddler whose five-year-old brother burned the family trailer park down after supposedly watching the episode (This was later disproved as the family didn't have cable television. Blame turned instead to the mother who had left her children unattended.) Judge responded to the controversy by changing Beavis's catchphrase in a later episode to "Fryer! Fryer!" thus subverting the original line and attacking the establishment in the process.

While Beavis and Butt-Head belong to the '90s and to popular culture, they remain on the outside, as dysfunctional adolescents who see everything as either "cool" or "lame" and prefer the comfort of the sofa to venturing out into society. They are scathing viewers of the media of their time, and mirror images of the *real* '90s youth culture that adults didn't want to acknowledge. The animated adolescent, in the show, had no interest in politics or adhering to social codes and groups; the duo simply exists, finding each other's company comforting and cable television entertaining. They embodied Generation X, which was typified as disaffected and directionless; Rich Cohen, a Generation X child himself, describes them thus:

> We've seen everything and grown tired of history and all the fighting and so
> have opened our own little joint at the edge of the desert, the last outpost in a
> world gone mad.[39]

He claims that they are the last generation to enjoy an "old-time childhood" caught between Baby Boomers and Millennials and seem to be
identified by their irony and sense of dread (2017). While the '90s children within this chapter are largely categorized as millennials, *Beavis and
Butt-Head* represent the door opening into the void between childhood
and adolescence, where youth culture was watching a decade descending
into anxiety and chaos, with calm, cynical detachment.

From the late '80s onwards, it became apparent that there was a market for niche audiences. *The Simpsons* became a prime-time sitcom for
Fox and an important vehicle for subverting political and societal issues
within a family-centric suburban setting, albeit through the medium of
animation. *Beavis and Butt-Head* pushed the trope of the dysfunctional
but happy adolescent to extremes and an animation renaissance followed,
with shows focusing on the family and particularly on the child, as a har-
binger of anarchy, resilience and freedom. Comedy Central's *South Park*
extended these themes much further, from 1997, and became what Cogan
calls "the cruder drawn and much ruder speaking kids" to naturally follow
Beavis and Butt-Head and *The Simpsons*, and that, just as Bart did, Eric
Cartman "caused similar tremors and moral panic in the cultural strato-
sphere."[40] Much has been written and debated about *South Park* since its
launch, but we must acknowledge the show's representation of childhood
here as significant in that it was able to follow the trends of the shows that
preceded it and also establish new territory in terms of the animated child
and what they do next.

Jonathan Gray raises the same point about the pioneering spirit of
children in the United States, where he discusses the idealization of children in the U.S. began when Twain conceptualized Huckleberry Finn as
representing the endurance of the American entrepreneurial spirit and
allowed the reader to see the problems of racism through a child's eyes.
He goes on to suggest that the sadistic child and the dark side of humanity depicted in William Golding's *Lord of the Flies* is also reflected in *South
Park*, with Cartman representing this trait in particular. *South Park* allows
us to see the world through the children's eyes, and they are confused by
what they see, and, like Golding's point that children are not lost souls,
Gray maintains that Parker and Stone's aim is to criticize adult life in the
show.

South Park also reflects the political and social tensions of its time
through the child and "works to dispel the myth … that childhood is
totally pure."[41] The *South Park* boys are adept at questioning the strange

and inappropriate behavior of adults, and mimicking it within their own play. Occasionally their questions and concerns hit close to home. For example, in the episode "Cartman's Mom is a Dirty Slut" (1998) Cartman's quest to discover the identity of his father mirrors Beavis's own earlier search. Parker and Stone intended the show to hone in on the innocence of children, amidst the satire, achieving this through the portrayal of friendships, particularly between Kyle and Stan. Note that through the series Cartman remains the unliked outsider who's demanded for attention and respect often relegates him to playing alone.

The Child in *South Park* became the most vociferous and vocal of the 1990s. Childhood becomes a force of nature here, at once appalling yet compelling, and the issues that affect the boys were current for the era. Because of the speed at which each episode can be created, there is often a topical immediacy in the show's attacks on politics and society, as was common in later seasons, but the first three seasons, airing between 1997 and 2000, were key in their focus on the misbehaviors of adults and the impact this had on the children. There is an innocence that permeates each episode, a thread that is tangible amidst the chaos of their world. The boys find comfort in each other to help them cope with the strangeness and toxicity around them; in the 1990s, they became fascinating representations of third grade kids trying to make sense of the world, often questioning adults about their decisions and finding little solace in their answers. *South Park* subverted, in extreme and surreal ways, how America viewed itself and how it was seeking and failing to find its own answers, about politics, society and family, particularly at the turn of the century.

Cartoon Network launched in the '90s as a division of Warner Bros., focusing on the child and teen audience, with shows such as *Dexter's Laboratory* and *The Powerpuff Girls* platforming child geniuses and superhero kids for Millennial and Generation X viewers, alike, to enjoy. A characteristic of the cable channel was childhood anarchy, and child-centric worlds. Kevin Sandler wrote that Cartoon Network didn't attempt to make emotional connections with kids' lives or target any specific demographic. It preferred to be "irreverent and rankish" and Sandler compares the network to Warner Bros. icon Bugs Bunny with its "mindlessly funny, oftentimes ironic, and playfully violent approach to animation."[42]

Cartoon Network was also a celebration of the successes and failures inherently connected to childhood, with its academically or physically superior protagonists, as well as its slower-witted or violent ones. One characteristic became the glue that held its animated child stars together; they were all outsiders. Just like MTV's Beavis and Butt-Head, or Fox's Lisa Simpson, Cartoon Network's children were the geeks or the dysfunctionals; those kids on the fringes of the neighborhood striving to be "normal" and to belong within a social group. Beavis and Butt-Head never achieve this at school and neither does Lisa (and, as discussed above, Bart is often relegated to being isolated or bullied). Dexter, while tormented by his older sister, is oblivious to how others perceive him, and Blossom, Buttercup and Daisy are too busy saving the world to notice, but one animated series to emerge in the latter part of the decade manages to tap into the complicated and real social circles of children in suburbia by dissecting who was in and who was most definitely not (and why) and, in doing so, subverted the anxieties of parents as the United States fast approached the turn of the century. That show was Danny Antonucci's *Ed, Edd n Eddy*.

Linda Simensky, executive producer at Cartoon Network at the time, recalled that Antonucci approached her with a drawing of three goofy-looking kids and the title, with the tagline that "they're friends because they have the same name." The channel had only produced shows through Hanna-Barbera up to that point, and this show would be the first to be created outside this system which would report to Cartoon Network directly. The producers believed that they needed to follow the model created by Termite Terrace back on the Warner Bros. lot in the 1930s, as they considered it to be the definitive, unbeaten model for the best cartoons.[43] Antonucci explains the nature of the show:

> [T]hey all create their own hell and learn absolutely nothing. That's the motto I live by. There's absolutely nothing to learn from the show, no morals, no lessons, nothing…. I used to come in, cause mischief, stir the pot and then leave. I see it all as kudos to the kind of toons I grew up with.[44]

Antonucci, as a Baby Boomer of the Golden Age of animation, understood the power of subversion and animated mischief, as honed by the likes of Avery and Jones. Atonucci's description of the three Eds creating their own hell and learning absolutely nothing could easily be applied to Porky, Daffy and Bugs, as could the character traits of the trio. *Looney Tunes* in the 1930s recognized the power of subversion, particularly at a time of recession following the Wall Street crash. The 1920s was an era of hedonism and excess, just as the 1980s was. In fact, the '90s seemed to mirror the '30s in the sense that it was intended to be the decade of restraint following a decade of spending. Antonucci, in a further interview, discussed the concept for his show and how he wanted to create characters like his Warner Bros. favorites, and to create "an animated world with a soul … it was less about creating a beautifully designed, pretty show than it was about characters and stories kids could hang onto."[45]

What is interesting about Antonucci's attitude is the lack of morality intended for *Ed, Edd n Eddy*. He taps into the disconnection of the time, and the dysfunction of the family unit as portrayed in *The Simpsons* and

Beavis and Butt-Head, as well as reflecting back to the Golden Age of cartoons, where characters waged war on each other and on the establishment, and nobody won. In the early 2000s, he stated that the big networks didn't have a clue what they were doing, and that success was about having the "chutzpah and the balls to keep pushing."[46] Antonucci created his characters to be ugly on purpose as a reaction to the shiny CGI outputs by the large studios that began in the '90s. The show that was to become Cartoon Network's own project embraced Simensky and Antonucci's nostalgia for the revolutionary, anarchic Termite Terrace cartoons, recapturing a moment of childhood that had shifted into rebellious anti-morality at the turn of the century.

Ed, Edd, and Eddy share more common traits than their names alone. They are the outsiders, lingering on the periphery of their neighborhood, where the other kids play together in a tightly knit, seemingly inadmissible group. The premise of the show focuses on the three Eds attempts to both infiltrate the group and to devise of various money-making schemes to enable them to buy jawbreaker candy, during their summer holidays. This is their only objective; they are unconcerned and unruffled by events around them and by the continual absence of any parental figures. The trio spend each episode creating a new scheme to solve a problem to ultimately make them money. Eddy is the leader, which is more due to his domineering personality than any other quality, while Edd (known as "Double D") is the brains behind the gang. Ed, meanwhile, represents the dysfunctional child, malleable and amenable, who simply goes along with everything that is devised by the other two. Like Beavis and Butt-Head before them, the three Eds exist in their own social bubble, watching others and offering their own views of what they see; and like the MTV duo, they often act with violence.

In the episode "Pop Goes the Ed" (1999), we are introduced to the trio who are attempting to harvest a beehive using baseball bats, and we are initiated into their characters, particularly Eddy's trait of self-preservation and his leadership, as he instructs Ed and Edd, and manages to evade being stung while his friends do not. The boys are enduring an intensely hot summer day, and their priorities become about finding shade and then water. They discover from cool kid Kevin that there is a sprinkler party being held in the neighborhood, but he announces, dismissively, to them, "You're not invited." Immediately their status is revealed, as outsiders, and undesirables. Unthwarted, Eddy decides that they will gate crash the party anyway, each wearing one of his brother's collection of swimming trunks ("We're hot," he tells his friends, excitedly, while the audience is aware that, due to the trunks being so ill-fitting, the boys are definitely not). Upon entering the garden, Ed promptly sits on the sprinkler, and then he and Edd regale the neighborhood kids with scary stories of zombies, to which Eddy remarks, "Stop talking shop. I said mingle." After a disastrous string of events, the boys' trunks fall off and they are forced to sit in the paddling pool until it is dark and the other children have gone inside.

The first episode of Antonucci's show clearly establishes the "in" and "out" crowd, as well as why the Eds are relegated to their position of loitering on the edge of their society. Their behavior is chaotic and careless, anarchic and hopelessly dysfunctional, and we understand at once that they are the outcasts and that the humor of the show is centered around this fact. Eddy is an ambitious leader and his ideas are occasionally innovative, but they never succeed due to their clumsy execution. Edd is intelligent and quiet, a reluctant accomplice to the events that befall the gang, while Ed is unaware of his surroundings, and of the instructions given to him; he simply represents the "other" and constantly sheds his human traits to mimic caterpillars and inanimate objects. When I asked my own teenage daughter if she remembered watching *Ed, Edd n Eddy* as a young child, she immediately recalled, with delight, laughing at Ed as he imitated an aircraft in one episode.

Ed's difference is further highlighted in the episode "Over Your Ed" (1999), in which Double D observes that Ed is "smelly, smelly, smelly" and Eddy decides that they should give Ed a make-over, starting with a bath. As he sits in a wagon, he asks, "Is sitting naked in a wagon cool? Am I cool now?" to which they reply, "No, you're naked." Eddy teaches Ed "cool moves" (the joke being that Eddy's own moves are far removed from being cool). They dress Ed up, give him a list of cool quotes and sit him on a bench to await passers-by, announcing, "Someone's coming!"

The idea that Ed appears "cool" to the other children, through his reading of his lines and his acting cool, is of course a signpost directly to his difference. He is momentarily accepted into the "in" crowd and Eddy manages to make money from *The Ed Show*, but this is short-lived as always, and Ed is revealed once more to be "other"—his comfortable status quo. Only Eddy is concerned about, and frustrated by, the lack of acceptance of himself and his friends. Edd and Ed are oblivious to their status.

In "The Ed-Touchables" (1999) Eddy is convinced that an invisible predator is stealing belongings from the neighborhood kids, signifying his anxiety about a thief in their midst: "Beware of the toucher! Serial toucher on the loose!" The connotations here could be seen as a metaphor for childhood concerns about being left home alone to fend for themselves and the danger of strangers, and this seems to be implied with the other children when they plead, "Won't somebody help us?" Childhood is momentarily rendered vulnerable here, until Antonucci reminds us that there is nothing for Ed, Edd, and Eddy to learn here. Eddy remarks to the other children, "Relax, we've got it all under control," snapping out of the vulnerable child mode, and launches a scheme to charge them for the capture of the serial toucher, his intention being to make enough money to buy as many jaw breakers as possible. He positions Ed on a bench, wearing a sign that reads "Don't Touch" (again a rather overt suggestion) and the first child that touches it is hauled in for interrogation.

Similarly, in "An Ed Too Many," (1999) the boys decide to make a giant pizza in Eddy's house and they do so uninterrupted; at one point, Ed's sister Sarah joins them and they tell her that her mother is calling her to get rid of her, but no parents are ever present in this child-centric universe. The chaos of creating and cooking a giant pizza remains one that is carried out without any parental supervision or reprimand. It reminds one of the scenes in *Toy Story* (1995) when Woody imitates Sid's mother to call him away, and seems a typical observation about the lack of parenting in a child's life. The nuclear family unit in the late twentieth century had become increasingly fragmented, with both parents going out to work, while other families consisted of children living with a divorced parent, and Wyness' view of children policing their own and becoming less reliant on their parents can be directly applied to *Ed, Edd n Eddy*.

The observations Antonucci made about childhood in the show were spot on. Regardless of parental absence during the long hot summers, the neighborhood kids are only intent on being entertained, launching money-making schemes, and deciding who belonged and who did not. Just as Piaget reflected in his observations at the beginning of the twentieth century, the child is self-obsessed and concerned only with its own attainment of pleasure and places itself at the center of its world. Gradually the child becomes aware of its own position in the universe and where it fits in; the three Eds are caught on the periphery between entertainment, entrepreneurial activities and "fitting in." Each boy seems to possess a fractured identity; Antonucci's claim that they were friends because they shared the same name could be extended to the fact that they each had a character trait that, when merged with the other two, formed a complete child, one that displayed the traits that a parent or teacher might imagine to represent "wholeness." Eddy's leadership qualities complement Edd's intelligence and Ed's innocence and playfulness.

Antonucci explained that he had aimed to create a series that had a "soul"; this seems to run contrary to his argument that there is nothing to learn within each episode but he achieved something very unique with this show. He created a connection, through realism, to these animated childhood representations in the '90s, that seemed to tap into the suburban world like no other cartoon had. The antics of the three Eds are exaggerated, emulating the slapstick violence of the *Looney Tunes* characters before them, but the message of the show was clear: kids were home alone, creating their own entertainment and mischief, forging relationships with each other and establishing who they were and where they could fit in.

Conclusion

The 1990s saw the United States transition into a new digital age; it was a time of great innovation, and an era that changed the world forever, but it came at a cost. Concerns about the adultification of children, with the launch of the World Wide Web, seemed to pale in significance compared to the news stories of children in Waco and Columbine becoming victims of shocking violence, and the cries about the loss of innocence were equaled by questions of where to situate childhood. The child is a symbol; it is a purveyor of the pioneering spirit of the United States, from the writings of Mark Twain to the adventures of Bart Simpson. The child, captured on screen by a generation who grew up on the Golden Age of animation, embraced a new anarchy that was a reimagining of an old one: that of the *Looney Tunes*. Youth culture viewed the decade with calm, cynical detachment. Reactive, bored and weary of the chaos that parents and politicians alike wrought on the decade, the animated child began to subvert situations that made no sense to them and to form opinions on the world around them, as they saw it. Bart's view of himself was one of immortality and his actions towards others were devious; Beavis and Butt-Head passed judgement on the media they watched, as they slipped unconsciously into the roles that would ignite a generation; the South Park boys constantly questioned their world and the inane decisions of the adults around them; the three Eds recognized themselves as outcasts and entrepreneurs but never as home-alone, vulnerable kids. Childhood became charged with anarchy and suburbia became a playground for outsiders.

Animation is able to render the child as both innocent, manipulative and appealing in ways that live action cannot. Violence is exaggerated into slapstick, bodies become airborne and expressions can be embellished. The Three Eds squirmed in embarrassment as they were ejected from society, Cartman was relegated to the outside because he offended more readily than he pleased others, and adolescents Beavis and Butt-Head sank deeper into their sofa as they launched their social missiles at the world. The animated child is an infallible, enduring being. At the turn of the century, these characters questioned, pitied, laughed at and turned their backs on the establishment and subverted everything that they saw and felt. In a decade of reflection, anxiety, violence and fear, these youngsters turned to subversion and mischief to find the answers and, in doing so, created a whole new world.

NOTES

1. Colin Harrison, *American Culture in the 1990s* (Edinburgh University Press, 2010), 3.

2. Jean Piaget, *The Language and Thought of the Child* (3rd edition) (New York: Routledge, 1959), x.

3. *Ibid.*, xvii.

4. Adrian Schroeber, Debbie Olsen, *Children, Youth and American Television* (New York: Routledge, 2018).

5. Neil Postman, *The Disappearance of Childhood* (New York, Knopf Doubleday Publishing, 2011).

6. Schroeber & Olsen, *American Television*.

7. Carol Stabile, *Prime Time Animation: Television Animation and American Culture* (New York: Routledge, 2003), 8.

8. Michael Tueth, "Back to the Drawing Board: The family in animated television comedy" in Carol Stabile (ed.) *Prime Time Animation: Television Animation and American Culture* (New York: Routledge, 2003), 138.

9. Piaget, xii.

10. Jean Piaget, *The Construction of Reality in the Child* (New York: Routledge, 1999), xii.

11. Caroline Field Levander, Carol Singley, *The American Child: A Cultural Studies Reader* (New Brunswick: Rutgers University Press, 2003), 4.

12. *Ibid.*

13. Brown, Gillian. "Child's Play," in Caroline Field Levander and Carol Singley (eds.), *The American Child: a Cultural Studies Reader*, (New Brunswick: Rutgers University Press, 2003), 22.

14. *Ibid.*, 26.

15. George Comstock and Erica Sharrer, *Media and the American Child* (Oxford: Academic, 2007), 1.

16. Michael Curtin, Jane Shattuc, *The American Television Industry* (London: BFI/Palgrave Macmillan, 2009), 10.

17. *Ibid.*, 12.

18. Comstock and Sharrer, *Media*, 42.

19. *Ibid.*, 61.

20. Harrison, *American Culture*, 7.

21. Marlene Targ Brill, *America in the 1990's* (Minneapolis: Twenty-First Century Books, 2010), 15–19.

22. Harrison, *American Culture*, 1.

23. Brill, *America*, 25.

24. Michael A. Grimm, "Unfortunate Reality, Fictional Portrayals of Children and Violence," in Harry Eiss (ed.) *Images of the Child* (Bowling Green, OH: Popular Press, 1994), 116.

25. Michael Wyness, *Contesting Childhood* (Falmer Press, 2000), 6.

26. *Ibid.*, 111.

27. Harrison, *American Culture*, 127.

28. Tueth, "Drawing Board," 135, 139.

29. David Perlmutter, *American Toons In: A History of Television Animation* (Jefferson, NC: McFarland, 2014), 3, 7.

30. Sila Kaine Ezell, *Humor and Satire on Contemporary Television: Animation and the American Joke* (New York: Routledge, 2016), 8.

31. Jim Reardon, dir. "Bart of Darkness." *The Simpsons*, season 6, episode 1, FOX, 1994.

32. Ezell, *Contemporary Television*, 1.

33. Tueth, "Drawing Board," 139.

34. *Ibid.*, 146.

35. Wyness, *Contesting Childhood*, 2.

36. Dave Itzkoff, 2020, "Beavis and Butt-Head Revived at Comedy Central." Last modified July 1, 2020. https://www.nytimes.com/2020/07/01/arts/television/beavis-and-butt-head-comedy-central.html.

37. Hadley Freeman, 2020 "'People opened up because I'm the Beavis and Butt-Head Guy': Mike Judge on his New Funk Direction." Last modified April 15, 2020. https://www.theguardian.com/tv-and-radio/2020/apr/15/mike-judge-interview-beavis-butthead-silicon-valley-tales-from-the-tour-bus.

38. Joe Sommerlad, "Beavis and Butt-Head at 25: How MTV's original dumbasses stormed America and changed comedy forever." Last modified March 7, 2018. https://www.independent.co.uk/arts-entertainment/tv/features/beavis-and-butthead-25th-anniversary-mike-judge-mtv-tv-comedy-animation-offence-a8243906.html.

39. Rich Cohen, 2017, "Why Generation X might be our last, Best Hope." Last modified August 11, 2017. https://www.vanityfair.com/style/2017/08/why-generation-x-might-be-our-last-best-hope.

40. Brian Cogan, *Deconstructing* South Park: *Critical Examinations of Animated Transgression* (Lanham, MD: Lexington Books, 2012), 3.

41. Jonathan Gray, "From Whence Came Cartman: South Park's Intertextual Lineage" in Brian Cogan (ed.), *Deconstructing* South Park: *Critical Examinations of Animated Transgression* (Lanham, MD: Lexington Books, 2012), 10.

42. Kevin Sandler, "Synergy Nirvana—Brand equity, television animation, and Cartoon Network" in Carol Stabile (ed.), *Prime Time Animation: Television Animation and American Culture* (New York: Routledge, 2003), 98.

43. Linda Simensky, "Ed, Edd n Eddy: Three Guys, One 'Toon,'" *Take One 24* (1999): 28.

44. Ramin Zahid, "The Boys are Back in Town," *Animation 18, no. 3*, 26–27.

45. "A Double Milestone for Antonucci and the Eds!" 2008. *Animation 23* (1): 44.

46. Zahid, "Boys," 27.

PART II
_____

Rethinking American Culture
Through Social Challenges

Rocko's Modern Life and the Pains of Early Adulting

Adrián García

> "I don't believe in life lessons learnt from animated cartoons."
> —Kowalski, from *The Penguins of Madagascar*

I strongly disagree with Kowalski; but I know for sure that my parents would agree with him. After all, I grew up in Mexico the youngest of three siblings—my sisters preceded my arrival by a decade—and pretty much every cousin in the family is much older than I am. I have been told for years how they used to play by climbing trees, spent time playing hide and seek, or played hopscotch. It was as though they were trying to make me feel bad because I did not play the way they did. But I found my own way. I spent my afternoons playing with toys and watching television, especially Nickelodeon's programming (although some anime has always been welcomed). I used to draw the characters I liked the most, and I remember making my own comic book about a frog and his friends when I was in elementary school. It still might be somewhere in my parents' house. I definitely believe that these narratives somehow shaped my personality, but not exactly in the way you'd expect them to, which would be during my childhood when I saw them as simple animated cartoons. Instead, I rediscovered them during my college years, especially Joe Murray's *Rocko's Modern Life*, when, thanks to social media and close friends, I was finally able to see the show as a sharp critique of contemporary issues.

Before diving into this inquiry, I think it might be useful to establish the context of Nickelodeon programming on Mexican television. In the early 1990s, the cable television industry in Mexico was flourishing due to recently developed digital technology, and to the also recent neoliberal policies which the country had just adopted. These economic policies dated back to the early 1980s, and intensified due to the 1994 North American Free Trade Agreement (NAFTA), which played a big role in the way the industry was able to work alongside of transnational entertainment companies.[1] Furthermore, by 1993, legislation surrounding the cable industry changed drastically, especially with regard to advertisements, whose amount of air time was directly proportional to that of local productions. This opened the doors for small local broadcasters to increase their income by selling time for publicity. Even when these local broadcasters still were not able to compete with Televisa, the largest broadcast company in Mexico, they had a chance to offer a wider variety of content and better transmission quality, which made the cable television industry grow quickly throughout the country.[2] As a consequence, Mexican audiences witnessed an increase in the availability of foreign media, especially from the United States, enabling the child-oriented broadcast company Nickelodeon to make its way into Mexican households towards the end of 1996.

At around the same time in the United States, Nickelodeon was trying to change the bulk of its animated programming, which consisted at the time of newly acquired reruns and old shows. As their new strategy was developed, Nickelodeon began hiring young cartoonists and independent studios and offering them the opportunity to produce pilots. The initiative was led by Vanessa Coffey and Linda Simensky, producers at the time, with the consent of the then president of Nickelodeon, Geraldine Laybourne.[3] According to John Kricfalusi, creator of one of the very first original hits of the company, *The Ren & Stimpy Show*, Nickelodeon's approach to the production of animated series differed from the normal tendency of toy-company-commissioned animated series, leading to the bold decision of producing creator-driven cartoons.[4] The decision paid off when the success of the first generation of Nicktoons, as they were called, arrived with titles like *Doug, Rugrats, Real Monsters*, the before-mentioned *Ren & Stimpy Show, Hey, Arnold!*, and finally, *Rocko's Modern Life*.

I've known these shows since I was around seven, when my family jumped into the cable television frenzy during its expansion into Mexico. This expansion was not just about the television industry but telecommunications in general; the already mentioned change in Mexican telecommunication legislation in 1993 allowed media network owners to expand their range of services and not limit them to television only. Phone and early internet services were offered from then on by these companies, too, which were at the time transitioning from public to private ownership.[5] Mexican households also experienced a drastic and sudden openness to communication networks and cultural products as never before.

In order to map a general overview of the way people interact with and read these shows, I conducted a series of e-mail interviews in 2018. These interviews show that the broadcasts of Nickelodeon's content was widespread throughout the country, given the fact that the interviewees are from Mexico City, the northern state of Nuevo León, the western state of Jalisco, and Guanajuato in the central region. Everyone interviewed was first exposed to these shows at around the same time in their childhood, sometime in the mid–1990s.

Besides the heavy emotional investment these interviewees have with regard to these cartoons and their childhood, they acknowledge some sort of assimilation of what they call *values* learned from the character's experiences. Said "values" allowed these once young spectators to have access to factors rarely experienced in Mexico at the time, such as diverse cultures, religions, races, and the respectful dynamics the characters create around these issues, things that were yet to come, and that even now, are uncommon outside the main urban centers of Mexico. Uncle Nick, whose interview is a key component of this research, said:

> I identify a lot with Arnold and the Rugrats, in the values I've acquired practically since I watched these shows. Arnold, for example, selflessly offers help to everyone even when they are not polite. I acquired a sensibility for cultural diversity with this show, too. Or as Rocko, I feel sometimes like a foreigner to the noise and chaos of life.[6]

Conversely, another interviewee (who decided to go by the name of Astarothe, age 28), remembers how her parents disagreed with her watching these shows, labeling them as rude, ugly, and a bad influence for her because of their portrayal of what her mother called *irreverent* characters. This vastly opposite reading, compared to Uncle Nick's, is especially rich when noting that Astarothe refers directly to her mother's opinion on Helga G. Pataki, the strong female co-protagonist of *Hey, Arnold!* Though she usually calls several other characters names, she is also a very nuanced and deep character with several dimensions to her personality. She is rude and mean, but at the same time gentle and sensible, standing well as one of the first female leading characters in the early Nicktoons era. However, Astarothe recognizes that her child-self was not aware of this reading; rather, she enjoyed the content for its child-like appeal, and these shows were nothing more than mere "cartoons" for her at the time.

There was a period for all the interviewees when they stopped watching these shows, due to the fact that the Latin American branch of Nickelodeon pulled them from its programming and replaced them with newer shows. The change in content was not appealing to some of the interviewees, but by the time they were approaching adolescence, there was a common theme felt, as Uncle Nick summarizes here:

> Many will agree with me, our childhood began with the splendor of the contents of Nickelodeon in Latin America, and ends with its decay.[7]

Uncle Nick describes himself as a natural born collectionist. Over the years, he has built a broad archive of Nickelodeon's hit '90s shows recorded in the VHS format. A couple of years ago, as he mentions, as live streams were increasing in popularity in social media, he discovered a website that transmitted general media content from the 1990s. This inspired him to make one of his own, streaming Nickelodeon's cartoons exclusively:

> I remember that night. I designed a profile picture and opened the website. It was Thursday, October 13, 2016. The idea was to broadcast those episodes that I treasured for so many years and share them with the nostalgic of the world, in real time. From the beginning I thought about it in these terms: the television of your childhood, that now you can watch on your smartphone or laptop. I prepared my own broadcasting center, using an old VHS player, an iMac, conversion wires, and lots of faith.[8]

The first transmission occurred the day after, with a final tally of seventy viewers. Over the next year, the project grew to almost a half-million followers before being taken over by hackers somewhere in the Philippines. Uncle Nick tried to get the website back and reported the case to Facebook. This was followed briefly but eventually the website was taken down for good. Uncle Nick remained loyal to his audience, and soon built a replacement for the fallen project that he called *Nickstalgia*, which today has over 700,000 followers. It exists across several social media platforms, where the community engages in conversations regarding the content, memes, trivia facts, or discussions of the shows themselves.

The most salient feature of the *Nickstalgia* project (in which I feel the sense of community is truly palpable) is that it is comprised of the recurrent livestream sessions and weeknight broadcasts, during which thousands of followers watch and comment directly on streaming episodes, interacting with other participants (as well as with Uncle Nick), an opportunity that I have had the fortune to witness by participating as a passive viewer.

Elaborating on this thought, I will briefly mention that I received several requests for interviews in my email shortly after he announced my research, some of them from other countries in Latin America. I have resorted to using only those coming from Mexico for the purposes of this investigation, but according to the flow of comments during the live streamings, people from all over Latin America have joined the community and follow regularly the transmissions. This has sometimes required Uncle Nick to publish the schedules according to different time zones, as requested by viewers from South America. This fact shows how big Uncle Nick's project is and its potential for further inquiries.

The case of Uncle Nick and the *Nickstalgia* project is outstanding in the context of participatory culture, especially when talking about shifts "in the power relations between media industries and their consumers."[9] Uncle Nick's project has produced new content, mainly in the form of memes, and the community of fans has shared related images and sometimes even fan art, a feature that Henry Jenkins originally argued participatory culture has,[10] a prosumer network, a sharing space for recirculations, interventions, readings and rereadings, reinterpretations, all drawn from the original media but at the margins of the official channels where they come from. Perhaps the most striking thing about *Nickstalgia* is the recirculation of old content. Moreover, the livestreams at *Nickstalgia* resemble television narratives, complete with defined schedules and a menu of shows that will be transmitted ahead of time. Another interesting feature worth mentioning is one regarding the graphic identity of Uncle Nick's transmissions: throughout the live streams old Nickelodeon bumper videos can be seen between episodes, adding to the resemblance and nostalgia for the old looks of the broadcast channel. However, these bumper videos are not simply and passively retransmitted; they have been modified by replacing Nickelodeon's classic splash logo with Uncle Nick's, reinforcing his input within the nostalgic project.

The whole process embodies a reenactment of the experience of watching television as these fans did around twenty years ago during their childhood years. But now, within the framework of social media, where live comments are shared as viewers watch in real time, fans request shows or particular episodes directly, subverting somehow the model of television programming ruled by advertisements and demographics. But even when *Nickstalgia* is a truly interesting example on its own, the recirculation of Nickelodeon's content in its Latin American version has a longer history.

Beginning with official reruns, Nickelodeon Latin America launched *Nick Hits* in July 2009,[11] a programming block airing classic Nicktoons at prime time. However, this is just an honorific mention, because full episodes uploaded by YouTube users date as far back as August 2008. And, by 2012, a blogger archived the complete *Rocko's Modern Life* series dubbed to Latin American Spanish to his website. (This is how I rediscovered the show.)

Rocko's Modern Life, originally produced between 1993 and 1996, portrays the life of a young wallaby called Rocko who has recently moved to the United States from his homeland of Australia. In four seasons across fifty-two episodes consisting of two 11-minute independent parts, Rocko faces normal, everyday problems such as doing the laundry, getting rid of the trash, falling in love with someone who doesn't feel the same, annoying neighbors, dealing with bureaucracy, paying debts, and having a crappy job.

In an interview for Nickelodeon's *Nick Animation Podcast* series which features current and former talent of the broadcast company, creator Joe Murray explained how he and *Rocko's* writers packed the show with actual anecdotes from their lives,[12] so it's no wonder that Rocko seems like a normal guy. Elaborating further, Murray stated that he and his team tried to make a show with "relevance to what people are going through."[13] Analyzing relevant excerpts from four episodes that show Rocko and his friends—Heffer and Filburt—in both labor and consumerist environments, I would argue that *Rocko's Modern Life* is a show about growing up and the pains of early adulting. Using this argument, I will sketch a parallel with several fan reflections on these topics within a brief summary of Mexico's current economic situation.

During the show's introduction, a baby Rocko in diapers drops from his mother's pouch, only to be immediately and literally beaten into adulthood by an angry clock. Shortly after, a pair of giant hands manipulates him, opens his head, and introduces a thick book simply labeled as "Knowledge," which then kicks out a jelly-like mass (presumably his brain) that gets eaten by his pet dog Spunky. The hands proceed to kick him out of the frame, reintroducing him next into a space where a neon sign advertises the "real world." The commentary on the usefulness of "official knowledge" to deal with the "real world" may pose interesting questions on its own in the context of education, but I will let it aside as a note to possible future inquiries. Heather Hendershot states that education is probably one of the most broadly debated aspects of television,[14] with myriads of both supporters and detractors, making it an aspect too complex to elaborate in further detail within this investigation. However, as a tangent topic to education, I will address a very prominent characteristic of *Rocko's Modern Life*: its satirical nature.

The Russian-American writer Vladimir Nabokov once compared satire with a lesson, recognizing the didactic value in it, as Matthew A. Henry remembers in *The Simpsons, Satire, and American Culture*.[15] Satire is then a vehicle for reflection, demanding from its audience awareness of the context.[16] And just as *The Simpsons*, acknowledged by Murray as a predecessor of Nickelodeon's first generation of creator-driven cartoons,[17] his work on *Rocko's Modern Life* is packed with keen critical observations delivered by a narrative of exaggeration that points out the flaws of both its characters and their environment. As my interviewee Astarothe describes: "it utilizes a hyperbolic language, exaggerated but precise, to illustrate the many absurdities of our lives."[18]

In the episode *Power Trip, Trip* (Season 1, Ep. 5a; 1993), Rocko's mean boss leaves town for a hair transplant and asks Rocko to take care of his business, a comic book store. While handing Rocko the keys to shop, he warns him to not press the green button in the armchair of his office. Rocko temporarily hires his friend Filburt as an assistant, and once Filburt is at the front desk, Rocko finally gets into the manager's office—a neoclassical room with Doric columns, a marble floor, and golden statuary—a stereotypical representation of wealth and power absurdly placed in a comic book store. He immediately walks to the armchair and tries its many applications: he plays some music and navigates the office with the apparently autonomous movement of a chair that even seems immune to gravity. Then, after hesitating briefly, he pushes the green button. The armchair vibrates and Rocko literally melts down from pleasure, the result of which turns him into a clone of his boss, mistreating Filburt because of his lack of efficiency. Things escalate to the moment where Rocko lectures Filburt about supply and demand, concluding that if his work does not render a profit, Filburt is useless to him. Rocko eventually fires him and kicks him out, where Filburt ends up lying in the street as several vehicles run over him.

The masturbatory rendering of the seduction of positions of power coded in the vibratory armchair has a vast potential for analysis on its own, but as was done earlier with the education debate, I will mark it as a side note. Rather, I will focus on the cold-bloodedness of the business language that Rocko uses to rationalize his decision to fire Filburt, dehumanizing him in the process, and add it to a previous episode in which Rocko himself is fired.

In the episode "Canned" (Season 1, Ep. 8b; 1993),[19] during the opening sequence Rocko is working at his previous job, selling comic books in a bigger store. A voice on the speakers calls him to see the boss, who refers to him as 1-4-5-6-9-10 upon his arrival to the office. The boss explains to Rocko that he has been promoted from the position 6-1-2 to the position 8-1-4 because of a restructuring of the company in order to enhance productivity. Rocko asks naively what that all means, and his boss flushes him through the armchair which turns out to be a toilet in disguise. Later, Rocko looks for new jobs in the newspaper, but finds only embarrassing situations: mouth tattoo artist (he gets swallowed); plumber's assistant (he has to prevent the plumber's pants from going down); and operator for a presumptive phone sex hotline (the service itself is never mentioned—the job is only referenced as "hotline." Still, he discovers that his neighbor, a married female frog, is presumably unsatisfied). Finally, he gets a job as a test subject for wacky inventions at Conglom-O, a monopolistic company that manages pretty much everything in the city, which goes by the slogan: *We Own You.* Fittingly, the logo is a martini in a glass with the Earth substituting for the olive. Rocko has to risk his life testing new and completely artificial candies capable of triggering mutations, or trying a new repellent spray amid a stampede of wild animals. No safety measures are taken, and ultimately it seems that this gigantic company could not care less for its newest and most disposable employee. Talk about dangerous work.

With the resurrection of *Rocko's Modern Life* in Mexico, thanks to YouTube users, bloggers, projects such as *Nickstalgia,* and Nickelodeon Latin America itself, fans that at first were drawn back to this show by feelings of mere childhood nostalgia (as my interviewees have stated) found themselves able to read the show differently as adults. "Nicktoons," and *Rocko's Modern Life* in particular, are packed with clever jokes, pop cultural references, and a colorful palette of innuendo. Joe Murray has implied that for him, animation should not be seen as a babysitter. Intentionally, *Rocko's Modern Life* was written with layers of meaning, something that Rebecca Farley calls *double-coding,*[20] the use of different densities of text that appeal to more than one audience at a time. Murray's intention was to have kids and parents watching the show enjoying it equally,[21] and at the same time to foster a further understanding of the show and the particular context it depicts. In an interview with the *Huffington Post*, Murray is quoted as saying: "My argument also was that kids were a lot smarter than most television execs gave them credit for."[22]

Or, as my interviewee Astarothe said:

> I rediscovered Nickelodeon with YouTube and my college friends. Suddenly I realized—or remembered—that they were incredible shows. We discussed them and then I started to download them (especially *Hey, Arnold!* It was the easiest to find). Many people uploaded full episodes to YouTube, where I watched a lot of them again. And it made sense to me, besides the feeling of remembrance, even if it was superficial, how simple life was. Apart from nostalgia, I understood this show more deeply. I laughed more. Particularly with *Rocko's Modern Life.* I think that was the one I recalled more things from. I super identified with its way to feel situations, frustrations, and hopes. Ingenuity against hard life.[23]

It is interesting how a wave of nostalgia, of revisiting old shows, and the possibility of more mature readings of them thanks to double-codedness, match the moment when several of the interviewees were about to experience the same phenomenon of becoming adults that the characters enact, in their final years of college, it became a point of identification. Fans found themselves in similar situations, and thus their reading of the shows progressed into a more comprehensive and nuanced one, rather than just the enjoyment of the goofy plots.

In "Who Gives a Buck" (Season 1, Ep. 1b; 1993), Rocko gets a credit card and uses it irresponsibly. This episode was extensively commented by a number of research participants who closely related to this topic and its depiction of dealing with rampant credit card debt. The exaggerated narrative escalates the situation to the point that the credit bureau empties Rocko's house, taking even his dog's bowl, the very item he used the credit card in the first place. As the punchline to address the precariousness of dealing with financial institutions, Rocko's closest friend Heffer (he is a steer) sells his second stomach to buy a new bowl for the dog.

The dark move of selling internal organs to pay debts plays brilliantly with the indifference with which Rocko mistreats Filburt during his power frenzy (leaving him in the street to be run over) and also with the flushing of Rocko through the toilet as if he were nothing but corporate crap. These representations of unemployment and hard financial landscapes map a grim but relatable scenario within the framework and constraints of satire. All of this resonates especially well for Mexican fans of the show (myself included), as the Mexican economy has not been the most welcoming environment to thrive, generally speaking, due to the fact that, according to scholars and INEGI (National Institute of Statistics and Geography translated to English), the average annual growth since 1993 has been 2.5 percent, far lower than the 6 percent promised by NAFTA's early supporters.[24] More recently, even when the availability of employment has increased, wages continue to shrink (INEGI, Vanguardia).[25]

The fact that the Mexican economy has grown so slowly since 1993, after a brief period of recovery in the late 1980s following a major crisis in 1982, drew critical attention to NAFTA, which was renegotiated as USMCA and implemented in July 2020. The agreement was considered at the time of its conception as a panacea to the problems Mexico was facing. However, another crisis hit the country in 1994, soon after the agreement was signed, and the overly optimistic expectations of NAFTA have not yet been seen, as it is increasingly visible that the Mexican market was not, and still is not, prepared to compete directly with highly developed economies such as those of Canada and the United States.[26] The effects were specially visible in contexts like agriculture, where Mexican producers, unable to withstand against cheap products from the United States flooding the Mexican market, found themselves financially vulnerable.[27]

The effects have worsened over time to the point that over the last three decades, the acquisition power in the country has dropped a shocking 80 percent, according to a research conducted by the National Autonomous University of Mexico (UNAM). This research takes as standard a group of forty basic edible products capable of properly feeding a family of four members (two adults, a teenager, and a child) at a cost of 245 Mexican Pesos per day, or 13 U.S. dollars.[28]

The study, fittingly named "Mexico 2018: Another social and political defeat to the working class, the wage increases that were born dead," one measuring income disparity across Mexico, stated that back in the 1980s just 4 hours and 53 minutes of work were enough to buy the recommended products. Yet, to this day, between inflation and the unwillingness of politicians to raise wages accordingly, is a questionable maneuver to keep workforce cheap to attract foreign investors. This move has kept buying power so low that to acquire the same goods today a person would have to work 24 hours and 31 minutes. Political initiatives have proved to be insufficient, with wage increases failing to match the inflated prices of basic, sustainable products.[29] Indeed, these "increases" are born dead—they are in fact nonexistent. Keep in mind that this just applies to food needs.

Moving forward, other research conducted by the Ibero-American University at Puebla (specifically comments posted by Esther Miguel Trula published to the World Economic Forum's website) foreshadows an interesting yet worrying coincidence. During the 2000s, while average wages were steadily decreasing, paradoxically the population in Mexico was becoming increasingly more literate. This has given rise to one of the most well-prepared generations in terms of life skills while at the same time remains one of the worst ever paid, also. Back in 2005, a Mexican degree holder of any given major earned in average 11,500 Mexican pesos (MX) per month, or approximately 1,045 U.S. Dollars (USD); by 2017, the average professional salary had fallen to around 7,365 MX, approximately 390 USD with today's currency exchange.[30]

This monthly amount renders a daily profit of less than 359 MX (19 USD), considered at the limits of poverty according to the National Council for the Evaluation of Social Development Policies (CONEVAL),* and according to Anna Portella, writing in the Mexican edition of *Forbes* as recently as the spring of 2018, two-thirds of workers between the ages of 15 and 29 years old meet this criteria.[31]

I would like to draw attention to the nuances of the statements. While CONEVAL states that the average wage of 19 USD would be enough to keep one above the line of poverty, they fail to address that 13 of those 19 dollars correspond to the cost of proper nutritional coverage only, which I explained earlier in the essay. The remaining 6 USD won't be enough to cover commuting, rent, or medical expenses, the latter supposedly being a labor right under Mexican law pertaining to social security coverage. But, as it turns out, an astonishing 61 percent of the working population in Mexico has no medical coverage, pointing to a generalized loss of rights.[32]

---

*CONEVAL, or the Consejo Nacional de Evaluación de la Política de Desarrollo Social, is a government-funded council founded in 2005 to measure income disparity across Mexico.

Socioeconomic mobility is not the only thing turning into a mythological creature for the younger generations of workers in Mexico, but the sole concept of financial stability is becoming increasingly meaningless. One of my former professors once told me that my generation could be defined by three markers: young, broke, and indebted (punchline: with study loans). It is the story of my life, and with irony at its finest.

It is particularly relatable to me now: currently residing in the United States, studying and working, is the result of finding little opportunities in my field in my home country. What's more, the parallels I draw as a fan of *Rocko's Modern Life* go beyond facing the absurd "modern life" of laundromats or the bureaucracy of a strange country, that in the end turns out to be the same old bureaucracy, leaving me as a stranger, no matter what country I find myself in; I have traced useful markers, life hacks, in the way I have conducted myself in a harsh job market environment, even if only in the identification of themes, let's say, *SpongeBob SquarePants'* Squidward Tentacles' realization of being stuck in a dead-end job, unrespected, underpaid, unchallenged, with cynicism as the only way out, to cite a more recent heir of *Rocko's Modern Life*. As Nicolle Lamerichs explains in his review of Rebecca Williams' *Post-Object Fandom: Television, Identity and Self-Narrative*, "fan objects create stability in one's life, or *ontological security*," borrowing a term from Anthony Giddens.[33]

These life hacks I refer to tend to gravitate around the adulting narrative, and particularly in how this is depicted in *Rocko's Modern Life*, as some sort of approach to maturity and stability that fails constantly. Often, Rocko finds himself trapped in absurd yet common daily activities, as in the episode "A Sucker for the Suck-o-matic" (Season 1, Ep. 8a; 1993), where the opening sequence shows the protagonist trying to clean his messy house with an old vacuum cleaner that eventually breaks down. His friend Heffer invites Rocko to sit down and watch TV, which is tuned in *Lobot-o-shop*, an advertisement channel. The television develops a pair of hands with which it literally washes their brains while airing an advertisement about the *Suck-o-matic*, a miraculous vacuum cleaner capable of a convenient range of skills from vacuuming (of course) to fixing hair, addressing personality issues, solving international politics, not to mention the machine's usefulness with aiding in liposuction. Rocko immediately buys it and cleans the house, but he cannot turn it off, eventually finding out that the *Suck-o-matic* has its own mind, and its purpose is to eat its owner (which finally happens, not just to Heffer and Rocko, but to everyone in town who bought a *Suck-o-matic*).

Rocko's constant failures spring from the challenges of basic adulting in the sense that the fruits of his labor are meant for him to keep his lifestyle as a single male living alone with his pet in the suburbs. However, his attempts to do so are frustrated by economic hazards, such as unemployment or debts. The irony, especially concerning debts, comes from the absurdity of consumerism, making his life wobble between vital things and banal shopping that at the end amounts to more debts. This is metaphorically pictured as the vacuum cleaner swallows its owners: the whole town, and possibly the whole world, eaten by the consumption of commodity.

The stern depiction of labor problems and endless bills to pay is sweetened by the many times Rocko and his friends play very different roles, such as going on road trips, having movie nights, rollerblading, or just having fun in general, blurring in that way the limits of the adult figure. Useful here is David Buckingham's reading on the inversion of the authority relationship between adults and kids in British television, as the "embarrassment about the fact of adult power."[34] My interviewee Astarothe summarizes that idea in this way:

> Deep inside I feel, even today, that every time I see *Rocko, The Angry Beavers*, *Hey, Arnold!*, that on the one hand we adults are concerned with so many things, things that at the end are ridiculous and absurd; that is precisely what I find so funny in these shows, how well they depict the absurdity of this anxiety of 'becoming.' On the other hand, there is the freshness of what really matters to a child: making a list of things to do on a Saturday (eat cereal, watch cartoons, biking), and the 'simple' triumphs of achieving those goals. The needs of the adult world oscillate between truly vital ones (eating, sleeping, paying the rent) and somewhat banal pleasures (having an attractive body, buying a new smartphone). But I think that these childhood triumphs are precisely the things that eventually become really meaningful for the rest of one's life. In some sense, childhood is uncommodifiable, I mean that the desire of becoming something fantastic cannot be experienced out of the self…. There are a lot of people who feel uncomfortable in the 'adult world,' same as me. And there is (in this show) some sense of reclaiming my desire to avoid becoming that 'kind of adult.' And it just makes me smile.[35]

Finally, I would like to draw again on Joe Murray's words, when at San Diego's 2017 Comic-Con, he stated that *Rocko's Modern Life* is still resonating, and perhaps is better known, today than when it originally aired in the 1990s.[36] This nostalgic phenomenon, exemplified by Uncle Nick's project is just one iteration of media recirculation, one originated from the fan base of the show rather than the corporate exploitation of nostalgia (which came later), something that in a broader sense has changed the landscape of television and content in general, in an age of social media and participatory culture.[37] "Through different transmedia installments, texts can become immortal," Lamerichs argues, thus giving media companies the opportunity to explode the nostalgic fan base of certain contents.[38] This is particularly important to mention when considering the *Rocko's Modern Life* reboot, a TV special called *Static Cling,* meant to be released in 2018 but streamed on Netflix in the fall of 2019. Murray stated in this interview that the series has aged well, yet I will argue that it has matured along with its fans, becoming more relevant for them as they grasp not just the sophisticated jokes they missed when they were children, but the similarities between Rocko's never-ending growing and learning processes and their own. The 20-year span that has passed has given the series an acquired visible relevance, to the extent that it was Nickelodeon executives who looked directly toward Murray to work on the reboot,[39] resembling the notion of "media virus."

The term, coined by Douglas Rushkoff, is a text that slowly introduces critical readings into mainstream media.[40] Going back to Henry's analysis of *The Simpsons*, cartoons are specially fitted to be rendered as such due to their seemingly innocuous appearance; for me, *Rocko's Modern Life* works neatly in this framework, having matured thanks to fans that recirculated it and kept reading into the critical subtext of the series, making it still relevant today.

The relevance of the show might be found in the realness of its conception, which pulls inspiration directly from the experience of its writers and its creator, as mentioned earlier. This close relationship with the mundane establishes solid ground for fans to find parallels with their own lives, contexts, and points-of-view. It is here where further questions should be posed: What are the constants of becoming an adult—individually so—that made it important enough to be featured within the writing of *Rocko's Modern Life*? What makes the show today, 25 years after its premiere, powerful enough to exert such meaningful influence in the lives of its fans? What are the nuances of early adulting across national borders? What are the differences? What has (or has not) changed economically over the two decades as the show's original viewers work to become independent adults? Why do Rocko's economic and labor struggles keep being so relatable? I pose these questions as a conclusion because I do not believe there is a final answer; at one time I thought I would not be able to see new episodes of Rocko anymore, yet (at least) one more is coming.

Static Cling (2019), *Rocko's Modern Life* TV special, begins with the comeback of the three major characters, Rocko, Filburt and Heffer, to Earth after 20 years of being lost in space. Throughout the trailer, they face a growing city that has swallowed the suburb they used to live in, they encounter new technology, social media, state surveillance, hyper-consumerism and its most disgusting mechanism: planned obsolescence, when they are buying the newest smartphone, and the employee of the store simply replaces the "9" for a "10" in the advertisement, and a river of people runs over Rocko to get the device. Fan comments on the video uploaded by Nickelodeon on July 2017 illustrate some points that have been discussed:

- "I have one thing to say: Nostalgia." (Animationwolfyumi14)
- "'The 21st century is a very dangerous century.' I can relate to this." (Crispy Toast)
- "Hey, Arnold! returns, Rocko's Modern Life returns, and Invader Zim returns. Nickelodeon has answered our prayers!" (Guy1891)
- "As a Rocko fan since the show's birth this has to be the greatest feeling in nostalgia I've ever had! This sneak peek has given me all the relief that the reboot is gonna feel like the 90's [sic] version and I am in love with the modern take! The kid in me is alive again and cannot wait to get into this show again! So excited!" (Sahido Serako)
- "This show was always ripe with social satire. It makes sense bringing it back." (Byron MacGreggor)

After a year of delays, silence and cancellation rumors, Nickelodeon announced *Static Cling Rocko's Modern Life* TV special wouldn't be broadcast on the channel but streamed on Netflix.

Humor and satire remain, all the characters were there (fan service throughout), yet Rocko's personality seemed off, even though his trademark nervousness and problem proneness still shine. He and his friends, Heffer and Filburt, come back to Earth after 20 years lost in space, but more importantly, in time.

They have spent two decades ruminating on their favorite cartoon, *The Fatheads*, on their VHS player and old fashioned TV set, antiques by our modern standards of media technology. The dynamics of the group come to fruition once they land and start exploring the new high-tech society their town has turned into. They find themselves with no option but to migrate to the digital world of the 21st century. Heffer and Filburt embrace it eagerly; the former tries virtual reality technology with childlike enthusiasm, the latter becomes an influencer streaming his entire life. Rocko, to the contrary, remains reluctant to change, and he finds out that *The Fatheads* are no longer running on TV and wants them back so he could feel like coming home at last. A meta-nostalgic Rocko, no one saw that coming.

The self-reflexive narrative escalates to baroque heights: Ed Bighead, Rocko's despicable neighbor, makes a major mistake while calculating profits for Conglom-O, the giant corporation that runs the city, taking it to bankruptcy. Ed gets fired, and when Rocko finds out *The Fatheads* were cancelled, their goals meet: Ed's son, Ralph, is *The Fatheads* creator, a reboot would save his job, the company, and give Rocko a sense of home.

Conglom-O likes the proposal, but decides to produce it on its own terms: labor exploitation and no regards for the original work. Disdaining the result, Rocko goes on a quest to bring Ralph back to produce a genuine *Fatheads* reboot: hand-drawn and true to its essence. Leavening details for the curious and jumping to the conclusion, Rocko gets to see his most burning desire coming true: *The Fatheads* come back, but something feels wrong.

Rocko's nostalgia is our own. What is wrong is not the media technology nor are the contents we scroll past endlessly, it is the time drag that slows him down in contrast to a world that moves fast and has forgotten him. *Static Cling* makes sense as Rocko's realization that no matter how behind he feels, he must grow up or be buried.

Static Cling is a brilliant title. It is as if Murray had in mind dust as a metaphor for nostalgia, the remains of pop culture clinging to our media technology, building up, burying us. By having Rocko accept change, for me, brings his character to back into place, a wallaby unbothered by the chaos around him.

I don't see *Rocko's Modern Life* coming back with new seasons, and *Static Cling* feels like a slap on the face of media companies and fans as well, or it might be a final lesson: for the former, produce new good content for God's sake; for the latter, grow up or be buried. Take that, Kowalski!

NOTES

1. Delia Crovi Druetta. "Televisión por cable en México: una industria en busca de nuevos rumbos." *Comunicación y Sociedad*, vol. 35. Universidad de Guadalajara. January-June 1999, 142.

2. *Ibid.*, 136.

3. Joe Murray. *Creating Animated Cartoons with Character: A Guide to Crafting and Producing Your Own Animated Series for TV, Web, and Short Film*. New York: Watson-Guptill, 2010, 38.

4. Wheeler Winston Dixon and John Kricfalusi. "Interview with John Kricfalusi." *Film Criticism 17, no.1.* (Fall 1992): 45.

5. Druetta, *Comunicación*, 138.

6. Uncle Nick. E-mail Interview. Chicago, April 8 2018.

7. *Ibid.*

8. *Ibid.*

9. Burgess, Jean, and Joshua Green. "How YouTube Matters." *YouTube: Online Video and Participatory Culture*. (Cambridge: Polity, 2010), 10.

10. *Ibid.*

11. "Nick Hits (Nickelodeon Latin America Block)." *Wikipedia*, 15 Apr. 2017. *Wikipedia*.

12. Nick Animation. "Episode 23: Joe Murray." December 2, 2016. *Nick Animation*, YouTube. https://www.youtube.com/watch?v=dGDlufo6CXs.

13. *Ibid.*

14. Heather Hendershot. "Children and Education," in *Television Studies*, Toby Miller, ed. (London: British Film Institute, 2002), 80.

15. Matthew A. Henry. *The Simpsons, Satire and American Culture*. (New York: Palgrave Macmillan, 2012), 33.

16. *Ibid.*, 28.

17. Nick Animation.

18. Astarothe. E-mail Interview. Chicago, April 18, 2018.

19. Introduced earlier on the text as a previous episode, *Canned* was in fact aired after *Power Trip*. However, the events presumably take place before *Power Trip* to make chronological sense.

20. Cited in Henry, *The Simpsons*, 33.

21. Nick Animation.

22. "Travel Back To 1990's Cartoon Heaven With 'Rocko's Modern Life' Illustrator Joe Murray." *Huffington Post*, 22 Jan. 2014. https://www.huffpost.com/entry/joe-murray-animator_n_4639041.

23. Astarothe. E-mail Interview. Chicago, April 18 2018.

24. Morales, Isidro. "The Mexican Crisis and the Weakness of the NAFTA Consensus." *The Annals of the American Academy of Political and Social Science 550, no. 1* (1997): 130–152.

25. *En Picada, Calidad de Los Salarios En México: INEGI*. Vanguardia._

26. Morales, *NAFTA*.

27. *Ibid.*

28. Manuel Hernández Borbolla. 2018. "Poder adquisitivo de los mexicanos cae 80% en 30 años, revela la UNAM." *Huffington Post*, January 15, 2018, sec. México. https://www.nvinoticias.com/nota/93279/poder-adquisitivo-de-los-mexicanos-cae-80-en-30-anos-revela-la-unam.

29. *Ibid.*

30. Esther Miguel Trula. 2017. "La Gráfica Que Resume La Indignación de Los Jóvenes Mexicanos: Estudiar Para Convertirte En Pobre." n.d. *World Economic Forum*. https://es.weforum.org/agenda/2017/06/la-grafica-que-resume-la-indignacion-de-los-jovenes-mexicanos-estudiar-para-convertirte-en-pobre.

31. Anna Portella. 2018. "Con salarios de pobre y sin seguro social: así viven los jóvenes mexicanos." *Forbes México*. May 4, 2018._ https://www.forbes.com.mx/con-salarios-de-pobre-y-sin-seguro-social-asi-viven-los-jovenes-mexicanos/.

32. *Ibid.*

33. Nicolle Lamerichs. "Post-Object Fandom: Television, Identity and Self-Narrative by Rebecca Williams (Review)." *Cinema Journals 55, no. 3* (Spring 2016): 172.

34. Cited in Hendershot, "Children and Education," 83.

35. Astarothe. E-mail Interview. Chicago, April 18, 2018.

36. AfterBuzz TV. *Charlie Adler, Carlos Alazraqui, & Joe Murray at San Diego Comic-Con*. July 20, 2017. YouTube. https://www.youtube.com/watch?v=3eVdah2hgqY.

37. Lamerichs, "Fandom," 171.

38. *Ibid.*, 175.

39. AfterBuzz TV.

40. Cited in Henry, *The Simpsons*, 38.

Shrek and the Art of Subversion

Chandrama Basu

Fairy tale as a cultural genre has come to occupy a significant position in society, and it continues to exert profound impressions on the minds of its readers and viewers, irrespective of age, class, and/or gender. The contention remains, however, in the fact that in recent times, not only do people "know fairy tales only through badly truncated and modernized versions,"[1] but "most children now meet fairy tales only in prettified and simplified versions which subdue their meaning and rob them of all deeper significance—versions such as those on films and TV shows, where fairy tales are turned into empty-minded entertainment."[2]

According to Jack Zipes, it was Walt Disney, who "cast a spell on the fairy tale and it has been held captive ever since."[3] He observes that Disney's fairy tale films follow a predictable schema where,

> 1. girl falls in love with a young man, often a prince, or wants to pursue her dreams,
> 2. wicked witch, stepmother, or a force of evil wants to demean or kill girl,
> 3. persecuted girl is rescued miraculously either by a prince or masculine helpers, [and]
> 4. happy ending occurs in the form of wedding, wealth and rise in social status or reaffirmation of royalty.[4]

Animations, especially those that are produced by Disney, have often been criticized for its banal portrayals of

- the hero as the stereotypically handsome, brave young man or prince,
- the princess or the young maiden as beautiful and innocent to the point of being passive,

93

- the society in which the characters inhabit as perfectly picturesque, and efficient, and
- all stories conclude with the rejoicing of the kingdom on the prospect of a happy and romantic marriage between the beautiful woman and the handsome hero who live "happily ever after."

Alan Bryman terms this overarching homogenizing phenomenon of Disney as "Disneyization" that "creates structures of similarity"[5] and is "associated with cultural homogenization."[6] This phenomenon precludes disparate experiences, endorses "sectionality," and offers an essentially exclusive purview of the society.

In recent times, Disney productions like *Brave* (2012), *Frozen* (2013), and *Moana* (2016), with their characterization and narrative, strive to subvert the ingrained social and cultural standards. Instead of representing only modified versions of prevailing modes of characterization and storytelling, these films furnish unorthodox characters harboring exceptional perceptions about the world. The characters are set against such predicaments that cannot be solved merely with magical intrusion from a fairy godmother or heroic intervention of a handsome prince but requires self-determination and resourcefulness. *Brave* features a unique narrative about princess Merida, who neither falls in love with either a young man or a prince, nor is rescued by active male heroes; on the contrary, she struggles to gain autonomy in her own life and becomes the savior of her mother's life. *Frozen* exhibits not a romantic love story but manifests a celebration of love shared by two sisters and illustrates that romantic love is not the only act of true love essential for restoring peace in life. In *Moana*, the eponymous heroine challenges tradition to preserve her own community and exemplifies the necessity to supplant deep-rooted customs to generate positive developments.

While these films have recently gained currency for deconstructing, primarily, the conception of the innocent, inactive princesses waiting to be saved by vigorous men by representing dynamic heroines, the very process of subverting the conventional features of fairy tales had initially been accomplished with success by Andrew Adamson and Vicky Jenson directed *Shrek*, based on William Steig's picture book *Shrek!* (1990). *Shrek* follows the regular Disney fairy tale narrative where a young damsel (Princess Fiona, apparently in distress) is saved by a young and brave knight (Shrek) following which they fall in love and live happily ever after. However, the film contends the expected notions of Disney's fairy tales by portraying a green ogre as its protagonist who does not fall in love with the beautiful Princess Fiona at first sight. The princess, on the other hand, fights ruffians, gobbles meat, and decides to embrace her physique of an ogress permanently by the end of the film. The innocuous villain

Lord Farquaad is portrayed as a dwarf knight, at whose behest commoners observe "revered silence," give "applause," and "laugh."

Shrek begins with the narration of a classic fairy tale where a cursed princess is locked in the highest room of the tallest tower, waiting to be rescued by her true love. But the expectations of a customary fairy tale are foiled when a hefty green hand rips off a page from a beautifully bound fairy tale book and bangs open the door of a toilet; an enormous green ogre emerges from there and cleanses himself with mud, moss and worms. That the film means to hurl a direct challenge to the popular retellings of fairy tales is explicated from the very outset of *Shrek*. The intention of the film to transgress the confines of formulaic representation is reinforced with the film's background soundtrack that "works on the viewer/listener ... namely [for] generic subversion. Jett's lyrics":

> I don't give a damn about my reputation
> Livin' in the past, it's a new generation,
> [...]
> I've never been afraid of any deviation

invite the audiences to an experience that is not fed by the dreary and formulaic ideologies of the world and suggests that both the film and its hero intends to "break the mold," thereby "consciously toying with and flouting the conventions, tropes and expectations of the fairy tale and the children's movie."[7]

Fairy tale movies are generally replete with beautiful fairy tale creatures and their breathtakingly magnificent world; but *Shrek* directly attacks the conventions by making an unlikely hero out of an ogre. Instead of portraying a handsome young prince, the film features "an outsider from the swamps, ugly and stinking"[8] and "challenges the cultural value of physical appearance by framing that value as part of a patriarchal ideology that needs to be dismantled."[9] In regular fairy tales an ogre is typically perceived and represented as "a bizarre and dangerous antagonist whose main ambition is to catch and devour humans"[10]; that *Shrek* satirizes and underscores the villagers, without any apparent provocation, as well as their plan to attack Shrek assumes that on grounds of being an ogre, he will "grind your bones for its bread." To frighten them away and protect his privacy, Shrek sarcastically supplements their knowledge with the information that "ogres ... they are much worse. They'll make a suit from your freshly peeled skin. They'll shove your liver, [and] squeeze the jelly from your eyes." This becomes apparent once again, when Donkey enquires of Shrek, "Why didn't you just pull some of that ogre stuff on him? You know: throttle him, lay siege to his fortress, grind his bones to make your bread? You know, the whole ogre trip." But this time, Shrek proclaims the unattended truth that "there's a lot more to ogres than people think."

Although ogres are primarily characterized by their "malicious behavior toward his human counterparts,"[11] the film rarely depicts Shrek as either an antagonist to human civilization or employing aggression and violence in aiming to satiate his cannibalistic appetite. On the contrary, in the scenes where Shrek encounters representatives of the so-called civilized society—like the Captain, the villagers, or the knights in Farquaad's court—it is Shrek who is manifested as the sane figure, harboring an attitude to avoid or control unpleasant situations. For instance, when Shrek visits Lord Farquaad in Duloc to demand his swamp back, he is the one who is inadvertently pulled into a brawl as Lord Farquaad whimsically declares: "Knights! New plan! The one who kills the ogre will be named champion! Have at him!" Shrek, in contrast to the expected reaction of ogres, exclaims: "Oh, hey now, come on, hang on now.... Can't we just settle this over a pint?" Again, when the villagers plan to attack Shrek, he does not exhibit any inclination to consume or pounce on them, and instead, advises them to run away, after terrifying them with a prolonged, huge, yet casual roar by way of validating and deriving amusement from the villagers' spurious ideation of an ogre.

However, as Shrek later confides to Donkey: "I'm not the one with the problem, okay? It's the world that seems to have a problem with me. People take one look at me and go, 'Agh! Help! Run! A big, stupid, ugly ogre!' They judge me even before they know me. That's why I'm better off alone." Shrek is squarely aware that, more than his nature, it is his physical attributes that make people fear, reject, misunderstand, and ridicule him. Shrek alarms the villagers with his scream, not because his basic intention is to unnerve them, but because he needs to protect himself from being ridiculed or feared, thus forcing him to "cover his awareness of feelings of inadequacy and loneliness."[12] Shrek utilizes his masculine qualities as "protective layers" and in the process challenges the concept of "macho idealism" or "ideals of masculinity" that considers possession of muscles, use of brute strength and/or force as mandatory for being a male.[13] The character of Shrek, with his internal and physical idiosyncrasies, represents an ideological space, where "the conflation of the [archetypical aspects of] monster and the hero [amalgamates] into one figure [and] parodies not only the structural expectations of fairy tale but its unambiguous morality and weight of cultural expectation."[14] Moreover, as Donkey and Shrek share a tête-à-tête where the former poignantly forces Shrek to accept the truth that he enshrouds his emotions like an onion because he is afraid of his own feelings, they subvert the relation of "hegemonic masculine characters."[15] This is firstly because "such a conversation among male characters is not typical of fairy tales,"[16] and more importantly, although recent fairy tales have started portraying and celebrating female-female relationship, as the relationship between two sisters in *Frozen* and mother-daughter relationship in *Brave*, male-male relationship either in terms of family or friendship has remained largely unrepresented.

The fact, however, remains that, in *Shrek*, almost all the lead characters make fun of or express dissatisfaction over the physical features of others, despite themselves being short of the ideal body type. For instance, although Shrek himself is a victim of the society that struggles to accept individuals whose physical attributes do not match the norm, he does not fail to make fun of Lord Farquaad's physical stature. While Princess Fiona herself suffers from her lack of exemplary physical perfection, she initially expresses her consternation at Shrek's unusual physiognomy. Although she tries to conceal her obvious disappointment with Lord Farquaad at their first encounter, by poking the miniature figure of Lord Farquaad as the groom deep into their wedding cake to reflect his true height, she relays her discomfort over having to accept a husband who does not conform to social standards of physical normalcy. Lord Farquaad, in fact, does not surprise the audience when he calls Shrek "hideous," nor when he says he finds the once "beautiful, fair, flawless" Princess Fiona disgusting as she changes into an ogre. *Shrek* subverts the cultural standard of physical appearance by playing on the ambiguous dichotomy of the beautiful and the ugly. By substituting the conventionally beautiful and accepted for the unconventionally hideous and repulsive, and by manifesting the commonplace reaction of the society at the atypical physical features, even if they are not perfect themselves, *Shrek* attempts to indicate that society cannot accept uncritically the deviant bodies of those who are often construed as outsiders in the society.

Until recently, animated fairy tales like *Snow White, Cinderella, Beauty and the Beast*, etc., provided an elevated space to encounter romance and love. As Jack Zipes underlines, the fairy tales produced by Disney "heightened the romantic aspects of the story. In contrast with the rather matter-of-fact treatment sex and marriage receives in traditional folk-tales, Disney's versions always emphasized true-love, with love-at-first sight the preferred type."[17] *Shrek*, in contrast, challenges this romantic idealism. Shrek, at the very beginning, refutes the concept of "happily ever after" with disdain by exclaiming sarcastically, "Yeah, like that's ever gonna happen" as he tears the page from the fairy tale book, which ironically bears the description of a "happily ever after" ending. This refutation not only implies Shrek's skepticism about the attainment of such a prospect in his own life in light of his debased social situation, but also enunciates his mistrust of the normative and improbable steps leading to a paradisiac future. But as the film shows, Shrek, in contradiction to his own expectations, attains a satisfactory resolution in his life—he gets the love of his life and also takes back his swamp. The film follows the contemporary cinematic trend of imparting the ostracized hero with a promising culmination (which again is often laden with the intent to subvert stereotypical portraiture of the figure of the hero), in the vein of *Can't Hardly Wait* (1998) or *Loser* (2000). The core of the matter, however, lies in the way *Shrek* challenges the orthodox worldview of a fairy tale. Although the protagonists achieve their desired outcome, the very suspiciousness the eponymous hero harbors towards a happy resolution because of his distinctiveness and consequent social segregation, identifies the essentially discriminating belief system that hackneyed representation of fairy tales has engendered.

In opposition to Shrek, Fiona, however, at least initially—expects that her life will be akin to traditionalistic fairy tale princesses. Like Rapunzel and Sleeping Beauty, Princess Fiona is imprisoned in the dragon's keep, hoping that her life will turn out as "it [usually] goes: a princess locked in a tower and beset by a dragon, is rescued by a brave knight and then they share true love's first kiss." Fiona expects that her savior should "sweep me off my feet, out yonder window and down a rope onto your valiant steed"; "charge in, sword drawn, banner flying"; and kiss her at the conclusion of the valiant enterprise. She hopes that she will be rescued by her true love, and when she sees Shrek (with his face covered by a knight's armor), she prepares herself for experiencing a romantic fairy-tale moment. She flops herself gracefully onto bed, arranges her dress, pretends to be asleep with a bouquet (clutched in her hands and resting against her bosom, no less) when Shrek leans toward Fiona, she puckers her lips, expecting to be kissed by her savior and true love. Shrek, however, negates any such possibility, exhibits no sign of romantic inclination towards the beautiful princess, shakes her vehemently, grabs her arm and hauls her away—that, too, without slaying the dragon. When Fiona, bewildered at the knight's unorthodox behavior, questions Shrek, "But wait Sir Knight! This be-eth our first meeting. Should it not be a wonderful romantic moment?" or exclaims, "But we have to savor this moment! You could recite an epic poem for me? A ballad? A sonnet? A limerick? Or something!" Shrek hampers her expectations by challenging the exaggerated priority given to romantic idealism in animated fairy tales, saying, "Yeah, sorry, lady. There's no time," and "I don't think so" and by doing so, directs "a sustained and irreverent attack on … the Disney animated fairy-tale that dominated the field throughout most of the twentieth century."[18]

The scenes depicting the first encounter between Shrek and Fiona, thus, present a dialogic conflict between the norms instituted by (Disney's) animated fairy tales and *Shrek*'s intention to subvert its acknowledged features. Where in *Snow White*, *Cinderella*, or *Sleeping Beauty*, the handsome young hero falls in love with the beautiful young heroine at the very first sight, Shrek and Fiona go against the grain by showing hardly any interest in romantic dalliance at their first encounter. Both Shrek and Fiona are acutely rooted in and motivated by their respective immediate circumstances—Shrek is not driven by any heroic or romantic impulse to rescue Fiona, but must accomplish Farquaad's challenge to retrieve his swamp, and Fiona is eager to kiss her champion and observe the rituals of fairy tales not out of any amatory desire, but to annihilate her curse. Far from being concerned about amorous involvements, the protagonists of *Shrek* are embroiled in their own cruxes, and they need each other not to satisfy their romantic yearnings and perceive each other as an end in itself, but only as a means to attain their own objectives and use one another as a tool to unlock their own quagmires. This shift in perspective subverts the normative aggrandizing of romance and establishes Shrek as a fantasy narrative preoccupied more with individualism and enterprise than with inscrutable supernatural activities often conjured to unite star-crossed lovers.

The romantic idealism of celebrated fairy tale animations is also challenged by the fact that, instead of being liberated of the curse, Fiona is permanently transformed into an ogress by the end of the film. According to Fiona's curse, she is supposed to be "by night one way, by day another. This shall be the norm. Until you find true love's first kiss. And then take love's true form." But, Shrek subverts the norm that magic spells are incontrovertible and indubitable, and surprisingly, even after Fiona is kissed by Shrek and she floats into the air, building up to the moment where she will be restored to her true self forever, Fiona does not change into her beautiful former self. She remains an ogre to the surprise of the audience that are acclimatized to experiencing such transformations in fairy tale films. The belief that kissing beholds the key to positive transformation and the negation of it in Shrek could be further studied in reference to *The Princess and the Frog*, where Tiana kisses Prince Naveen, the frog, in the hope that he would be transformed into his real handsome self. But, to their utter astonishment, Prince Naveen not only remains unchanged but Tiana herself is also magically altered into a frog. While in *The Princess and the Frog*, Charlotte was ready to kiss "a hundred frogs, if I could marry a prince or be a princess," in *Shrek* Fiona's obsession with kissing the knight/true love has been logically explained, as her want to stop her nocturnal transformation into an ogress every night.

When Shrek confesses his feelings for Fiona, she chooses to manifest her appearance as an ogress to Shrek, instead of concealing a defining aspect of her selfhood, like she has always done, first by being secluded in a remote castle away from human society and then by hiding herself at night away from Shrek and Donkey on their journey back to Duloc. By choosing to exhibit a contentious aspect of herself to the world, she rebels against her fear of rejection by the society and disentangles herself from the hitherto confining and incomplete identification to which she was subjected. By doing so, she also rebuts Farquaad's contemptuous yet ubiquitous remark when the latter says: "Oh, this is precious! The ogre has fallen in love with the Princess.... Who cares! It's preposterous!" She clarifies Shrek's misconceptions about Fiona's impressions on love and beauty, attests that the idea of an ogre falling in love with a princess is not altogether a preposterous one (since she realizes, "you shouldn't judge people before you know them"), and affirms that prescriptive ideas of beauty, as adverted by her case, are delimiting and subject to time and mutability.

Shrek also satirizes and subverts the pejorative and constraining circumstances in which Disney installs its female protagonists like Snow White and Cinderella. As the mirror exhibits Cinderella as one of the eligible bachelorettes, he describes her "as a mentally abused shut-in.... Her hobbies include cooking and cleaning for her two evil sisters," thereby underlining the fact that her inherently virtuous and generous qualities have made her a "mentally abused" person who continues to render unacknowledged and tedious services to her evil sisters and fails to assert herself even when wronged. Popular versions of fairy tales often portray the female protagonists as inordinately positive characters who undertake exceptional measures to reach gratifying and laudatory ends. They are illustrated as essentially righteous characters who are driven to aid and comfort others to the extent that their tolerant and compassionate attitude takes precedence over their personal needs and desires. In Shrek, the scene where Princess Fiona sings to a bird is a close replication of Snow White singing to a little bird. But whereas the latter sings innocently to mend things that have gone wrong, the former sets out softly before making the bird burst into feathers with her unbearably shrill-pitched tune, and she avails the opportunity to lift the eggs and uses them for their breakfast, understandably, as she herself explains: "We kind of got off to a bad start yesterday and I wanted to make it up to you." Unlike puritanically steadfast female protagonists like Cinderella or Snow White, Fiona is a practical and utilitarian princess who does not offer unconditional benevolence to the world. She tries to retain her integrity only to the point where it does not become an obstacle to obtaining her personal objectives. In this way, Shrek not only criticizes and satirizes Disney's romantic idealism, but through its visual reference to Disney characters, it "deliberately set[s] out to deny the saccharine morality and overtly family atmosphere associated with Disney productions."[19]

To posit a critique of the female protagonists commonly presented in fairy tale animations, *Shrek* depicts a heroine who subverts the normative conception about women in nefarious ways. *Shrek* plays with the visual representation of fairy tale characters by challenging the classical version of ivory complexioned, smooth-skinned, slim women and tall, muscular, white, clean shaved, starry-eyed heroes. While Shrek expresses his dissatisfaction over his physical features, Fiona too expresses her disgust over her ogress-body; and a substantive portion of their revulsion stems from the fact that they do not possess physical attributes that match the ideal body conventions. Fiona lacks an exemplary body in the form of an ogress—she is not white and fair with sharp and proportionate features, but greenish with a flat nose, large jawline, imperfect teeth and protruding ears. Both Shrek and Fiona are plump with a flabby waistline (Fiona) or a big belly (Shrek) and are often qualified using negative terms, like ugly or gross. Nevertheless, their so-called imperfect physical features never interfere with their physical fitness and agility, counter to the presumption that "among women, the ideal body representation emphasizes slimness, youth and a well-groomed appearance, [and] the ideal body image of men emphasizes health and muscles."[20]

However, when Donkey exclaims, "Shrek is ugly twenty-four seven," he misses the truism that "to accept a woman whose appearance does not meet the cultural standard … is perhaps more challenging than accepting an 'unattractive' male."[21] As underlined by Debra Gimlin, "the link between the body and identity is more explicit among women, because, for them, more than men, the body is a primary indicator of self to the outside world,"[22] an observation that becomes explicit when Fiona exclaims: "I'm a princess—and this is not how a Princess is meant to look." She is content with her beautiful, shapely, sexually attractive body, but the moment she transforms into an ogre and lacks exactly these bodily features that she lauds, she grows to detest herself. As she loses her ideal body and beauty every night (and permanently at the end of the film) she becomes "vulnerable to outside approval, carrying the vital sensitive organ of self-esteem exposed to air."[23] She even starts doubting whether Shrek is really her true love. But, once she learns to accept her new bodily identity, which comes primarily through Shrek's appreciation of her beauty, she accepts herself and becomes a representative of "an alternate concept of femininity."[24]

According to Naomi Wolf, "the beauty myth is always actually prescribing behavior and not appearance,"[25] and it is directly associated with one's outer manifestation of identity. This is especially true in Disney's representation of women, where:

> The teenaged heroine at the idealized height of puberty's graceful promenade is individuated in Snow White, Cinderella, Princess Aurora, Ariel, and Belle. Female Wickedness—embodied in villainous characters such as Snow

White's step-mother Lady Tremaine, Maleficent and Ursula—is rendered as middle-aged beauty at its peak of sexuality and authority. Feminine sacrifice and nurturing is drawn in pear-shaped, old women past menopause, spry and comical as the good fairies, godmothers, and servants in the tales.[26]

Shrek subverts the dictation of women's appearance on their behavior by portraying Fiona as a princess, who does not adhere to the "prediscursive"[27] notions of being a female or a princess. The film satirizes the inactive damsel in distress, which is further contrasted in more recent Disney productions that feature resilient female protagonists.

Princess Fiona, like her diligent successors, shows little adherence to either the dictums of elite society or the inveterate norms of elegance and composure. The proficiency with which she runs with Donkey and Shrek from the castle, and the dexterity with which she rips apart some bark from a tree to give "a few homey touches" to the cave and the spontaneity with which she fights the Merry Men and Robin Hood single-handedly, not only amazes Shrek but presents Fiona as one of the subversives, yet delightful heroines along with Rapunzel, Moana, Anna and Elsa. Fiona also debunks Queen Elinor's definition of a princess in *Brave*, according to which:

> A princess must be knowledgeable about her kingdom. She doesn't make doodles.... Princesses don't chortle. Doesn't stuff her gob! Rises early! Is compassionate, patient, cautious! Clean. And above all, a princess strives for ... well, perfection.

Princess Fiona, quite contrastingly, is "as nasty as" the swamp-dweller Shrek, belches loudly, and shows no sign of sophistication. She sits carelessly; gobbles meat in an unladylike manner; uses a spider's web to trap flies and create makeshift cotton-candy; and swiftly grabs a snake, inflates it, and presents it to Shrek as a gift. She employs her expertise in martial arts to defend herself and does not rely upon Shrek's agency to protect her from Robin Hood, who in turn, attempts in vain to protect her from the beast. Fiona does not let her elevated status as a Princess or her beauty to govern either her personality or her behavior.

Shrek's subversive embodiment of female characters is not limited to the characterization of Princess Fiona only and extends to subhuman characters as well. The film follows ancient fairy tales and folktales by featuring a fire-breathing dragon, responsible for guarding the locked—away princess, but its treatment is markedly exceptional. In *Shrek*, the dragon is initially introduced as a ferocious creature, hindering knights from rescuing the innocent princess in keeping with "Western folklore, [where a dragon is] a fabulous animal generally represented as a monstrous winged and scaly serpent or saurian with a crested head, enormous claws, and a barbed tail."[28] In Western mythology as well as in scriptures, dragons are mostly "either masculine or gender-neutral"[29] represent "the combination of every bad feature in nature-the sum of every creature's worst,"[30] and it is only by slaying the evil dragon that harmony can be restored. A major departure takes place, when the audiences in anticipation of a terrifying combat between Shrek and the dreadful dragon are surprisingly amused with a pink-colored, female dragon, who bats her eyelashes, tries to seduce the donkey, and displays more interest in courtship and a potential romantic relationship than breathing fire and eating knights. This intentionally diverting and somewhat comical rendition of the dragon as "both female and 'feminine,'"[31] dismisses long-established western and eastern folkways of branding a dragon as "jaws of hell,"[32] and a "symbol of male ruler."[33] By characterizing Dragon as an affectionate and friendly persona, *Shrek* attests the idea that gigantic and apparently savage beasts can be more considerate and gentle than the inhuman and brutal Lord Farquaad, whose diminutiveness has been unambiguously correlated with simplicity and amicability in character.

Shrek's subversion of platitudinal representation of characters is also extended to its account of Lord Farquaad. The film characterizes the so-called perfect bachelor of Duloc as a dwarf, thereby inverting the idealized image of male handsomeness promoted by Disney films. In films, as much in fairy tale films, a dwarf is rarely represented as "an ordinary human being, but rather a mischievous being, happy to be ridiculed and always to be laughed at rather than with."[34] Erin Pritchard argues that while dwarfs have been prominent parts of films such as *Snow White and the Seven Dwarfs* (1937), *The Wizard of Oz* (1939), *Willy Wonka and the Chocolate Factory* (1971), and *Charlie and the Chocolate Factory* (2005), their dwarfism has mainly been "played upon in a comedic or fantasy way."[35] But in *Shrek*, Lord Farquaad is portrayed as an extremely cunning and brute tyrant who is neither funny nor adorable. While his "neat, clean and beautiful ... court ... masks the ugliness and violence of his empire,"[36] Lord Farquaad's choleric spirit can be understood as a classic case of Napoleonic complex, as he employs his fiery spirit, dominating behavior and aggressiveness to extenuate and compensate his inferiority complex due to his short stature.

Fairy tale movies are generally replete with beautiful creatures and their utopian world, but *Shrek* directly attacks the conventions by exhibiting a sectarian repulsion against fairy tale creatures. As the film depicts, it is due to Lord Farquaad's eviction notice that the poor and helpless fairy tale creatures are forced to take refuge in Shrek's swamp. While in traditionary fairy tales, fairies, nymphs, and fair godmothers act as sources of aid to helpless protagonists like Cinderella and Sleeping Beauty, the agents of assistance in *Shrek* are themselves portrayed as helpless victims of Farquaad's tyranny. His cruelty is further emphasized in the scene of torturing the Gingerbread Man, where Lord Farquaad uses the latter's severed limbs to torment him and seek information about the "rest of that fairy tale trash poisoning my perfect world." Lord Farquaad, who aims to be the idolized ruler of Duloc, perceives the fairy tale creatures as a threat to the perfection of his kingdom and commands them to be arrested and banished from the kingdom. This staunch aversion of Farquaad towards fairy tale beings highlights his intention to eliminate the so-called perfect and faultless fantasy characters who threaten to accentuate his imperfection, challenge his authority, and thereby implicates his actions as a derivate of his inferiority complex.

Lord Farquaad's malicious nature is also underlined by the episode that he does not intend to marry until he realizes that he can gain something from the relationship. He decides to marry Princess Fiona not because he falls in love with her, but because he intends to exploit the princess's social position to achieve his ambition of becoming the perfect King. In contrast to Shrek, "who ultimately resists the patriarchal traps of the ideology of romance and hegemonic masculinity,"[37] Lord Farquaad is portrayed as a villain who is essentially "sexist and misogynistic."[38] When the mirror provides Lord Farquaad with the opportunity to choose a Princess from among Cinderella, Sleeping Beauty, and Fiona, suggestively enough, the "princesses are presented [not as beings with humane qualities, but] as objectified commodities"[39] advertised with their prominent features and further as companions that suit Farquaad according to his own needs and discretion. The truth is that Lord Farquaad does not need anyone for himself but is willing to choose a partner only to escalate his social position to that of a King. This becomes explicit in the way he chooses a bride for himself. Like a consumer who gets dazzled and puzzled at the prospect of getting to choose from various alluring products, he is shown to have become confused with more than one option until, at last, he chooses almost randomly, and in conformation to Thelonius' choice of number three bachelorette, Princess Fiona.

Fairy tale films are also customarily set against aesthetically appealing backgrounds and its photogenic kingdoms induce one "to wonder about the workings of the universe, where anything can happen at any time, and these happy and fortuitous events are never to be explained."[40] In a similar vein, Duloc is portrayed as a kingdom that is programmed to be beautiful and perfect and its absolutely neat and arranged artistry stands in sharp contrast to Shrek's savage and disorganized swamp. As Shrek and Donkey enter the castle for the first time, the glockenspiel welcomes them to the town of Duloc where "we have rules let us lay them down.... Duloc is, Duloc is, Duloc is a perfect place." Such mechanical eulogy and forced imposition of rules serve only to articulate its very opposite, and the ambiguity soon becomes distinct. Firstly, as Lord Farquaad announces: "If, for any reason, the winner is unsuccessful, the first runner up will take his place, and so on and so forth. Some of you may die, but it's a sacrifice *I* am willing to make," providing testimony to his sense of narcissism. While the prevalence of justice is regarded as one of the pivotal cornerstones of an ideal kingdom, the notion gets a severe blow as Farquaad projects a distorted sense of justice and administering the kingdom by exhibiting his nonchalant willingness to sacrifice his subjects to meet his selfish aspirations.

Secondly, one unique feature of Duloc is that the inhabitants of the land are "instructed" to give "applause," cheer, show reverence and so on to Lord Farquaad, thereby implying that the commoners are not allowed to express their own opinions and against the authority. If anyone dares to express his/her opinion, such as when the mirror clarifies that Lord Farquaad technically is not a king, their intention is curbed at the very outset with violent threats. Thelonius crushing a mirror indicates his fate, forgoing any further speech that is not desired by the authority. Therefore, Lord Farquaad is obeyed by his servants and subjects alike, not out of love but from fear of punishment. Eventually, when "the Lord is exposed as a petty tyrant and made into a laughingstock while the ugly Shrek and Fiona can retire to the messy swamp,"[41] *Shrek* provides an alternative image to the loveable image of dwarfs in animated films and subverts the cult that has generally portrayed aristocratic lords, knights, and princes as brave and courageous, responsible for bringing about the resolution in the narrative by rescuing the distressed damsel. As Lord Farquaad sends Shrek as his champion to rescue Princess Fiona, without participating in the process himself, he is essentially represented as a subversion of fairy tale heroes who undertake impossible quests for the sake of their true love.

The function of subversion has also been carried out by its background score. Music has always played an evocative role in Disney produced classic animated films like *Cinderella* and *Snow White* and to more recent films like *Tangled, Moana,* and *Coco.* As Jessica Tiffin observes, "The fairy tale has always been a particularly good fit with the musical genre, perhaps because both narrative traditions rely on a degree of stylization and deliberate removal from realism. The willing suspension of disbelief of the audience can be applied as much to the taken-for-granted magic of the fairy tale as to the unlikelihood of characters breaking into song to express their feelings."[42] I maintain that the narrative of *Shrek* does not intend to suspend the audience's disbelief in unexplainable magical events, and as such, the music of the film also functions, not to provide the audience with a route to escape the real, but to pronounce and make the audience accept the alternative of deep-rooted norms.

The film "goes on to employ its soundtrack for very specific thematic, character-development and plot-development purposes."[43] For instance, *Shrek* is introduced with American band Smash Mouth's "All Star" and it intends to establish both the film and the character of Shrek as agents of "little change" to the entrenched norms, and not one to be "fed to the rules," and questions "so what's wrong with taking the back streets?" The film employs Vincent Cassel's "Merry Men" to describe Monsieur Hood as one who "rescue[s] pretty damsels," and gets "awfully mad" when a beauty is accompanied by a beast and he takes upon himself the responsibility to "take my blade and ram it through your [ogre/ here Shrek's] heart." The song here is used ironically to subvert the concept of a damsel in distress, in need of male protection, as Princess Fiona's combat with Merry Men and Robin Hood soon proves her to be capable enough to protect herself. Further, while fairy tales like *Tangled* employ a combination of folk-rock and medieval music, a substantive number of *Shrek*'s songs belong to the genre of punk-rock that took the form of a social rebellion against the norms. Therefore, it is obvious that *Shrek* "simultaneously employs and exploits the rebellion of punk-rock. It taps into its discordant theme of subversion against the establishment, but at the same time, *Shrek* commodifies that rebellion in a good-humored children's film, thus ultimately flipping the dynamic and subverting the subversion."[44]

Cyrille François notes that when Hans Christian Anderson wrote fairy tales "in colloquial language…[his] unique style was much criticized by his contemporaries, who often accused him of writing poorly."[45] However, the "language of the tales has been altered over time, particularly as part of the effort to present 'cleaner,' more refined and less earthly versions."[46] Subsequently, the language in which the characters of fairy tale speak and converse with each other, irrespective of their class and background, is refined, without either any admixture of crudeness or references to any obscenity or sexual innuendos. As Angela Carter points out, such alterations were markedly common in the nineteenth century, "largely as a result of class consciousness. Removing 'coarse' expressions was a common nineteenth century pastime, part of the project of turning the universal entertainment of the poor into the refined pastime of the middle-class."[47] Consequently, Princess Elsa and the working-class commoner Kristoff in *Frozen* or the thief Flynn Rider and Princess Rapunzel (in *Tangled*) speaks in a uniformly refined language, despite the fact that they are from different social backgrounds and that language is "mediated by material, economic and social conditions, including class location and cultural history."[48] *Shrek*, however, subverts Disney's attempt at unifying the use of refined language by fairy tale characters and thwarts the expectations of audiences.

The film exhibits a marked difference in the employment of language by Lord Farquaad and Princess Fiona, who are representatives of the aristocratic section of the society, and Shrek, Donkey and the rest of the working class as marginalized section of the society. The intent is not only to emphasize the difference between their social classes but also to subvert the leading animated fairy tales' discriminatory tendency to uphold the cultivated and courtly language used chiefly by the social elites. Princess Fiona, for instance, concludes that Shrek is "a little unorthodox" not only from his behavior but also from his use of colloquial language that does not conform to a sophisticated knight's manner of speaking. This becomes distinct when, to Fiona's question, "Where are you going?" Shrek replies in his usual manner: "I have to save my ass!" More expressions like:

- "Together we'll scare the spit out of anybody that crosses us!";
- "You almost burned the hair off my nose";
- "I'll whup their butt";
- "you're just reeking of feminine beauty";
- "stubborn jackass";
- "I'm the talkiest damn thing you ever saw"

and so forth have been allotted to such characters who do not belong from the sophisticated elite class of the society, but are commoners and working-class individuals. On the other hand, the dialect used by Lord Farquaad and Princess Fiona resonates with the formal and decorated courtly language that is bereft of any indecency or vulgarity. Lord Farquaad's (formal) eulogy of Fiona: "You startled me for I have never seen such a radiant beauty before.... Princess Fiona, beautiful, fair, flawless..." and Princess Fiona's initial use of archaic language like: "This be-eth our first meeting" or "Thy deed is great and thine heart is pure" or her ceremonious praise of "Sir Shrek. I pray you that you take this favor as a token of my gratitude" or "You rescued me! You're amazing, you're wonderful...!" and so on contrasts the indecorous language usage of the commoners.

Shrek subverts the homogeneous constitution of popular retelling of fairy tales by causing a rupture in its picturesque neatness and stable social structure. While fairy tale films have not been bereft of spillovers and accidents, they have always been beautiful and elegant without making people cringe with a feeling of disgust from its viewers. To posit itself as a direct opposite to Disney's "perfect clean and orderly world,"[49] Shrek embodies an intrinsically grimy and flustered world. The eponymous character of the film cleanses himself with mud, uses slimy extracts from worms and bugs to brush his teeth, jumps into a sludgy swamp pond, picks out leeches and tastes them, pulls out wax from his own ears to light candles, soaks knights in the dirt, uses eyeballs for cocktails, and dines over bugs and slugs. Giroux views Disney's animated films as "teaching machines" that "inspire at least as much authority and legitimacy for teaching specific roles, values, and ideals [as] more traditional sites of learning such as public schools, religious institutions, and the family [do]."[50] By depicting an essentially crude world that shows little concern with neatness and cleanliness, compassion towards fellow beings and animals, use of appropriate language and behavior, *Shrek* undermines fairy tales' moral education about acting in conformation to esteemed principles of decorum and propriety.

One of the most notable functions served by fairy tales is that they make people believe in the achievement of otherwise improbable objectives without substantial individual agency. In fairy tales, the

> persecuted scullery maid is able to marry a prince or escape from the kitchen into the castle. A slow-witted swineherd marries a princess and inherits a kingdom. A woman is forced to take a beast as her husband, and he turns into a handsome prince.... Helpless children are abandoned in a forest, then threatened by a cannibalistic witch, but they survive. A wolf entices a naïve girl into bed, where he devours her; but she is miraculously rescued, and afterward inflicts fitting revenge upon the beast.[51]

Such incredible events are so arranged in a fairy tale that it not only serves the "specific functions to induce wonder"[52] but also operates as standardizing machinery that normalizes unproblematic materialization of fantastic events and fluent acquirement of solutions to persistent problems. But the narrative of *Shrek* does not unfold per the norm and does not feature auspicious and inexplicable events but culminates with the sustenance of a curse. The entire narrative of *Shrek* is woven with participation and action undertaken by its characters, especially by Shrek. When his swamp is incidentally populated with undesired individuals, rather than depending on fate or on the agency of anyone else (as the fairy tale creatures do in the film), he undertakes a quest that transforms his life and that of Princess Fiona's forever. The film negates the "fairy tale solution" that suggests one "to fall asleep and let nature take its course; [or that] fate will make the right decisions"[53] and exemplifies the relevance of action and autonomy in life.

Nevertheless, the story features a happy and romantic ending, where Shrek finds Fiona beautiful (despite her being an ogress), and they marry. While *Shrek* does refute and criticize idealization of romantic love, the ritualistic happy conclusion of the film "indicates possibilities of overcoming the obstacles that prevent...[individuals] from living in a peaceful and pleasurable way."[54] The film questions the parochial concept of happiness as manifested in fairy tales by presenting an unrestored Snow White closed in a glass coffin, and again by showing Sleeping Beauty and Snow White quarreling with each other over who will catch the bouquet tossed by Fiona. Further, fairy tale films generally conclude with the marriage of the immaculate couple whose eternally happy life begins with the rise in social status of either one of the partners, their settlement in an opulent aristocratic family and an extravagant castle. In this respect, "apart from deviating from the standard of presenting a beautiful appearance, the ogre couple also subverts the traditional notion of a prince's and a princess's central position in society by opting for a marginalized existence in the swamp, thus self-confidently living 'ugly ever after.'"[55]

Shrek provides an alternate narrative to the recurrent, yet constricted, perceptions popularized by contemporary adaptations of fairy tales. While most fairy tale films have perpetrated and normalized a set of generic criterions, deemed essential to achieve a favorable resolution, the film challenges the proverbial presentation of animated films and endorses the essential multiplicity and relativity that underlies complex social discourses. In this context, Jack Zipes's opinion about *Shrek!* aptly extends to the cinematic adaptation of *Shrek*, when he asserts that:

> *Shrek!* is a fairy tale that radically explodes fairy tale expectations and fulfills them at the same time: the utopian hope for tolerance and difference is affirmed in an unlikely marriage sanctified by a dragon. The ogre and his wife will continue to frighten people, but they will be happy to do so in the name of relative morality that questions the bias of conventionality associated with evil....[56]

This subversion of the principles regularized by society, fairy tales or Disney productions serve to "offer storytellers and their audiences a socially acceptable platform for the expression[57] of aspects that have been constructed as an antithesis to recognized norms and draws attention towards fairy tale's social uses and effects in increasingly nuanced ways."[58]

In contrast to the wonted messages delivered by popular fairy tales, *Shrek* asserts that beauty, love, friendship, and villainy comes in all shapes, colors and sizes and caters to all, regardless of their social backgrounds. The film conveys that women need not conform to socially expected and accepted perceptions of beauty, irrespective of which they find their true love, who, again, might not be a Prince Charming, but finds beauty in what the world thinks to be detestable; and that what has been acknowledged as amicable and helpless in society could be equally tyrannical and spiteful. Most significantly, happiness or love does not discriminate anybody based upon their physical and social conditions and can happen to individuals as ugly and imperfect as Shrek, Fiona and Donkey and desert as perfect and powerful a human being as Lord Farquaad. The film underscores the importance of accepting oneself with all his/her idiosyncrasies, advocating individualism, respecting the Other, and especially, celebrating the heterogeneity of the society.

Notes

1. Jack Zipes, *Breaking the Magic Spell: Radical Theories of Folk and Fairy Tales* (Lexington: The University of Kentucky Press, 2002), 5.
2. Bruno Bettelheim, *The Uses of Enchantment: The Meaning and Importance of Fairy Tales* (New York: Vintage Books, 2010), 24.
3. Jack Zipes, *Fairy Tale as Myth/Myth as Fairy Tale* (Lexington: The University of Kentucky Press, 2013), 72.
4. Jack Zipes, "Introduction," in *Fairy Tale Films: Visions of Ambiguity*, Pauline Greenhill and Sidney Eve Matrix, eds. (Logan: Utah State University Press, 2010), xi.
5. Alan Bryman, *The Disneyization of Society* (London: Sage Publishers, 2004), 168.
6. Bryman, *The Disneyization of Society*, 168.
7. Glenn Jelennik, "Quiet, Music at Work: The Soundtrack and Adaptation," in *Adaptation Studies: New Approach* (Madison: Fairleigh Dickinson University Press, 2010), 227.
8. Zipes, *Breaking the Magic Spell*, 227.
9. Mark Stoner and Sally J. Perkins, *Making Sense of Messages: A Critical Apprenticeship in Rhetorical Criticism* (New York: Routledge, 2015), 268.
10. Thomas Geider, "Ogre, Ogress," in *The Greenwood Encyclopedia of Folk Tales and Fairy Tales, Volumes 1–3*, ed. Donald Haase (London: Greenwood Press, 2008), 743.
11. *Ibid.*, 703.
12. Stoner and Perkins, *Making Sense of Messages*, 269.
13. *Ibid.*
14. Jessica Tiffin, "*Shrek and Shrek II*," in *The Greenwood Encyclopedia of Folk Tales and Fairy Tales, Volumes 1–3*, ed. Donald Haase (London: Greenwood Press, 2008), 860.
15. Stoner and Perkins, *Making Sense of Messages*, 269.
16. *Ibid.*
17. Jack Zipes. *The Oxford Companion to Fairy Tales* (Oxford: Oxford University Press, 2015), 157.
18. Tiffin, "*Shrek and Shrek II*," 860.
19. *Ibid.*
20. Shraga Fisherman, "Body Image and Wellbeing in Religious Male and Female Youth in Israel: An Educational Challenge," in *Gender and Diversity Issues in Religious-Based Institutions and Organizations*, ed. Blanche Jackson Glimps and Theron Ford (Hershey, PA: Information Science Reference, 2016), 57.
21. Stoner and Perkins, *Making Senses*, 270.
22. Debra Gimlin, *Body Work: Beauty and Self-Image in American Culture* (Berkeley: University of California Press, 2002), 4.
23. Naomi Wolf, *The Beauty Myth: How Images of Beauty Are Used Against Women*. (New York: HarperCollins, 2002), 14.
24. Martin Butler, "Negotiating Gender in the *Shrek* Movies," in *Gendered (Re)Visions: Constructions of Gender in Audiovisual Media*, ed. by Marion Gymnich, Kathrin Ruhl, and Klaus Scheunemann (Gottingen: Vandenhoeck & Ruprecht, 2010), 69.
25. Wolf, *The Beauty Myth*, 14.
26. Elizabeth Bell, "Somatexts at the Disney Shop Constructing the Pentimotos of Women's Animated Bodies," in *From Mouse to Mermaid: The Politics of Film, Gender and Culture*, ed. by Elizabeth Bell, Lynda Hass and Laura Sells (Bloomington: Indiana University Press, 1995), 108.
27. Judith Butler, *Gender Trouble: Feminism and the Subversion of Femininity* (New York and London: Routledge, 2011), 10.
28. Kathleen Kuiper, ed. *Merriam Webster's Encyclopedia of Literature* (Springfield, MA: Merriam-Webster, 1995), 344.
29. Unger and Sutherland, "Gendered Discourses," 465.
30. Elizabeth Edwards Goldsmith, *Life Symbols as Related to Sex Symbolism* (New York: The Knickerbocker Press, 1924), 151.
31. J.W. Unger and Jane Sutherland, "Gendered Discourses in a Contemporary Animated Film: Subversion and Confirmation of Gender Stereotypes in *Shrek*," in *Discourse*

and Contemporary Social Change. ed. by Norman Fairclough, Giuseppina Cortose and Patrizia Ardizzone (Bern: Peter Lang, 2007), 465.

32. Goldsmith, *Life Symbols*, 152.

33. Quingyun Wu, *Female Rule in Chinese and English Literary Utopias* (Syracuse, NY: Syracuse University Press, 1995), 34.

34. Erin Pritchard, "The Social and Spatial Experiences of Dwarfs within Public Spaces" (PhD diss., Newcastle University, 2014), 162.

35. Pritchard, "The Social and Spatial Experiences of Dwarfs," 162.

36. Jack Zipes, *Fairy Tales and the Art of Subversion* (New York and London: Routledge, 2006), 211.

37. Stoner and Perkins, *Making Senses*, 268.

38. *Ibid.*, 269.

39. *Ibid.*

40. Zipes, *Dreams*, 5.

41. Zipes, *Subversion*, 211.

42. Tiffin, "*Film and Video*," in *The Greenwood Encyclopedia of Folk Tales and Fairy Tales, Volumes 1–3*, ed. Donald Haase (London: Greenwood Press, 2008), 347.

43. Jellenik, "Music at Work," 227.

44. *Ibid.*

45. Cyrille François, "Teaching Hans Christian Andersen's Tales: A Linguistic Approach," in *In New Approaches to Teaching Folk and Fairy Tales*, ed. by Christa Jones and Claudia Schwabe (Logan: Utah State University Press, 2016),165.

46. Nancy A. Walker, *The Disobedient Writer: Women and Narrative Tradition* (Austin: University of Texas Press, 1995), 49.

47. Walker, *The Disobedient Writer*, 49.

48. A. Luke and P. Graham, "Class Language," in *Concise Encyclopedia of Pragmatics*, ed. by J.L. Mey (Oxford: Elsevier, 2009), 62.

49. Zipes, *Subversion*, 193.

50. H. A. Giroux, "Animating youth: the Disneyfication of children's culture," *Socialist Review* 24 (1995): 25.

51. D.L. Ashliman, *Folk and Fairy Tales: A Handbook* (London: Greenwood Publishing Group, 2004), 2.

52. Jack Zipes, *When Dreams Came True: Classical Fairy Tales and Their Tradition* (New York: Routledge, 2013), 5.

53. Ashliman, *Folk and Fairy Tales*, 2.

54. Zipes, *Dreams,*6.

55. Butler, "Negotiating Gender in the *Shrek* Movies," 68.

56. Jack Zipes, "On re-reading William Steig's book *Shrek!*" Accessed August 15, 2018. https://www.tor.com/2010/02/05/on-re-reading-william-steigs-book-shrek/.

57. Ashliman, *Fairy Tales*, 50.

58. Christina Bacchilega, *Fairy Tales Transformed? Twenty-First Century Adaptations & the Politics of Wonder* (Detroit: Wayne State University Press, 2013), 28.

"Once again, the day is saved"

How the Subversive Feminism of The Powerpuff Girls Permanently Changed Television Animation

David Perlmutter

In 1998, towards the end of a remarkably creative decade in the history of television animation, one of the most remarkably creative shows of that time premiered, opening with these words, spoken in a deceptively serious and stentorian fashion:

> Sugar. Spice. And everything nice.
> These were the ingredients chosen
> To create the perfect little girls....

However, the creation process was altered when an "extra ingredient" was "accidentally" added, a mysterious brew known only as Chemical X. From that point on, nothing in the city of Townsville was ever going to be the same, to say nothing of the genre of animation as it would be presented in the medium of television.

Just as the show's heroines repeatedly save the day before bedtime at the end of their respective narratives, it can be said that this program provided a similar role of "savior" for the superhero sub-genre in television animation, helping to spawn the remarkably diverse world of action-comedy series aimed at children that has come in its wake. This essay explores the importance of *The Powerpuff Girls* (*PPG*) to the history of television animation in the United States in both creative and technical terms, with an emphasis on how it subtly subverted many of the established tropes of both television animation and the wider multi-media superhero narrative to achieve its aims. By situating the program within its historical context, and exploring the content and construction of some of its most audacious episodes, I will explore how this series, in spite as well as because of its great popularity, came to be a ground-breaking series in many important respects.

Television animation in the United States has never had an easy existence. From its earliest days, it was condemned to critical shunning for its supposed lack of production values by fellow animators, and because it was supposedly used as a means to lure children in to both the benefits and deficits of television viewing. This latter view, in particular, remains a hold-over from the days of theatrical animation, has often been used as a form of attacking the genre and its producers even when this was not the intended case, and as, since the 1990s, children ceased to be the only perceived target audience, if they ever were that at all.[1]

While a number of highly accomplished series were produced in the 1950s and early 1960s, particularly by Hanna-Barbera and Jay Ward studios, television animation came under more severe censorship later in the decade as a consequence of it being labeled a contributor to growing violence on television. This was an accusation based more on querulous speculation and political protectionism, as the major television networks wished to expediently distance themselves from the violence debate as much as they could. Yet, between the late 1960s and the early 1990s, television animation was subjected to an unprecedented amount of censorship that was arguably applied because it was valued only for economic rather than aesthetic terms. Very little that could be considered violent was allowed to be presented, effectively tying the producers' creative hands. Tying them tighter still was the insistence on the promotion of positive social and hygiene traits in the narratives, as children were considered to be the default audience. What resulted was a series of programs that, while technically competent, left much to be desired creatively.[2] (The lingering effects of this can still felt in some modern programs aimed at the very young.) However, the genre as a whole was quick to evolve past this point by the beginning of the 1990s.

The network monopoly that instituted censorship began to falter with the establishment of the Fox Network in 1987. Fox was supported by a series of liberal-minded and edgier series aimed in particular at young adults, which the conservative-minded traditional networks had either ignored or avoided. *The Simpsons*, the new network's flagship, was a series that turned the majority of television animation's clichés on their heads, insistently suggesting that there was much more to be explored in the context of the genre and medium than had previously been thought. Over the following decades, production of television animation expanded rapidly, airing not only network outlets but on new cable outlets such as Nickelodeon and the Cartoon Network, not to mention the Disney Channel. However, while many producers were willing and able to offer more liberal, edgier fare to these outlets, others remained initially at least more conservative, not willing to abandon earlier business models until it was absolutely necessary to do so.

The impact of the restrictions on programming content was no more strongly felt than at Hanna-Barbera. Studio founders William Hanna and Joseph Barbera had kept their studio afloat between the late 1960s and late 1980s by abandoning the subtly witty and insouciant programs they had first produced in the late 1950s and early 1960s in favor of backing the anti-violence, pro-social line. While Barbera in particular resented the imposition of the regulations (he famously called it "legislated television" and compared it to football without tackling),[3] the producers knew that if they did not abide by the regulations they would not be able to produce material for the networks, their only real outlet at the time. Whereas the early work of the studio was produced under conditions of adopted and maintained respect for the individual staff members,[4] by the early 1970s, the increased volume of production and added demands made on staff turned the company into a regimented factory working towards solitary, impersonal goals. The degree to which this had been accomplished, and how much productivity was harmed, was suggested in 1979 when the local animators union—The Motion Picture Screen Cartoonists Guild—went on strike against Hanna-Barbera in a bitter campaign with lasting effects.[5] Not surprisingly, the company increasingly began to work more often with overseas studios in "runaway" arrangements than its own staff to produce series, creating a further sense of resentment and distrust among the workers. The quality of what was produced at the time reflected this creative entropy. By the time *The Simpsons* debuted, Hanna-Barbera programming was as inconsequential as FOX's new offering had been deemed monumental. It might have stayed that way had it not been for some momentous changes.

First was a change of the executive guard. In 1991, Hanna-Barbera was purchased by the flamboyant and controversial media mogul R.E. "Ted" Turner and folded into the operations of his company. Turner was attracted by the studio's wealth of material, which could easily be used as programming fodder for his cable outlets, though he was as much motivated by what he saw as the need to halt Disney from forcibly taking it over.[6] Turner synchronized Hanna-Barbera's assets with the animated ones of the film library of Metro-Goldwyn-Mayer, which he had briefly owned in the 1980s, before selling it again *sans* the film library. To make the acquisition useful, he established a unique cable outpost: Cartoon Network. Turner had earlier established the highly successful Cable News Network (CNN), the first successful all-news television outlet. Cartoon Network, which launched in 1995, was largely an extension of the CNN strategy applied to television animation. It proved to be a highly lucrative brand that continues to thrive, in modified form, today.[7]

Hanna and Barbera, who were both entering their eighties, retired from active management of their eponymous studio during this time.

In the immediate pre–Cartoon Network era, David Kirschner largely retained the status quo-oriented management of his predecessors in producing unexceptional material, yet his successor would not be content with this. Fred Seibert was not an animator by trade when he became head of Hanna-Barbera in 1994, having previously been an engineer and producer of jazz records, an advertising executive, and a founding member of the MTV staff. However, he was a passionate fan of animation and felt things could be improved upon from the way things were. The need and desire to produce original programming for the fledgling cable channel simply provided an official impetus for the plans he had in mind.

Seibert, with the assistance of Cartoon Network president Betty Cohen, devised a radical experiment. The series *World Premiere Toons*— which would later gain popularity under its new title *What a Cartoon!*— filled a programming hole while also serving (in a way) to reconnect television animation with its roots in an unrestricted environment. Short films were commissioned (with lengths between seven and ten minutes), each with the promise that they could act as pilot episodes for full-length series. Management would not and did not interfere with the creative process, which was a radical departure from the studio's established protocol. The original plan was to produce 48 films over three years, but this format was overhauled as the producers were buried by a massive number of submissions, reflecting the idea's wild appeal. As historian Michael Mallory notes, "[w]ell over a thousand artists presented storyboards, sketches, [art] school projects, or privately produced 'seed' cartoons to a studio selection panel, each hoping to land a development deal, which carried with it access to studio production resources."[8] Standards were quite high, as the creator of one of the chosen projects would find out.

Born in Charleroi, Pennsylvania, in 1971, Craig McCracken had, like many animators, shown signs of artistic skill from his youth. After attending high school in his native state, he headed west to further his education at California Institute of the Arts. During that time, he met and befriended Russian-born Genndy Tartakovsky, and developed his first films, which were good enough to be featured at a popular independent animation festival. However, McCracken was destined not to finish his schooling. During his third year, a friend advised him that Hanna-Barbera was looking for an art director for its animated series *2 Stupid Dogs*. McCracken went to the studio, pitched himself, and was hired. Remarkably, he had never worked in the animation industry before that time,[9] but this was typical of the hiring practices under Seibert's watch. Not only did Seibert hire McCracken and Tartakovsky, but several other future movers and shakers of television animation came into the studios as young apprentices among the animators, writers, producers and directors then. This young blood was just what the ailing television animation practices of Hanna-Barbera required for rejuvenation.

Naturally, McCracken was aware of the *What a Cartoon!* project when it began and was eager to be part of it. Drawing initial inspiration from an animated serial called *The Adventures of Stevie and Zoya* (produced by Joe Horne for MTV) he developed a superhero narrative, one resurrected from an idea he toyed with during his student days. His heroines were a trio of prepubescent schoolgirls that were originally known as The Whoopass Girls. After completing the pilot, titled "A Sticky Situation," he became so confident in the idea's potential that he then proceeded to start work on four separate films with the characters, though only one was seen to completion.[10] Despite this, he was able to convince the management of the idea's worth. This resulted in two films with the characters aired as part of *What a Cartoon!* during 1993.[11] The installments were well-produced, in spite of McCracken's DIY approach to animation, but were nowhere near the potential they would ultimately achieve.

McCracken was then sidetracked. Tartakovsky had successfully pitched his project *Dexter's Laboratory* (1996–1998, 2001–2003)[12] to the network as a full-length series, and he recruited McCracken to serve as the art director and chief character designer. Working under Tartakovsky, McCracken sharpened his skills with on-the-job training. Tartakovsky's background and influences covered both American and European influences, which *Dexter* displayed in the juxtaposition of a non–North American, angular approach to character design with a largely American approach to belly-laugh humor. What was perhaps most unique about it, however, was that Tartakovsky and McCracken chose to dispense with some of the more repetitious elements of the process of writing and directing television animation. Rather than rely on stock backgrounds, recycled character moves and poses, and particularly limited and repetitive storylines, they treated each episode as an independent unit as opposed to the traditional identical field of thirteen approach of the past. Particularly, they liberated the camera.

Technology, as well as creative restrictions during the network censorship era, had until the 1990s restricted the potential for camera movement during and between shots in animation, restricting the camera chiefly to a passive, impartial recorder of events. Tartakovsky and McCracken were not interested in presenting material in this manner (as, indeed, many of their contemporaries were not, either). They brought many of the techniques of live-action filmmaking into television animation in ways that enriched their visual scope and served to provide the punch necessary for their jokes. Zip pans, extreme zooms both in and out, lingering long shots and short cutaways replaced the traditional static camerawork of earlier eras. Given the emphasis on action and comedic elements of the series, it was necessary to develop a new approach to cinematography that matched the increasingly ambitious aims of the producers. The approach paid off, as *Dexter* proved to be a highly popular series with a long run, and acted as a curtain-raiser for what McCracken would accomplish with his own *PPG*.

When production finished on *Dexter's Laboratory*, the unit that had produced it remained intact, with McCracken now assuming leadership and Tartakovsky becoming the silent partner. McCracken had retained interest in developing *PPG* as a series, trying to interest other entities but received little interest. Furthermore, the original idea and concept had not been attractive enough to the desired young demographic when it was pitched to them in focus groups.[13] So McCracken retrenched with support from the network and proceeded to develop a detailed background and backstory for his supporting cast. As he later recalled:

> When I did the first shorts, I was more focused on developing weird concepts than developing characters.... That was my biggest mistake. I knew the characters so well because *I'd* been working with them for years, but I forgot that I wasn't telling the virgin audience [i.e., those who were tuning in to the show for the first time] who they were. [emphasis in original][14]

The solution McCracken came up with was to introduce the characters and concept in a short but efficient way in the main title sequence; this helped to dispose of the excess baggage of introducing and re-introducing the idea over time in the narratives proper. This would allow McCracken and company to concentrate first and foremost on the development and execution of those on their own terms.

Animation is a collaborative medium, so it is rare that a single individual's insight and will can come to dominate an animated film or television series. McCracken indicated such himself when he spoke about the ways and means by which story ideas were developed for the project:

> It's an open, creative process.... We'll have story meetings ... kick around ideas and see what gels, and we'll write up an outline that gives the main [idea] of a story, where it's going.... That is given to the storyboard guys, and...[they] are the ones [who are] really making the show. They're the ones coming up with the shots, the gags, writing the dialogue, and doing a major part of the work. Then they'll put it on the wall and pitch it to the whole group, and we'll go through and make notes on it, tighten it up, and make it work better.[15]

Still, an element of tight control over the process, not unlike that of a live-action film director, resided with McCracken himself. A great deal of the notetaking (which could become very complicated and detail-oriented), tightening up and "making it work" was done by the creator himself. He co-directed many of the episodes in tandem with Tartakovsky, later employing several line directors. He was an exacting perfectionist, sometimes scrapping or redoing entire sequences if they did not match what he wanted. This was not done in a tyrannical fashion but simply through his function as the program's executive producer; but, it is noticeable to the viewer. As with other television animation producers of the period, he was enacting his belief as to how television animation *should* be produced to be at its most effective. Consequently, McCracken was able to develop a highly personal approach in a genre that had previously been highly impersonal. His idea was his alone, and it would only be under his guidance that it would survive and thrive.

That *PPG* was a success after it began is putting it mildly. It would ultimately run during its original production for the better part of seven years, far longer than the majority of animated programs manage to do, and was nominated for and won the highest awards of excellence in both television and animation. And, as with many a popular television animation program, it became the foundation of a small empire of licensed merchandise. What is most remarkable about *PPG* is that it achieved this success—as well as altering the fundamental nature of both television animation and the wider media superhero genre—in a most unobtrusive fashion. McCracken may not have intentionally tried to challenge the status quo in developing his setting and characters, but he did so just the same.

Historically, the superhero genre, in both comics and animation, has a well-earned reputation for existing primarily as a boys' club, one in which women were not allowed to participate in unless certain specific qualifications were met. From the beginning of superhero comics in the 1930s, and continuing until at least the end of the twentieth century, creative power (in terms of writing and drawing) was held almost exclusively by men. Likewise, the vast majority of the heroes of this period were men, or, at the very least, masculine in nature. While there were some exceptions amongst the heroes from time to time, women who became or acted as heroines were restricted in a number of respects.

First was the fact that they were often the creations of men (Wonder Woman, for example, was famously devised by psychologist William Moulton Marston) and thus did not entirely reflect a truly genuine feminine mindset. Second was the fact that, unlike the men, female super-heroines have often had to face an ingrained level of sexism, the idea being that a truly powerful woman could exist only as a novelty item rather than as a full-blooded "masculine" hero. Third, and perhaps what was the most limiting factor of all, was the fact that female heroes were frequently made to enact tropes that reinforced their supposedly typical "femininity" (i.e., screaming, fainting) and therefore established that they were somehow "inferior" to the men. Even when editor/writer Stan Lee introduced a greater level of narrative and character complexity to comics in the 1960s, the advances still served to benefit male heroes at the expense of female ones. The case of the Invisible Woman from the Fantastic Four is a good example, as she never developed an identity distinct and separate from the male members of the group.[16]

When superheroes first began emerging as part of television animation in the mid–1960s, there was no perceived need or desire on the part of television animation producers to fundamentally alter the playbook that the comics had handed them in any way. Animation, like comics, had largely been a male preserve and likewise tended to reflect a masculine depiction of what women were supposedly "like" rather than what women truly knew they were. If anything, the anti-violence backlash of the late 1960s served to compromise any genuine creativity in television animation super-heroics as it did for the entirety of television animation. Thus, any attempt to truly explore the potential of super-heroics would have to wait until such censorship was less limited. This is where the historical importance of *The Powerpuff Girls* lies.

The number of pre-adolescent superheroes in the canon to this point was rare; the number of ones who were girls was even less so. The persistent, almost corrosively "masculine" nature of the superhero genre denied them a place for so long. So, to have kindergarten-age girls as the heroines of his narrative was a rule-breaking, audacious act on McCracken's part. This was chiefly because it obliterated and erased one of the biggest obstacles needed for taking female super-heroics seriously. The objectification of the adult female body by men has always been a major obstacle in Western society. No more so than female superheroes, whose attire has always seemed to encourage voyeurism in male readers, as practical as it may be in doing their duty. But, pre-adolescent girls do not have bodies that can be objectified in the same way, allowing McCracken and company to focus on other issues. This was a subtle but extremely important shift in the portrayal of superheroes in television animation, and it would be one that, in the following years, would help make the genre of television animation a place where the female voice could increasingly be respected rather than degraded or shamed.

It helped, too, that the world had changed considerably since the 1960s. As they had in the wider world, women emerged as a stronger presence behind the scenes in both comics and animation, particularly in the creative roles once denied them. This further strengthened the appeal and viability of McCracken's concept at the time of its debut. McCracken's production team for the series was, not surprisingly, a co-ed one, with many women playing prominent roles. Most notable was writer Lauren

Faust, who scripted some of the more startlingly feminist statements made throughout the series. She would ultimately end up developing one of the more startling successes of the 2010s with *My Little Pony: Friendship Is Magic*, not to mention working on other series developed by McCracken, whom she later married.

Just by existing as they did, the Powerpuff Girls came at a remarkable time in the historical evolution of television animation, and their subtle words and deeds reinforced their importance while sowing the seeds of their future media influence. In particular, it shows how the subversive way it presented its feminist subtext would be one of its greatest and lasting cultural legacies. As with most superhero narratives, *PPG* at its heart deals with the conflicting issues and concerns that superhuman beings are perennially caught between: (1) what makes them human; (2) what sets them apart from others; and (3) what roles they must play in society. McCracken foregrounded the uniqueness of his heroines with an equally unique approach to enacting their adventures:

> Nothing set McCracken's approach to the series apart more than his heroines themselves. No other television animation characters have been more prominently featured in a series. Their delight is to be savored; their rage feared. Even at their most helpless, the viewer is never allowed to forget what they are capable of doing at their most powerful, benevolent or otherwise…[W]e are never allowed to assume, likewise, that because they are "heroes," all their actions are therefore just. Indeed, their patience is frequently tested, and their wrath brought out, by the epic levels of stupidity they have to confront.[17]

That most of this stupidity is committed by the largely dull-minded male characters in the series speaks for itself.

McCracken's need to develop the series beyond the one-dimensional action-centric approach used in the earliest episodes of the series required him to develop his leads as multi-dimensional figures who could both attract and sustain audience attention. The trio therefore came to assume the personalities they acquired:

- Blossom (voiced by Cathy Cavadini), the group's red-haired "leader," is notable for her formidable intelligence. She conducts herself with a prominent mental superiority that can calcify into an iron will at the worst of times. Her assumed responsibility of the group's public persona and battle director, belies her chronological age and plays a prominent part in the stories. Her conduct at its worst does not go unpunished, and she can be contrite on the occasions when she is shown to be in the wrong.
- Blonde-haired Bubbles (Tara Charendoff Strong) exists as another type entirely. Her personality is equal parts naiveté, exuberance,

and paper-doll fragility, which her high and extremely "feminine" voice does little to distract from. She is the most sensitive emotionally of the trio, driven to tears more than once in the course of the series by what she hears and witnesses. The trio's enemies often try to play on this as a means of destroying them all. However, Bubbles can rouse herself with a startling fury when called on in the most startling of ways, doing so in the name of vindication.

- Black-haired Buttercup (E.G. Daily) is equally remarkable. Taking pride in her ability to fight in a far more stereotypically masculine way, she can be hell let loose when allowed to pummel her opponents into submission. Her trouble comes with knowing when to *stop* fighting. She and Blossom, not surprisingly, are in conflict regularly and often, both verbally and occasionally physically. Even on the rare occasions when Buttercup allows herself to be "sensitive" enough to reveal her inner feelings, they are explored in the same explosive fashion as her fisticuffs.

Each, in a way, comes to assume some aspect of a particular feminine stereotype but behave in a way that challenged and debunked it.[18] These conflicted, highly emotional personalities are what drive the program, and McCracken gives them free reign to do so. Furthermore, he increases the level of interaction the viewer has with them (and everyone else in the narrative) by a highly cinematic filming approach. The editing of the show is fast and furious, with images coming from an astonishingly wide number of camera positions, placements, and movements, particularly on the occasions when the Girls fight with villains. The involvement of the viewer in these situations is both unavoidable and undeniable to the point that they can sometimes feel the impact of explosive punches thrown on their own body.[19] No other animated program has had this kind of immersive feel to viewing it, before or since.

Prior to *PPG* it might have been enough to take a basic superhero situation, such as a villain battle, and replay it a few times to create a series. McCracken, however, was not satisfied with this; neither was his team. Unlike their predecessors, they chose to use the series to challenge many of the set assumptions on which the superhero narrative was based upon, providing both comic and dramatic means elements of a more equitable and arguably feminist narrative in its place. It is in these sorts of narratives that many of the most memorable moments of the series occur.

On a basic level, subtle feminism is reflected in the fact that the majority of the male characters the Girls interacted with—friend or foe—are ones they can easily fool or beat. They tend to embody a range of masculine stereotypes (e.g., stubbornness, stupidity, obliviousness) in much the same fashion as the Girls reflect feminine ones, but the males are not allowed to show such a wide range of feelings as the Girls are. Only the Girls' creator, Professor Utonium (Tom Kane), was able to be seen on equal terms to them in this regard since, as their "father," he is able to use a modicum of patriarchal affection and authority to keep them in line. He, however, could be charmed too, beguiled and dominated by them as he often was by some of the adult females in the series. As a consequence, it was often the case that the Girls were often more befuddled by female villains, who fought them on their own terms, and more apt to look up to friendly female adults for guidance. This formulation, constructed in tight eleven-minute episodes, was what the show existed as for the balance of its run, and how it exists in its current form on DVD.[20]

While not all the episodes had a feminist agenda, the ones that did are notable for such, and, as always with the series, were remarkable for the matter of fact manner in which they asserted the plurality and diversity of women's voices in what had once been a masculine playground. Take for example the 2001 installment "Equal Fights." Here, the Girls are confronted by Femme Fatale, a personification of the radical nature of feminism and the misandry that often comes with that political viewpoint. Earning the Girls' confidence, only after convincing them the men in their lives have given them a raw deal, the villain converts them to their cause, and causes them to act in highly misandrist way themselves. It is only when the Girls are confronted with the fact that (1) Femme Fatale's view of the world is highly limited and that (2) she notably does *not* speak for all the women in the world that the Girls are able to take measures into their own hands again and defeat her. The 2001 episode "Members Only" presents an equally uncompromising inner message. In it, the Girls attempt to join the masculine-centric superhero organization The Justice Friends. However, while they meet the physical requirements for the job, they are denied membership because of the membership's sexist bias against "little girls." Revenge comes when the members are attacked by a villain capable of draining their "manliness" from them. The Girls, having none of that in their systems, defeat him easily.

Other episodes of the series underlined the unique super-heroic status of the Girls while at the same time acted as cautionary tales for those who became too infatuated with them. The 1999 episode "Collect Her" involves a stereotypical comic-book aficionado who imprisons the Girls in "power packages" (oversized versions of the Mylar bags in which comic-book collectables are stored) so that he can have them "forever." In a just form of payback the people of Townsville rescue the Girls for all the times they saved the town from destruction. The 2004 episode

"Documentary" involves a similarly obsessive filmmaker trying to make a film about the Girls. However, they barely appear in the episode, and he has to ironically try to cobble something together about them by the most amateurish of means.

Nothing served to highlight the uniqueness of the series and its lead characters better than the brilliant 2001 episode "Knock It Off," a scathing and ironic satire of the sort of mass media merchandising of which *PPG* had by this time irrevocably become a part of. Dick Hardly (a college classmate of the Professor's) meets the Girls and discovers their secrets. This prompts him, with some stolen Chemical X, to create a variant of the Girls which he creatively calls The Powerpuff Girls X-Treme. But he's not done there. He then clones them *ad nauseum*, positioning his clones around the world. Cornered by the Girls, he ingests the remainder of his supply of Chemical X, becomes a monster, and nearly kills them by draining the chemical from their bodies. It is only when the Professor sincerely declares his love and affection for the Girls that Dick and the clones are finally destroyed. It is a haunting lesson about the destructiveness of greed but also a vindication of how love and affection are necessary in the world. It further reaffirms the brilliance of this series and its storytelling method.

The achievement of *PPG* begins with a unique approach to storytelling, presenting a style that had become hackneyed only to utterly transform it by approaching the form from an entirely new point-of-view. By bringing a decidedly feminist perspective to something that had been almost drowning in a corrosive masculinity, McCracken changed the way television animation approaches super-heroics permanently and certainly for the better. *PPG* proved that heroics, super ones and otherwise, are not and cannot be something for white men alone. Many shows in the coming years would adapt *PPG*'s dramatic, cinematic storytelling to a wide variety of narratives, carrying on the work started by McCracken and his company in following decades. As unique as these followers have been, it will always be apparent just where and from whom certain tricks in their bag had been learned from. By showing how effectively super-heroics can better reflect the realities of the world, *PPG* made it safe for anyone to dream of the occasions when they, too, could conquer their limitations and "save the day."

Notes

1. For a wider analysis of this concept, see David Perlmutter, *America Toons In: A History of Television Animation* (Jefferson, NC: McFarland, 2014).

2. For a discussion of the violence debate and its legacy, see Perlmutter, *America*, 116–129.

3. Joseph Barbera, quoted in Gary Grossman, *Saturday Morning TV* (New York: Dell, 1981), 358.

4. Joseph Barbera, *My Life In 'Toons* (Atlanta: Turner, 1994), 136.

5. Tom Sito, *Drawing the Line: The Untold Story of Animation Unions From Bosko To Bart Simpson* (Lexington: University of Kentucky Press, 2006.) 258–261.

6. Ted Turner and Bill Burke, *Call Me Ted* (New York: Grand Central, 2008), 290–292.

7. Turner and Burke, 292–294. The assets of both Hanna-Barbera and Cartoon Network are today owned by Time Warner, to which Turner sold his company in 1996.

8. Michael Mallory, *Hanna-Barbera Cartoons* (New York: Hugh Lauter Levin Associates, 1998.) 196.

9. Craig McCracken, quoted in Joe Murray, *Creating Animated Cartoons With Character* (New York: Watson-Guptill, 2010), 106–107.

10. Allan Neuwirth. *Makin' Toons: Inside the Most Popular Animated TV Shows And Movies.* (New York: Allworth, 2003), 72–78.

11. Craig McCracken, quoted in Murray, 106–107.

12. David Perlmutter, *The Encyclopedia of American Animated Television Shows* (Lanham, MD: Rowman and Littlefield, 2018), 153.

13. Neuwirth, *Makin' Toons,* 75.

14. Craig McCracken, quoted in Mallory, 208–210.

15. *Ibid.*

16. For some historical overviews of the evolution and development of superhero comics in twentieth century America, see in particular Gerard Jones, *Men Of Tomorrow: Geeks, Gangsters And The Birth Of The Comic Book* (New York: Basic Books, 2004.); Jordan Raphael and Tom Spurgeon, *Stan Lee And The Rise And Fall Of The American Comic Book* (Chicago: Chicago Review Press, 2004.); Ronin Ro, *Tales To Astonish* (New York: Bloomsbury, 2004.); Sean Howe, *Marvel Comics: The Untold Story* (New York: HarperCollins, 2013.); Tim Hanley, *Wonder Woman Unbound* (Chicago: Chicago Review Press, 2013.); and Jill Lepore, *The Secret History Of Wonder Woman* (New York: Alfred A. Knopf, 2014.) For a study of super-heroines in particular at this time, see Trina Robbins, *The Great Women Superheroes* (Northhampton, MA: Kitchen Sink Press, 1996.).

17. Perlmutter, *America,* 270.

18. *Ibid.,* 271.

19. Perlmutter, *Encyclopedia,* 479.

20. The most comprehensive collection available is the *10th Anniversary Collection* (Cartoon Network/Warner Home Video, 2008), which offers the "complete series" in a fully accessible fashion. Other collections, containing smaller numbers of episodes, are also available from the same source.

We Need to Talk About
The Lego Movie!

Social Commentary and Consumer Culture in the LEGO-verse

Sasha Dilan Krugman

Using the popularity of the brand and the recognizability of the medium itself, Chris Miller and Phil Lord reached global success in 2014 with their hit animated film *The LEGO Movie*. Blending animation, consumer culture, and a nuanced sense of humor, the film seemingly targets younger audiences while self-reflexively speaking against a growing consumer and capitalist culture. Using the implications of the LEGO medium's materiality,[1] the directors use the LEGO blocks directly as an animated vessel through which social commentary can be problematized. Presenting the LEGO-verse in the film as a totalitarian, capitalist, and utilitarian dictatorship under the not-so-subtly named "Lord Business/Mr. Business," the hero of the film—"an ordinary LEGO citizen" named Emmet—must use his creativity in order to protect his world from a "Kragle"[2] -induced stasis. At first glance the film operates under a double metaphor, utilizing firstly the fight of individualist expression against capitalist and utilitarian societies, and secondly the creative stunting of children in the face of adult exceptionalism. Spawning after its release spin-off films, video games, custom LEGO sets, and a TV-series,[3] the LEGO films have enjoyed a success similar to that of the toy that inspired its inception. However, based on the LEGO business model alone, a system that simultaneously supports free play while providing step-by-step instructional manuals for its users, it is naïve to consider the film as simply a subversive champion of free expression and individualism. The LEGO business model is contradictory in and of itself as it is problematic to assume the ability of free play within a system of play.

125

Based on the abbreviation of the Danish words "*leg godt*," meaning "play well,"[4] the LEGO brand has enjoyed international success throughout the years as a powerhouse of the toy industry. Although the company initially produced both wooden and plastic toys, their success came in 1949 with the birth of their patented interlocking brick system, eventually leading to their global success.[5] After spawning the second largest theme park corporation in the world in the 1960s, the LEGO company revolutionized the industry with their introduction of the mini figure.[6] With over four billion mini figures currently in existence,[7] the LEGO company owes its global success to their business model based on their "system" of play. Although the company has suffered financial setbacks over the years, and a series of failures within the global toy market,[8] their financial recovery can be attributed to its return to their original system of play. Focusing on the importance of story and narrative in order to foster child involvement, the company produced a varying array[9] of sets modelled after short films and TV series. Basing the company's core on the interlocking brick system that made it famous, LEGO became the largest toy company world-wide in 2014.[10] As bricks from the 1950s can interlock with bricks produced today, the LEGO system of play allows its users a seemingly infinite set of possibilities.[11]

Taking the LEGO toy as a medium for expression, this chapter will first introduce the LEGO medium's system of play, its use as a multi-media form of expression and the expanding culture that surrounds this system that has formed a community based on its creative consumption. Second, this chapter will highlight the theoretical underpinnings of animation, play, and consumer capitalism that deems this product simultaneously productive and problematic in context to its use in the film. Such an approach allows for a close analysis of the language and rhetoric the film uses, revealing the contradictory societal critiques initially conveyed in the film. Last, this chapter will theorize the implications of the LEGO media universe that the film has created in tandem with tie-in productions released after the first film.

The System, the LEGO Community and Brick Films

Fascinated by the idea of a system himself, the third son of the original LEGO founder, Godtfred Kirk Christiansen, spent "several weeks" defining the attributes of the system, arriving at six core features.[12] The system of play was therefore defined as limited in size without setting limitations for imagination, affordable, simple/durable and varied, fun for every age and gender, a timeless classic, and easy to distribute.[13] David Gauntlett defines the LEGO system of play as:

> The idea that any LEGO element, or any LEGO set, is not an isolated or complete object, but comes with the potential, and the promise, that it is part of a much larger whole. The system of interconnecting studs and tubes, patented by the LEGO Group in 1958, means that any LEGO object can be connected with others and almost endlessly extended. The System is good for users, because the value of their LEGO collection is increased as it grows—because they are able to do more diverse and more interesting things—and obviously this works well for the company too, providing customers with a rational motivation to make more purchases from the same range of products.[14]

This not only implies a human dimension, but also that the system has less to do with the objects within the system but is more motivated by what "humans *do* with the objects."[15] Central to this conception is then the dynamic relationship the company has with its users, fostering ecosystems and common identities between cross-cultural consumer groups. For Gauntlett, this can be extended into a "broadly-understood system to embody a democratic philosophy of things fitting together, and empowering people to build."[16]

Connecting its users under a system ethos[17] the LEGO system of play constitutes itself as a creatively inspired tool of thinking, "using LEGO bricks to support the representation of ideas, and the organization of thinking."[18] This means that the medium itself can be used to represent abstract experiences, feelings and ideas, contributing to a process of creative problem solving allowing the physical object to have a tangible relationship with the creator.[19] Gauntlett suggests we recognize "that culture always signifies both a context for experiences, and actual experiences themselves," implying that culture exists in a site within which people are creative and simultaneously exist in spaces influenced by creativity.[20] The model therefore suggests that culture is a system through which "people build meanings, and develop community, through the four dimensions of *having, doing, being* and *knowing.*"[21]

Within this frame we must accept the LEGO System as a kind of culture and therefore assess it through the cultural model presented above. The *having* dimension connects LEGO products to culture as tangible tools, while the *doing* dimension concerns cultural and relational practices, while the LEGO system creates a community of doers who can share their work through various platforms.[22] The *being* dimension of the cultural model then concerns ritual and sentimental practices as well as group characteristics, which in the case of LEGO culture refers to the collective practices of its users and the company's general ethos.[23] Lastly, the *knowing* dimension highlights the connection between knowledge and shared meanings that support a culture, in the LEGO context "dimension is well integrated with *doing* and *being*, which as we have seen, both involve networks of knowledge-sharing and mutual support."[24] Gauntlett concludes that the LEGO medium can therefore be seen as a "convivial" tool that allows for it to function as "flexible to different people's needs, enable individual self-expression, and encourage conversation."[25]

The cultural implications of a medium such as LEGO cannot be undermined, especially considering that "there are over 100 LEGO pieces for every person on the planet."[26] LEGO culture therefore spans across multitudes of fields and communities. Multiple user conventions such as BrickCon, Brickworld, and BrickFair have gained prominence in America based on user participation; other such events take place in Europe, Asia and around the globe. These conventions host large gatherings of users who have created their own language and currency based on LEGO bricks.[27] In terms of user engagement, these are occurrences that have spawned independent of the company itself, becoming self-sustaining communities catering to individual builders.[28] The LEGO Architecture Series was created by a singular LEGO user, and other LEGO sets such as their CUUSOO series, is based on the creation of a crowdsourcing platform born from community interest and support.[29] Now rebranded as "LEGO Ideas," the platform allows LEGO enthusiasts to design, brand, and market their original LEGO designs on an interactive platform. The competing designs are then narrowed down, ultimately leading to the mass production of one of the designs; allowing LEGO consumers to become Master Builder's in their own right.[30]

The LEGO medium is one based on a systematic creativity, meaning that the creativity it inspires within its users is based on a simple system, giving it a form and means of communication. The way the system of play works is then embedded within the system itself, both as a creative tool and a language. Mathematically speaking, although the LEGO system is finite in its practical conceptions, it is a medium that is "infinitely probable."[31] This is evident in the varying usage of LEGO outside of the building community, as bricks can be seen anywhere from patchwork projects and "LEGO bombing" of buildings (where repairs to cracks in buildings and infrastructure are made using LEGO blocks) to their usage in art and museum exhibitions and their scientific usage in community planning and even at institutions such as NASA.

Most notably the emergence of Brickfilms' stop motion of CGI films—featuring LEGOs as the predominant material of choice—in the late 2000s cemented LEGO as not just a toy, but a versatile medium of expression.[32] A Brickfilm can be defined as "a film made using LEGO bricks, or other similar plastic construction toys, primarily created with stop motion animation."[33] Individuals who create Brickfilms note that LEGO provides a recyclable medium that does not limit creativity, and is nostalgic, colorful, tactile, and modest in size, making it easier to tell stories.[34] Based on a large, mainly online, community born in 2001, Brickfilms have existed since 1973, reaching mainstream status in the late 1970s to 1980s, and were first featured in *Wired* magazine before becoming increasingly mainstream.[35] Spawning an expansive online community that remains active today, Brickfilms remain a popular choice of medium for creatives looking to share their unique narratives. Philip Heinrich's 2016 documentary film *Bricks in Motion*[36] highlights an array of international brick filmmakers and their experiences working in the medium. Their discussions on this specific branch of stop motion animation isn't limited to the messages they want to convey or avoid but also explores larger arguments surrounding the interpretation of their films. The filmmakers argue that due to their chosen medium, their work is seen as products of lighthearted entertainment, and therefore taken less seriously as an art film, creating a disconnect between the audience and the filmmakers themselves.[37]

The LEGO Movie

Although aesthetically reminiscent of a Brickfilm, *The LEGO Movie* provides audiences with a CGI LEGO-verse, allowing Lord and Miller further artistic control over how to animate their narrative, but most importantly humanize their mini figures. As the film opens, we witness the wizard Vitruvius trying to protect the "Kragle," (what audiences will recognize as Krazy Glue), from the evidently evil Lord Business. As Vitruvius fails to do so on his own, he warns Lord Business of a prophecy where an individual named the "Special" would discover the "Piece of Resistance" and stop the Kragle. Fast-forwarding to eight and a half years later, we are introduced to Emmet Joe Brickowski, an "ordinary construction worker" with "no special talents." After staying behind at work one day Emmet is introduced to Wyldstyle as she searches for something after hours. Investigating her intentions, Emmet falls through a hole, inadvertently leading him to discover the "Piece of Resistance." After experiencing intense visions, Emmet regains consciousness in the custody of Bad Cop, Lord Business' lieutenant and second in command. Upon learning of Lord Business' plans to induce a Kragle stasis on the World, effectively fixing citizens in their designated places permanently, Emmet is rescued by Wyldstyle and taken to Vitruvius. There Emmet learns about the existence of other Universes and Master Builders, and how Lord Business came to power, resulting in the regimented Universe Emmet resides in today.

As the "Special," Emmet is destined to defeat him, yet Wyldstyle and

Vitruvius are disappointed to find Emmet displays no creativity. While being pursued by Bad Cop across Universes, Emmet and Wyldstyle are taken to a meeting with the last remaining Master Builders. As Emmet fails to impress them with his lack of creativity, the Master Builders refuse to join Emmet in the fight against Lord Business and are eventually captured by Bad Cop and taken to Lord Business' headquarters. In an attempt to infiltrate Lord Business' office, Emmet and his allies are captured and Vitrivius killed. In his dying words, Vitrivius confesses to manufacturing the prophecy of the "Special," eventually returning as a ghost to tell Emmet that the prophecy is made up because everyone has the ability to be special. This leads Emmet to attach himself to a self-destruct mechanisms battery flinging himself off the edge of the LEGO-verse. Inspired by Emmet, the Master Builders escape, eventually rallying with the help of Bad Cop. Soon, LEGO citizens across the LEGO-verse begin building their own creative weapons, the Master Builders leading the rebellion against Lord Business.

The LEGO Movie garnered great success with its global audience, creating an innovative universe for children while simultaneously moving adults with its surface critique of consumer capitalism and contemporary society through its use of the nostalgic children's toy. In this regard, the LEGO medium's use as an animated vessel allowed Lord and Miller to convey their intended (and unintended), messages within the narrative through a "non" threatening and recognizable medium. What is important in further analyzing the film is to recognize the theoretical underpinnings that complicate the surface reading of the film. It does not suffice to simply argue that the film is either an advertisement or a subversive work; it is the dialectical tension between these two poles that makes the film a text that requires deeper analysis.

The first theoretical complication can be located within the understanding of what the animated medium is and how it functions. If we are to take the definition of animation to be a "film made by hand, frame by frame, providing an illusion of movement which has not been directly recorded in the conventional photographic sense"[38] then we treat animation as a code, or a system of organizing sings in a manner that produces meaning.[39] This treatment is illusory in context of the Brickfilm, as this mode of animation is a byproduct of a separation from the intended LEGO system of play. In context to *The LEGO Movie*, this definition creates a contradictory space of existence, as while the film itself is modeled on Brickfilms, and incorporates segments from famous Brickfilms. However, the film is made through CGI-Animation techniques and simultaneously resides in a system of codes while the narrative of the film seemingly champions a transgression of codes and systems. What complicates its placement in animation is the film's homage to a system of animated filmmaking aimed at subverting systems and codes of expression while simultaneously operating within its own set of literal systems and codes that allows for the film's metaphysical reality to take shape. Therefore, *The LEGO Movie* further complicates our understanding of the animatic apparatus.

Raaz Greenberg defines the animatic apparatus as one based on the absence of objects, meaning the medium functions through the creation of a "metaphysical reality," that allows for "the creation of reality instead of an attempt to reflect it."[40] This suggests that representation within animated texts can be based on the absence of a nonspecific representation of the object in metaphysical reality. The very presence of *The LEGO Movie* then subverts this trait of animation as the recreated object at hand is more than familiar to audiences which imbues the film with a meaning that isn't completely metaphysical. Although the LEGO's are animated in the film, the physical form of the object is directly replicated on screen. However, the self-reflexivity of the film itself allows for the audience to suspend disbelief, mediating between the synthetic and the analytic.[41] This allows for the film to reflect upon its own construction and "its relationship to the context out of which it has been created, it deconstructs the imposed reality of cinematic discourse signaling an awareness of its 'means and motives of construction.'"[42]

The LEGO Movie makes the audience explicitly aware of the medium in which it is representing, continuing this self-reflexivity of medium throughout the film. The film focuses on building and other intrinsically LEGO oriented concepts, while the animators themselves chose to animate the film brick by brick, As Emmet showers, tiny blue LEGO pieces fall through his shower head; similarly, the bubbles that appear as he brushes his teeth are also from LEGO pieces. As Emmet and his fellow Master Builders are stranded at sea, their ship is rocked by waves; however, the water here, much like in other parts of the film, is a sequence of animated blue bricks. The self-reflexivity that the film utilizes can be further understood through Lindvall and Melton's analysis of the self-reflexive cartoon. They argue that self-reflexivity can been conveyed within the animated film through three general and overlapping methodologies. Firstly, the film comments on filmmaking and the film industry by "unveiling the raw materials and methods of the filmmaking process."[43] By incorporating the final live action sequences and revealing the parallels between "reality" and the LEGO-verse in the film, as well as other references to (1) LEGO products, (2) LEGO materiality, and (3) LEGO consumption, the film frequently comments on its own textuality. Secondly, Lindvall and Melton argue that animated films have the ability to function as a discourse as they speak directly to their audience and reflect explicit relationships to their creators.[44]

Jordan uses the expository scene between Wyldstyle and Emmet as an example of this relationship. As Wyldstyle and Emmet enter the first world after the audience's introduction to Bricksburg, Wyldstyle explains: "Your home, Bricksburg, is only one of many worlds in the universe. There's also this one, Pirates' Cove, Knights Club, Clowntown, a bunch of others we don't need to mention." As Wyldstyle names these worlds, extradiegetic still photographs of them fill the frame in rapid succession. The stills used in the film are not only sold by the LEGO group as individual sets, "but every picture appears to have been taken from actual LEGO box art and promotional materials."[45] Jordan attributes this reference to the self-referential and authorial voices of Lord and Miller; as LEGO Universes that are marketed to children by the LEGO company are represented, the LEGO film then must have a diegetic purpose in using these universes in order to support a narrative that transcends beyond a simple advertisement.[46]

Using a cinematic self-consciousness, the film then has the ability to comment on societal discrepancies through humor. This "confirms an unconscious awareness of the tacit rules of conventional and classic film production by breaking our expectations in the act of watching film."[47] Since the animated medium does not require an internalized and consistent logic like a live-action film, new codes can emerge when a reader encounters the unpredictable articulations of the cartoon. The super-textual can break into the text at any moment. It might even be planted as an integral part of the text, derailing it from the inside to transform the narrative into discourse, into dialogue with the reader.[48] This cinematic self-consciousness is what allows the text itself to acknowledge the presence of its reader. Although there is a narrative logic to the construction of the film, an internalized and consistent logic is not required for the messages within the film to be conveyed. Lindvall and Melton consider the animated film to be disruptive of the "diabolical seduction of images," arguing that these films do not even pretend to be referent, in turn functioning as "referents for a legion of simulacra that have become consumer products, seducing innocents into a reading of reality that is only cartoon illusion."[49] This approach implies that animated films can be seen as "deconstructing agents that have subjects who created them," allowing the authors of these texts to "communicate not only with themselves but with spectators who play along with them in their inter-textual games."[50]

The film's introductory scenes operate in a playful but telling manner, the city set in a rigid yet vibrant system: "LEGO mini figures walk in straight lines; their jerky strides are both functionally entailed by their stiff LEGO joints and emphasized by stop-motion-style CGI."[51] When Emmet reaches the construction site where he works, a giant LEGO construction manual is erected in front of him and his fellow workers, the sheer size of the instruction manual abstracting the mini figures' spatial presence. Lord and Miller playfully remind the audience the application of LEGO in children's game play.

The notion of play connects the *LEGO Movie* in a multitude of ways. Firstly, there is a theoretical play that takes place between the audience and the animated text as highlighted above. Secondly, the concept of play isn't only evoked through the very obvious use of a children's toy but is used in the live-action sequences of the film as means of commenting on, and then therapizing, the relationship between Finn and his father, one contaminated with notions surrounding the semantics of "proper" play, adult exceptionalism, and the self-expressive implications of the act of play. Some of the earliest theoretical work on play implies a polarizing relationship between accommodation and assimilation, assimilation occurring when "an individual applies his/her 'existing way of thinking' to a familiar object or situation" and accommodation referring to "the new object of situation."[52] Play can be further theorized as an affective by-product of real life tensions, motivated by behavior and "intrinsically related to what the child knows about the world and the rules governing relationships in the original situation."[53] Similarly, scholars have also equated play behavior to a means of metacommunication that is fostered within a perceptual relationship between text and context, arguing that "play aids in learning about learning."[54]

I argue the film further utilizes theories surrounding play by inadvertently drawing parallels between the "as if" characteristic of play and its fractal quality, one that allows for a mode of self-realization. The "as if" characteristic of play refers to the importance of substitution in child's play "whereby children treat things or people 'as if' they were something else" manifested in the film through Finn's use of his father's LEGOs as toys, as opposed to a "sophisticated system of interlocking bricks," like his father suggests.[55] However, when Finn's father acknowledges the creativity behind his son's creations, he subconsciously recognizes the "expressive opportunity for the fractal self."[56] As such, play must then be read as "not a flight from the world" but as an "inquiry into the challenges and responsibilities of social living."[57]

According to Henricks, this quality of play allows for the individual to select and solidify behavioral strategies as we experience and express selfhood through play, creating a dialogue between self and societal forms of otherness.[58] Within this frame, play then becomes a pathway for the construction of self, as consciousness is contained or consumed by these moments of making.[59] On one level, then, the film also deals with Finn's need for an outlet for individualist expression and his subconscious placement and re-enactment of his role within society, thus the importance of his father being placed as, in the LEGO-verse "as Lord Business, and The Man Upstairs" imposing a standardized norm on to his son. Finn's creative outlet for his emotions then are resolved through Emmet within the LEGO-verse as opposed to his unbounded "reality."

It is revealed in the final sequences of the film that Finn is projecting personal parental conflicts into the narrative. As the audience, we can link Will Ferrell, who plays Finn's father and voices Lord Business, to his both metaphorical and physical need to link the LEGO Universes into static and contained genres, equating "totalitarian rule with regimented, genre-divided difference."[60] Indeed, the citizens of the Old West cannot recognize Emmet's face in a line up until Bad Cop can draw a cowboy hat and mustache on his mugshot. An intertextual exchange is only possible in the film's constructed universe if the figures in question are Master Builders. The Master Builders seem to be presented in opposition to other LEGO citizens who follow manuals religiously. In this sense, these creatives are juxtaposed with LEGO consumers who explicitly follow the manuals. Master Builders captured by Lord Business are placed in a "think tank" and are responsible for the creation of the manuals Lord Business uses to develop his city. The LEGO company has an array of employees named Master Builders who are responsible for building new sets and larger LEGO projects for advertisement, even building the LEGO Universe in the film for the live-action sequences.

Emmet's difference from the Master Builders is highlighted throughout the film. When Emmet and Wyldstyle first meet, and she realizes that he is the "Special," she congratulates him on pretending to be a "useless nobody" so well. In fact, Emmet only falls through the hole in the first place because he is running after his manual. When Vitrivius and Wyldstyle enter Emmet's brain, they come across a literal blank slate, a surface of interlocking LEGO pieces and conclude that "he has never had an original thought in his life." When Emmet suggests something to build, a double decker couch, he is told multiple times that it is the "worst idea ever," even though the double decker couch rescues Emmet and his allies from drowning. Finn's father re-enforces this notion by noting that the LEGO Group intended for Emmet to be a mere construction worker.

Although Emmet is presented as a nobody, the film uses notions of self-realization to recognize the hypocrisy present in the Master Builders identity, the reasoning that leads Vitrivius to invent the prophecy in the first place. Within the company Master Builders are tasked with following the set instructions, eventually building the model intended by the designer. As a construction worker in Bricksburg, Emmet occupies the same position, tasked with building LEGO structures based on their exact directions. However, as the Master Builders in the film are high-lighted as renegade pioneers, Emmet's affinity for following rules is consistently undermined. When Emmet is first juxtaposed with Wyldstyle, a clear stylistic difference is present. Early on in the film Vitrivius brings up Wyldstyle's insecurity, evident in her tendency to change her name, frequently to something "cooler" than Lucy. Wyldstyle defines herself by living against the grain and standing against everything mainstream— in this case, everything Octan. Lord Business's prolific and far-reaching company, mass produces food, media and entertainment; in short, every consumable product, even down to voting machines. This additional homage to a connection between big business and politics is one that an audience of a certain age group may be able to expect when watching the film. However, as Jordan notes, she is dating Batman, an extremely popular pop-culture icon, thereby intrinsically and rather ironically tying one of the main facets of her nonconformity to a pop-culture icon.[61] This deems the individuality the film seeks to promote suspect, as identities surrounded by a material resource bind this individuality to LEGO itself.

As in the case of the film, child's play is connected to the materiality of LEGO; therefore, a deconstruction of the child as consumer and the connection between material culture and children's texts needs further explication. Robin Bernstein argues that as the historical relationship between material culture and play are integrated within children's literature. An emphasis of such texts ultimately allowing for a deeper understanding of the genre, as this is the only genre written by one group, adults, for another group, children.[62] Bernstein calls for a reading of such texts through multiple dimensions as children's play is simultaneously "compliant and unruly," noting children's ability to adapt mass-produced material products to their own wills.[63]

In tandem with Bernstein, Susan Honeyman argues that the industrialization of the toy narrative can be seen as a consequence of an increasingly manufactured agency that is present in commodified objects, or toy fictions, therefore making "these themes, and consumer culture anxieties, explicit for an assumed audience of children."[64] Honeyman further argues that consumer culture thrives on the myth of manufactured agency, "preserved by the distracting promise of authenticity, which is more or less a panacea for feeling real without the risk and responsibility that comes with true agency. By embracing the inauthentic, we unload the burdens of desiring agency."[65] Honeyman attributes this treatment of agency, particularly in reference to tie-in-toys, as manufacturers of a consumer agency as these inadvertently effect modes of play.[66]

Indeed, while Finn directs the "ordinary" citizens of his universe as compliant team players, it is the Master Builders who are the agents of creative anarchy. Grobovaite suggests that the intent behind the film, i.e., the intent to foster imagination and individuality cannot be read in real life, and the film itself offers no tangible solutions to this dilemma, "unless one is able to buy preposterous amounts of LEGO bricks and start constructing the LEGO worlds."[67] Citing a study on empathy and textual interaction in children's texts,[68] Grobovaite argues that a child's interaction with the text would appear at a more pragmatic level, therefore, a fan of the film could be able to recite Emmet's speech and conclusions without necessarily registering the lesson itself.[69] Grobovaite further writes:

> [in play] children are given the opportunity to create their own environment with their own rules; while their creations will inevitably be informed by certain influences they encounter in their lives, they do not have to speak on adult terms the way they are asked to in verbal surveys.[70]

In tandem with their invitation into the consumer market, through the encouragement of franchise toys, toys used as medium, the "large scope of the consumer culture touches their creative abilities [...] but more importantly, it effects their view of family, and their view of themselves." Arguing for context over text in children's entertainment, one can conclude that the film simultaneously champions individualistic creativity while serving as an elaborate advertisement, an intrinsic part of consumer culture itself.[71]

Citing a study by Shirley Steinberg,[72] Grobovaite argues that child focused consumer marketing pushes children towards a type of "adulthood that doesn't quite mix with the societal image of childhood."[73] While neither I nor Grobovaite fully concur with this conclusion, the fact that Finn, the only actual child to appear in the film, has invented LEGO characters that are adults is telling. After all, Emmet has his own apartment, car, and job. These are traits assigned to Emmet through the LEGO play system. As these mini figures come with implied narratives, even in gameplay there are segments of this conditioning that Finn cannot escape. Simultaneously, although Finn is constructed as a believable child in the filmic universe, he has an undeniably large access to LEGOs and LEGO universes—unlike many consumers and audiences—implying that "creativity is not achieved by any resource other than LEGO."[74] This alignment of creativity with the medium itself also bases Finn's identity on the products in the basement. Grobovaite writes:

> Just as Finn's creative ability only functions in the context of the LEGO brand, so does his relationship with his father. This is an even greater concern to be considered when analyzing the deeper implications of *The LEGO Movie*.

> Because Finn uses his creativity to communicate to his father his discontent-ment with the way the LEGO's are monopolized, their relationship is repaired. The entire father-son relationship hinges on the way the LEGO's are used in their household.[75]

Finn and his father are in turn only able to reconcile their relationship through their mutual love of play. In context of Grobovaite's work on the film, this is controversial, as the perquisite for the father/son bond seems to be the LEGO brick itself. This allows the film to be read as "liberation from the culture industry hegemony and further integration by the use of its products."[76] In fact, LEGO bricks became increasingly popular after the film's release, further becoming symbols of consumption.

Inadvertently reading the film through the capitalist lens adds another dimension to the film's narrative, as it is Finn's ability to adapt the material at hand that leads to the inception of the film's main narra-tive and his conflict with his father. If we take Finn's father's placement as Lord Business literally, then we can read the director's overt use of capital-ist critique as a metaphor delivered through both the fictional LEGO-verse and through Finn's almost anarchic mode of play. It is then possible on one level to argue that the film, through its metaphysical reality, creates a cap-italist metaphysics as well. The fictional city of Bricksburg, as well as the rest of the LEGO-verse, seems stuck in a cyclical sameness, each citizen trapped within their respective societal roles, repeating actions dictated by a singular capitalist entity.

If we take global capitalism as constituted through space and time, as in through its mitigation of the spatio-temporal dimensions, then it inad-vertently engulfs social life. Consequently, sustaining capitalist practices through a globalized system "in its totality."[77] A capitalist metaphysics therefore refers to:

> [T]he coordination of social and economic life through the organization or production of time and space in late/global capitalism. The term implies uni-versality, not always in its effects but its scope that extends toward all spheres and relations. It is in and through time and space that capitalism extends its reach, its power. Capitalism has a contradictory relation to spatio-temporality, both expanding and delimiting time and space at once.[78]

The entire LEGO-verse is limited spatially through borders and "no entry" zones, allowing for a minimalization of space in which capital is there-fore circulated.[79] The production of space limits mobility, orienting soci-ety toward a spatial stagnation, or through the use of the Kragle into a literal paralysis. Through the management of space, and time—distribut-ing time in regards to "labor time" and "free time"—and reducing sub-jectivity through spatiotemporal orientation, capitalism "circumscribes the possibilities of action through its production and organization of time and space."[80] This becomes evident in the construction of the LEGO-verse itself, sanctioned and ornately separated into quadrants with borders that are clearly labeled. As Emmet and Wyldstyle escape Bricksburg, they fly past an array of signs including "No Entry," "One Way," "Dead End," "Danger," and "Right Turn Only," signs that are later revealed to mimic the ones Finn's father has hung around his intricate LEGO collection: "In other cases, signs are similarly deprived of their function…. Over exit booths on a LEGO highway is written 'Color Inside the Lines,' and Bad Cop draws his Good Cop face back on with a huge 'D-Gray' marking pen, allowing for a full-on psychotic pun on *degraded*."[81]

Roberts further argues that by combining the titles of "Lord" and "Business," Lord and Miller have found a way to "conflate dictatorial, totalitarian omnipotence with the dominion of multinational capital-ism," foreshadowing a satirical connection embedded in the narrative that "there is no difference between the private sector and the public sec-tor: Megaruler and Megacorporation are one in the same."[82] Indeed, Pres-ident/Lord Business is followed by an army of robots and works on the highest possible floor of his office building. While his corporate drones cater to his every need, he remains simultaneously in control of every public aspect of life within the LEGO-verse presented in the film. Aptly named "Micro Managers," the robots at Lord Business' are "incapable of perceiving any negative repercussion their actions might have on their audiences."[83] Towards the end of the film, the Micro Managers are seen rebuilding destroyed parts of Bricksburg, mirrored soon after with Finn's father "micro-managing" his son's gameplay by "fixing" what he has done to the city with superglue.

While the capitalist undertones in the film are undeniably subver-sive in the message Lord and Miller seemingly aim to present, the film also functions as some sort of advertising myth, one that holds a "service-able and operational" story that "people can use to turn the contradictions they live with in everyday capitalist reality into an enjoyable experi-ence," or "therapeutic relief."[84] In this context, the *LEGO Movie* oper-ates within the idea of a "creative-yet-contained prosumer capitalism," embedding both prosumer and consumer into its narrative.[85] By provid-ing a re-arrangement of the ossified LEGO universe at the end of the film, the LEGO symbolically established itself as "metaphor for all the bad and all the good in contemporary capitalism."[86] Constructing itself around an "anti–Fordist, and bureaucratic liberation myth in which the joys, frustra-tions and rebellions of LEGO-playing children coincide with those of the grown-up employees and consumers," *The LEGO Movie* serves the creation of an idyllic advertisement myth.[87] Producing myth from commodity, the film slates pre-existing societal concerns and myths appropriated from varying ideological and theoretical traditions.

It is most productive to view *The LEGO Movie* as a film that presents multiple dialectical tensions within its narrative. As the film is therefore the site of multiple, coexisting ideological aims and functions, the film itself functions within a distinct discursive moment, blending both Warner Brothers and LEGO. Simultaneously however, it is evident that the film's directors allowed the narrative itself to self-reflexively mirror their own ideological aims through the unique representational use of the LEGO medium. After all, "LEGO bricks are the ideal material for the bricoleur who weaves harmonies of shape and color, and meaning and stories, into the productive chaos of available material, thereby also affirming the productive role of disorder."[88] Indeed, it is the message of productive disorder and individuality that drives the protagonists of the film. However, we must also keep in mind the guided constructional element that drives the LEGO system of play itself. It is naïve to assume that after seeing the film, children will exclusively purchase singular or plain bricks, since the LEGO consumer has been introduced to a world that "has been marginalized by construction sets."[89]

Merchandise based on popular cinema productions fuel LEGO Universes, and although these sets are not necessarily meant to be static models their narratives are pre-determined by their franchise partner. Linking consumer creativity to the "reclamation" of the brick,[90] the film provides a complicated yet elaborate universe functioning on the interplay of consumer and child capitalism and social critique. Similarly, through the very use of these increasingly familiar social phenomena, the film problematizes itself within the theoretical realm of animation, materiality and play, becoming as a result a brilliant case study in understanding the subversive nature of cinema and how a mass-produced subversive animation film can exist so successfully in contemporary society.

Since the very successful release of *The LEGO Movie*, Warner Brothers has capitalized on the overwhelming acceptance of the animated LEGO medium, this time joining the films to follow with larger cultural franchises in a much more explicit manner. It is important to note however, that such films are not new in the LEGO-verse. Over the years, LEGO has worked with producers and created a total of thirteen direct-to-video films, eight short films, ten television specials, and thirteen original television series.[91] Although I was unable to gather information regarding LEGO's use in advertisements not pertaining to their own products, Turkish Airlines recently started airing its LEGO Instructional safety video on different aircrafts and Turkish television.[92] Unsurprisingly, many of these products are based on a LEGO series such as Bionicle, NinjaGO and other miscellaneous LEGO sets, serving much like *The LEGO Movie* as both narrative product and advertisement. However, when the product is very explicitly linked to LEGO, such as in the case with what I refer to as LEGO co-productions, the subversive nature of the texts takes a backseat within the narrative and does not represent an explicit message meant to be conveyed to the audience.

In 2017, two more LEGO franchise films emerged, *The LEGO Batman Movie* [93] and the *LEGO Ninjago Movie*,[94] respectively. These films were also hugely successful; however, I argue their success had less to do with their subversive nature or innovative medium. Instead, their success lies in the humorous means by which the LEGO medium has been combined with popular franchise films, creating animated spectacles for audiences of all ages. Indeed, the aforementioned films once again present differing heroes' journeys tightly knit with action sequences and an all-ages understanding of humor, leaving bread crumbs of trans-medial and inter-textual references for its adult audiences. Although these films do not overtly critique the society they are produced for, they do make self-referential comments to the franchises they are attached to, using humor once more in a self-reflexive manner.

In light of the film's success, it is not surprising that the second installation of the original *The LEGO Movie 2: The Second Part* was released in February of 2019.[95] Set five years after the team's initial adventures, the film is based on the final seconds of the original film in which the city of Bricksburg is invaded by LEGO Duplo figures, or aliens from the planet Duplon. Based on the inclusion of characters from other LEGO films from the past years, it seems like the sequel has not only successfully followed in the path of its predecessor but also has inspired a new generation of spin-off films that employ the same format. Regardless of which LEGO film comes next, one thing is certain: we will be able to find the matching sets in stores.

NOTES

1. I.e., one can use instructions exactly or create their own.
2. The Kragle is revealed to a tube of Krazy Glue with certain letters obscured due to frequent use.
3. For a comprehensive list, see: https://en.wikipedia.org/wiki/List_of_LEGO_films _and_TV_series#TV_specials.
4. "Lego," *Wikipedia*. Last modified July 30, 2020. https://en.wikipedia.org/wiki/Lego.
5. *Ibid.*
6. Known as "minifig" for short, a now hugely popular collectible.
7. Wikipedia, "Lego."
8. The company initially hired the entire population of the city of Billund, creating a literal LEGO Town. After the expiration of the 1980s copyright, in order to compete with

the emerging market, the company invested in LEGO TC Logo, combining computer code and the LEGO system of play. This would eventually become LEGO Mindstorms. Investing in a series of computer games, new themes, failed theme parks, and a string of failed TV series the company found itself in a crisis of identity. Attempting to use the creation of Bionicle (which angered LEGO purists), and franchise sets (which failed as there were not enough toys produced and certain films did not reach audiences every year), the company was saved by a return to their original system of play ("LEGO").

9. Ninjago, LEGO Friends, Bionicle etc.

10. Wikipedia, "Lego."

11. Based on calculations, there are 102, 981, 500 different ways to combine LEGO pieces. Wikipedia, "Lego."

12. David Gauntlett, "The LEGO System as a tool for thinking, creativity, and changing the world," in *Making Media Studies: The Creativity Turn in Media and Communications Studies* (New York: Peter Lang, 2015), 2.

13. *Ibid.*

14. *Ibid.*, 1–2.

15. *Ibid.*, 2.

16. *Ibid.*

17. "…interconnecting set of parts, low level entry skills, a medium for mastery, the ability to create something where previously there was nothing, an open system with infinite possibilities, a belief in the potential of children and adults and their natural imagination, a belief in the value of creative play, a supportive environment, the system grows with the person, the system grows beyond the person." *Ibid.*, 3.

18. *Ibid.*, 4. Gauntlett further writes: 'We can arrange ideas in the external memory field'—by which he means, in the physical realm, when we have represented them somehow—'where they can be examined and subjected to classification, comparison, and experimentation.' He continues: In this way, externally displayed thoughts can be assembled into complex arguments much more easily than they can in biological memory. Images displayed in this field are vivid and enduring, unlike the fleeting ghosts of imagination. This enables us to see them clearly, play with them, and craft them into finished products, to a level of refinement that is impossible for an unaided brain. (Donald, 2001: 309).

19. *Ibid.*

20. *Ibid.*, 5.

21. *Ibid.*, 7. The creative mindset is supported when there are stimulating environments and resources (*having*), when there is a lot of inspirational activity and the engaging support of peers and mentors (*doing*), when there is an ethos which supports the passions of makers (*being*), and where there is a solid body of expertise and knowledge, and support for learning (*knowing*). These dimensions are all parts of culture, continuously in play together, and so they should not be considered as separate things. These four dimensions are driven by *playing*, *sharing*, *making* and *thinking*—the active processes through which people learn and form meanings together—and so these processes appear in between the four dimensions in our diagram, driving this windmill of continuous cultural creation.

22. *Ibid.*, 7. The *doing* dimension concerns the relationships and practices which are the lifeblood of a culture. In terms of LEGO culture, children are typically eager to exchange inspiration and stories around their creations, and this is supported by the LEGO.com website, YouTube videos, the LEGO Club magazine, LEGO's collaborations with museums, and so on. Communication and networks are vital to the *doing* dimension—especially for Adult Fans of LEGO (AFOLs), whose networks have exploded with the rise of the internet (and are typically independent of the LEGO Group). These cultures really take off when people are *doing* things together, sharing ideas and inspiration, and learning from one another.

23. *Ibid.*

24. *Ibid.*

25. *Ibid.*, 9. Ivan Illich, the philosopher most famous in the 1970s, makes a powerful case for the do-it-yourself approach to life and culture in his book *Tools for Conviviality* (1973). He outlines a distinction between "industrial" tools, which are one-size-fits-all things that only convey the identity of the organization that produced them, and "convivial"

tools, which are flexible to different people's needs, enable individual self-expression, and encourage conversation.

26. *A Lego Brickumentary*. Kief Davidson and Daniel Jung, dir. (Global Emerging Markets, HeLo), 2014.

27. *Ibid.* Currency is based on the rarity of the LEGO piece while abbreviations such AFOL (Adult Fan of LEGO), have spawned other terminology such as TFOL, KFOL, and Non-LEGO Significant other.

28. *Ibid.*

29. *Ibid.*

30. "How It Works." LEGO IDEAS. Last modified July 31, 2020. https://ideas.LEGO.com/howitworks.

31. *A Lego Brickumentary*.

32. *Ibid.*

33. *Bricks in Motion*. Philip Heinrich, dir. (Cinemation Studios), 2017.

34. *Ibid.*

35. *Ibid.*

36. *Ibid.*

37. *Ibid.*

38. Raz Greenberg, "The Animated Text: Definition," *Journal of Film and Video 63, no. 2* (Summer 2011): 4. Paul Wells, in his book *Understanding Animation* (1998), uses the following definition as a basis for further discussion: "A film made by hand, frame by frame, providing an illusion of movement which has not been directly recorded in the conventional photographic sense" (10).

39. *Ibid.*

40. *Ibid.*, 5.

41. Terrence R. Lindvall and J. Matthew Melton, "Towards a Post-Modern Animated Discourse Bakhtin, Intertextuality and the Cartoon Carnival" In *A Reader in Animation Studies*, Jayne Pilling, ed. (London: John Libbey), 204. "The animated film mediates between two competing epistemological methods, between what Paul Ricoeur designates in hermeneutics as *synthetic* and *analytic*. C.S. Lewis expresses it as the difference between 'looking along' and 'looking at,' corresponding respectively to the French verbs *connaître* and *savoir*. The first is a knowledge by acquaintance; the latter a knowledge by description. One might define them as a hermeneutics of faith and a hermeneutics of suspicion—both being necessary for a full knowledge of the object."

42. *Ibid.*

43. *Ibid.*

44. *Ibid.*

45. Jordan Treece. "The Double-Sided Message of The Lego Movie: The Effects of Popular Entertainment on Children in Consumer Culture" (2015). *English Seminar Capstone Research Papers 28*, 11. https://digitalcommons.cedarville.edu/english_seminar_capstone/28.

46. *Ibid.*

47. Lindvall and Melton, "Animated Discourse," 209. The rules referenced are the following: "This self-consciousness about textuality exhibits itself in several ways: (1) exposing and dismantling the filmmaking process; (2) alluding to other texts and contexts beyond itself, thus grounding itself in reality; or (3) addressing the plastic nature and raw material of celluloid and the frame itself."

48. *Ibid.*, 209–210.

49. *Ibid.*, 217.

50. *Ibid.*

51. (Jordan, "Message," 7.

52. Jean Piaget, qtd. in Mehri Takhvar, "Play and theories of play: a review of the literature, in *Early Child Development and Care 39, no. 1* (Oct. 1988): 227. Application of thinking is better defined by Piaget as "pure assimilation or primacy of assimilation over accommodation. Activities with an assimilative orientation fall under three headings, each of which take place in parallel with the child's level of cognitive development."

53. Lee Vgotsky, qtd. in Takhvar, "Play and theories," 229.

54. Gregory Bateson, qtd. in Takhvar, "Play and theories," 231–32.

55. Brian Sutton-Smith, qtd. in Takhvar, "Play and theories," 232.

56. Thomas S. Henricks, "Play as Self-Realization—Toward a General Theory of Play," *American Journal of Play 4*, no. 2 (Summer 2011): 192. "In this light, play—including the activity of play therapy—lives in the space between its participants. Play's materiality also helps children distinguish imaginative activity in the world from private fantasy. Russell Meares (2005) took a similar approach, stressing that play is an effective means to build the self, especially as a means of negotiating the relationship of aloneness to togetherness through dialectical participation with others. Terry Marks-Tarlow (2010) extended such ideas even further, linking the therapeutic tradition with themes from post structural thought and nonlinear science. Seen in this light, play seems an expressive opportunity for the fractal self."

57. *Ibid.*, 194.

58. *Ibid.*, 197, 200, 206.

59. *Ibid.*, 208.

60. Jordan, "Message," 12.

61. *Ibid.*, 13.

62. Robin Bernstein, "Toys Are Good for Us: Why We Should Embrace the Historical Integration of Children's Literature, Material Culture, and Play," in *Children's Literature Association Quarterly 38, no. 4* (Winter 2013): 459–460.

63. Bernstein, "Toys Are Good."

64. Susan Honeyman, "Manufactured Agency and the Playthings Who Dream It for Us," in *Children's Literature Association Quarterly 31, no. 2* (Summer 2006): 110.

65. *Ibid.*, 120.

66. *Ibid.*, 126.

67. Dalia Grobovaite, "Politics of Bricolage and the Double-sided Message of *The LEGO Movie.*" *Canadian Journal of Media Studies* 15, no. 1 (2017): 73.

68. Treece, "Message," 20. "Be Kind to Three-Legged Dogs: Children's Literal Interpretations of TV's Moral Lessons" by Marie-Louise Mares and Emily Elizabeth Acosta. "To an adult viewer, the episode's moral message is quite clearly one of accepting those with uncommon handicaps; in this case, the characters meet a dog with only three legs. After watching the episode, children were questioned on what they believed was the moral of the story. Mares and Acosta's study discovered that only a small minority of the children accurately comprehended the moral lesson of the show. Even though the point of the story was stated clearly by the characters' actions and words, most children watched the episode and concluded that it was simply a show about dogs playing together."

69. *Ibid.*, 18.

70. *Ibid.*, 20.

71. *Ibid.*, 20, 23.

72. *Ibid.*, 3, 10.

73. *Ibid.*, 24.

74. *Ibid.*, 24.

75. *Ibid.*, 25.

76. *Ibid.*, 26.

77. Grobovaite, "Politics," 69.

78. Stephanie Cheng, "Radical Democracy Conference at The New School for Social Research in NYC." In *Radical Democracy*, 2018. https://www.radicaldemocracy.org/conference/2018-conference/.

79. *Ibid.*

80. *Ibid.* "Marx explains, is its seeking "to capture the whole world as its market" while striving "to destroy space by means of time, i.e., to restrict to a minimum the time required for movement from one place to another." Space is minimized to accelerate exchange and the circulation of capital."

81. *Ibid.*, 2–3.

82. Richard Burt. "What Is Called Thinking with ShaXXXspeares and Walter

Benjamin?: Managing De/Kon/Struction, Toying with Letters in The Lego Movie." *Journal for Early Modern Cultural Studies 16*, no. 3 (2016): 100.

83. Lewis Roberts. "'It's a Dangerous World out There for a Toy': Identity Crisis and Commodity Culture in the Toy Story Movies." *Children's Literature Association Quarterly 42*, no. 4 (2017): 6.

84. Jordan, "Messages," 5.

85. Matthias Zick Varul. "The Cultural Tragedy of Production and the Expropriation of the Brickolariat: The Lego Movie as Consumer-Capitalist Myth." *European Journal of Cultural Studies 21*, no. 6 (December 2018): 2.

86. *Ibid.*

87. *Ibid.*, 10.

88. *Ibid.*, 12.

89. *Ibid.*, 7.

90. *Ibid.*, 8.

91. ("List of LEGO films").

92. See: https://www.youtube.com/watch?v=zQtod9801j0.

93. *The LEGO Batman Movie.* Chris McKay, dir. (Warner Bros. Pictures, 2017).

94. *Ninjago Movie.* Charlie Bean, Paul Fischer, and Robert Logan, dirs. *LEGO.* (Warner Bros. Pictures, 2017).

95. *The LEGO Movie 2: The Second Part.* Mike Mitchell and Trisha Gum, dirs. (Warner Bros. Pictures, 2019).

PART III

Modern America and the Transformation of Social Order

"This is me now!"

Gene's Gender Play in Bob's Burgers

Dan Abitz

Bob's Burgers is at its most subversive when Gene Belcher is play-ing with gender. In the season two finale,[1] a quick montage of four dif-ferent scenes of Gene yelling "This is me now!" as four different versions of himself exhibits how frequently Gene plays with gender. The montage includes Gene as Beefsquatch (a hybrid Burger Boy/Sasquatch look), Joe Buck from *Midnight Cowboy, Ziggy Stardust*-era David Bowie, and a Hare Krishna, and the montage's rapid repetition collapses into a palimpsest of Gene's history of momentary identities. These multiple Genes repre-sent an array of genders and sexualities. Beefsquatch (an amalgamation of a mythical creature and a hamburger) ostensibly lacks a gender, while *Stardu*st-era Bowie drags masculinity into a far more feminine arena. Bowie and Buck both have sexualities that do not remain strictly straight, while Beefsquatch's sexuality remains unknowable.

This montage—with its array of recognizable figures underscored by the repetition of "This is me now!"—undermines the stability of "me" and "now" for Gene, his family, and the show. By stacking these moments on top of one another, the montage offers us a glimpse of how many selves and how many temporalities Gene accumulates across his childhood, queering any sense of a stable (straight) subject successfully marshalled by "chro-nonormativity."[2] While it is true that the montage derives from the Belcher family's collective memory of Gene's various declarations of selfhood, Gene can only play with his identity in this way precisely because he for-gets his previous masquerades. Each new "me" and new "now" can only occur because they replace the old and thus forgotten ones, freeing Gene to repeatedly experiment with who or what he might desire to be.

The scene's humor lies in the juxtaposition of how seriously Gene takes these multiple selves with how silly they are to his family. Louise's

147

response of "Heard that before" suggests that, for her and the rest of the Belchers, *this* Gene is just another frivolity in a long list of them. I, however, want to take seriously Gene's frivolities, and to do so, I am going to take seriously someone else who asks us to avoid any such undertaking. Jack Halberstam believes that "being taken seriously means missing out on the chance to be frivolous, promiscuous, and irrelevant,"[3] so what could be more irrelevant, not to mention irreverent, than failing to take seriously the admonition against being taken seriously by taking seriously the content of that admonition? Moreover, what could be more suitable for making relevant the irreverent promiscuity of Gene's gender play? While I hope that readers will take seriously my arguments in this chapter, I agree with Halberstam that "the desire to be taken seriously is precisely what compels people to follow the tried and true paths of knowledge production."[4] Halberstam, in his injunctions to resist traditional or institutional forms of mastery, to privilege naïveté or stupidity, and to be suspicious of memorialization,[5] aims to "map a few detours" around such paths of knowledge production. By following those detours, I will try to map a few of my own and, hopefully, Gene's gender play is just silly enough a topic to learn something truly valuable about gender, identity, and childhood.

I plan to trace Gene's gender play through his forays into femininity and his masculine un-masking, as well as how Gene resists the various technologies of heterosexuality that attempt to make him a "normal" (legible, straight) child. I see Gene's play and resistance as moments or circumstances of failing that "offer more creative, more cooperative, more surprising ways of being in the world."[6] This approach to Gene's gender play and resistance involves exploring how the non-linear and non-serialized *Bob's Burgers* subverts chrononormativity and instead offers an anti-normative model of temporal and developmental delay. Because of this, my reading practices will take on at times the cascading, condensing effect of the montage with which I opened this chapter (though I do not avoid sticking to certain episodes or scenes). As well, I consider Gene as an example of Kathryn Bond Stockton's "ghostly gay child."[7] "Such a child," Stockton argues, "has been a child remarkably, intensely unavailable to itself in the present tense," and this chapter considers how Gene experiences and potentially embodies "an asynchronous self-relation"[8] through his various forms of play, resistance, failure, and success.

In this sense, Gene is the perfect guide for such a journey, for what makes Gene's gender play and resistance—and thus Gene himself—such a failure is precisely what makes him so queerly successful. I cannot promise an adequate definition or formulation of what it means to succeed queerly by the end of this chapter, but I hope that my failure to do so will, like Halberstam's "low theory," constitute a "theorization of alternatives within an undisciplined zone of knowledge production."[9] As a walking, talking, and farting undisciplined zone of knowledge production, Gene might provide us with an alternative compendium of childhood experiences to help us dislodge and unlearn the rigid forms of heteronormativity so often mapped onto children in the hopes of producing legible and predictable citizens.

"The girls' bathroom is nice!"[10] *Frolicking in the Feminine*

But, wait. What is *Bob's Burgers* and who the hell is Gene Belcher? By withholding any summary of either the show or the character, I have failed to follow one of Halberstam's detours. Another name for Halberstam's monograph might be *The Queer Art of Plot Summary*, as Halberstam uses the "rejected methodology" of plot summary to, in the case of *Dude, Where's My Car?* specifically, and her archive of silly texts generally, to reveal "the stakes in repeating, looping, summarizing, forgetting, and knowing again."[11] For Halberstam, tracing the intricacies of the plot of a movie that is as stupid as it is brilliant provides a queered set of narrative, aesthetic, temporal, and figural markers for her analytic peregrinations to follow or disregard. While length restrictions will prevent me from offering detailed plot summaries of every *Bob's Burgers* episode referenced or cited in this chapter, stopping here to plot out *Bob's Burgers* for voracious viewers, part-time partakers, and those missing out will be our first meandering detour.

On air since 2011 and with two Emmys[12] tucked in its greasy apron, *Bob's Burgers* follows the misadventures of the Belcher family as they try to eke out a living in Wonder Wharf.[13] Bob Belcher, the son of a diner owner, runs Bob's Burgers—an almost always-empty restaurant—with the help of his wife, Linda, and three children: Tina, Gene, and Louise.[14] Unlike the middle-class families of *Bob's Burgers* predecessors *The Simpsons* and *Family Guy*, the Belchers are a working-class family that frequently confront and contend with their material limitations. The family lives in a one-bathroom apartment above their restaurant, and, though the kids all have their own rooms, we learn early in the series that Louise's room used to be a closet.[15] While the kids never go hungry (they live above and work in a restaurant, after all), the parents frequently fail to pay their rent on time or in full. Living precariously under the near-constant threat of eviction and the bankruptcy of their family business (events often staved off solely by their landlord Mr. Fischoeder's attachment to Bob)[16] the Belcher family lives under a regime of failure, stuck with Bob's cruelly optimistic[17] attachment to life as a struggling burger chef.

Gene is the eleven-year-old middle child, sandwiched between his older sister Tina and his younger sister Louise. Theatrical, musical, gassy, and flamboyant, Gene first appears on *Bob's Burgers* wearing his "Burger Boy" hamburger costume, worn to lure customers into the failing family slop shop.[18] This initial obfuscation of Gene's body foreshadows Gene's inscrutability throughout the thirteen seasons of the show, making prominent—if not primary—his ability and desire to try on different identities and genders. While all three Belcher children are disruptive and awkward, Gene's variations on these themes frequently play out along the gender divide, making quite the spectacular mockery of its supposed rigidity and universality. In mocking gender difference, Gene accumulates identities, a sense of self predicated on incoherencies, and "an anti-ontological state of being" that, in its "state of indifference," interrupts any "line that automatically connects soma with self or dress with identity or opinion with body."[19] Ontology, like telos, cannot mean anything to Gene because he is a child, and this ignorance, a freeing form of failure, "preserves some of the wondrous anarchy of childhood"[20] for him, an anarchy he repeatedly exploits and figures through his gender play.

"Failing is something queers do and have always done exceptionally well,"[21] and it does not take Gene long to forget his gender coding and start frolicking with and in femininity. In "Spaghetti Western and Meatballs,"[22] Gene confronts his joke-stealing bully Choo Choo with Linda's sun-hat on his head and Louise's pink Little Princess toy guitar slung around his shoulders. In his drag performance of Banjo, the titular star of Bob's favorite Spaghetti Western film series, Gene finds himself face-to-face with the shirtless Choo Choo, hoping to stop the ensuing violence with atonal sounds from his plastic instrument. Mimicking Choo Choo during their *Banjo* standoff, Gene takes off his shirt as well, covering himself with the toy guitar. As the two shirtless boys face each other, one successfully embodies normative masculinity while the other improvises and fails. The scene, which ends mercifully with Gene and Bob fleeing Choo Choo and his also-shirtless father, is the culmination of Gene learning lessons with uneven ends. While Gene puts an end to Choo Choo's joke thievery using the guitar, thus finding his confidence in his feminine *accoutrement*, he fails to understand that the Little Princess guitar cannot protect him from more immediate and more normative expressions of violent masculinity. Failing to be the type of boy required by the situation, Gene flees, now encumbered by the pink toy guitar, experiencing what for many children are the familiar lessons of childhood: humility, awkwardness, and limitation.[23]

Throughout this exchange with Choo Choo, Gene finds his confidence through the Little Princess guitar, bonds with his father Bob, and ultimately ditches his responsibilities to normative gender formation while failing to be a "real boy." Thus, Gene begins what Halberstam calls a "queer form of antidevelopment" that "requires healthy doses of forgetting and disavowal and proceeds by way of a series of substitutions."[24] If "the child is always already queer and must therefore quickly be converted to a proto-heterosexual by being pushed through a series of maturational models of growth that project the child as the future and the future as heterosexual,"[25] then Gene's gender failure can be viewed as beating a path towards an alternative developmental model. We can thus re-interpret Gene's flight-not-fight response as both a running like hell away from any such conversion or proto-heterosexuality and as a moment of growing sideways. "Growing sideways," writes Stockton, "suggests that the width of a person's experience or ideas, their motives or their motions, may pertain at any age, bringing 'adults' and 'children' into lateral contact of surprising sorts."[26] Endearingly, Bob shepherds Gene away from this crisis of masculinity, and the two bond further (much to Louise's chagrin) over the resonant smells of their respective farts while hiding in a tube on a playground. Here, Bob's own gender failure, set in relief against Choo Choo's shirtless father's gender success, buttresses Gene's non-normative antidevelopment. The whole Belcher family is sideways in some manner, out of step and disjointed from the rest of Ocean Avenue, giving Gene a unique opportunity to grow howsoever he pleases.

Following the lines of antidevelopment set forth in "Spaghetti Western and Meatballs," Gene continues to flirt with femininity so extensively that the rest of this section could simply be a near-endless litany of gender-bending moments in Gene's life. While I certainly have most, if not all, of these moments committed to memory, it better suits the thrust of this chapter to forget all but a choice few. In "Synchronized Swimming,"[27] Gene's queerness is on full display, from covering his breasts while playing shirts-and-skins dodgeball in PE class, to lamenting about not being valued as a woman, and chastising Bob for not wearing a woman's bathing suit. At the center of these moments is Gene's body. As he is a fat child,[28] it is implied, though not exactly drawn, that he has breasts, and his breasts become a site for frequent gender play, functioning in this episode as the boundary between masculine and feminine that Gene crosses so gleefully.[29] Bodily comfort and sartorial aesthetics blend, too, as Gene disavows the needlessly cruel normativization mechanism of shirts-and-skins ("I hate the whole skins/shirts thing") while avowing the comfort and style of a woman's bathing suit ("I like it. It holds things in in all the right places"). Gene even tells Bob that his men's suit "looks ridiculous," further establishing that Gene has found the gender expression that best suits him.

While out of sync with Bob in this episode, Gene is in sync with his mother and sisters. "Synchronized Swimming" also involves the Belcher children convincing their guidance counselor Mr. Frond to let them out of gym class to take an independent study class in synchronized swimming. The episode's main story concludes with Linda successfully leading Gene and his fellow PE class-deserters in a synchronized swimming routine based around pre-natal yoga. Bob is even taken aback by Gene's pre-natal yogic aptitude, complimenting him on his ability to follow his mother's directions. In a pool emptied of its water thanks to Louise, in Bob's phrasing, "[pulling] a *Caddyshack*,"[30] Linda, Gene, and his fellow misfits perform their synchronized routine well enough to barely pass and avoid summer school. Growing sideways, often bringing children and adults into unique configurations of learning, development, and growth, thus involves lateral lines of relations as opposed to normative hierarchal relations that shoot upwards. The children's ill-conceived synchronized swimming class is the opportunity for Gene and the gang to find an alternative pathway to (barely) succeed. The lateral movements of the synchronized swimmers parallel the lateral lines of relation between Gene and his mothers and sisters, evincing a synchronicity between Gene's foray into the feminine and the entire group's ability to escape, however briefly, from the normative hierarchal relations of traditional school activities and teacher-parent-student dynamics.

This relationship between bodies and time, rendered here as synchronized swimming's arrangement of temporalities and movements, returns us to Elizabeth Freeman's concept of chrononormativity. "Chrononormativity," writes Freeman, "is a mode of implantation, a technique by which institutional forces come to seem like somatic facts. Schedules, calendars, time zones, and even wristwatches inculcate ... forms of temporal experience that seem natural to those whom they privilege."[31] Though Gene and his synchronized swimming troupe receive passing grades from the school board, they are D's and D-minuses: enough to avoid summer school but not enough to legitimize Independent Study. In this sense, the school board functions as an institutional force for chrononormativity, re-scheduling the normative PE class and eliminating Independent Study in order to preserve the chrononormative school schedule. With Linda and Bob failing to martial Gene and the other children in time with chrononormativity, it is easy to see why the school board must re-set the clock: chrononormativity relies on cyclical stability and on the "gender binary [organizing] the meaning of this and other times [cyclical time] conceived as outside of—but symbiotic with—linear time."[32] Gene's play with and in the gender binary threatens to undo that dialectic and thus its linearity.

Gene's feminine feats and masculine mistakes do more than threaten the gender binary required by chrononormativity; they make light work of "the unbearable heaviness of the gender binary."[33] Part of why Gene can play, fail, and succeed over and over again can be found in the show's own non-linear, non-serialized format. As an animated sitcom, *Bob's Burgers* forgets far more often than it remembers, and this serial forgetting provides Gene with a *tabula rasa* of gender exploration rarely, if ever, offered to those of us bound by straight time.[34] For Halberstam, forgetting "becomes a way of resisting the heroic and grand logics of recall and unleashes new forms of memory that relate more to spectrality than to hard evidence, to lost genealogies than to inheritance, to erasure than to inscription."[35] Ignoring that Gene has already snuck himself into Halberstam's definition of forgetting, the show's forgetful format resists inscription while doubling down on erasure, as Gene's status as an animated character on a non-linear sitcom means he is constantly drawn, erased, re-drawn, re-erased, and as a consequence, simply cannot be engraved. None of his gender play remains, and it thus resists reification, codification, or telos. Gene starts each episode anew, in a yellow shirt and blue shorts, with no traces of his play, failures, or successes, stuck to him. Rather, in the show's structured anti-chrononormativity, Gene can explore gender and childhood in ways that cannot solidify into a legible, stable identity. These moments of exploration include Gene yelling, "Tell that to my vagina!" at Mickey the bank robber,[36] fantasizing himself as Kate Winslet's "Rose" being drawn by Leonardo DiCaprio's "Jack" in *Titanic* (the same fantasy both Linda and Tina have),[37] and proclaiming, "I'm just a girl with a dream who got tired of hearing the word 'no!'" while wearing a sequined dress, white gloves, and a feather boa in a makeshift kids-only casino.[38] For Gene, gender is a malleable form of improvisation and desiring, a veritable "Sands from Exotic Lands" exhibit of playfulness and experimentation,[39] and while that play might sometimes make a pair of breasts,[40] it can always be erased and reshaped again.

"I'm ready to be the man of this family!"[41]
A Masculine Masquerade

Gene is not the only character in *Bob's Burgers* who plays with Gene's gender. In "Bad Tina," Louise attempts to console Linda over Tina's recent bad behavior by telling her, "It's time to focus on your good daughter: Gene," to which Gene replies, quite approvingly, "I'm pretty."[42] In the triptych episode "The Gayle Tales,"[43] wherein the grounded Belcher children attempt to win their aunt Gayle's favor with stories that feature her eventually kissing Scott Bakula, Tina's story, an imaginative mishmash of *Cinderella*, *Lady Chatterley's Lover*, and the plots of several Jane Austen novels, features Gene as Eugenia Chatterteeth, one of three younger sisters hoping to marry off their oldest sister so that they, too, can marry. Gene's enthusiasm for marriage almost outpaces Tina's characteristic desire for romance, as he yells out, "I want a wedding! But instead of a wedding cake, I want to get a bunch of cupcakes because it's a long time ago, and that idea is still good."

Embedded within Tina's literary fantasy, Eugenia's dream wedding takes place in the past but with a modern twist to show that straight time, refreshingly, is nowhere to be found. That Eugenia's petticoats are "unspeakable" in Tina's story only queers the episode further, reminding us, in case we have forgotten, that queerness often goes unspoken in the domain of straight time but can find expression in queerer temporalities. Even Linda figures Gene as a woman in her brunch fantasy in "Brunchsquatch,"[44] his yellow shirt now a sleeveless blouse and his blue pants now rolled-up jean capris. "Oh, honey. If you're fungry, I'm fun-*starving*," drolls Gene with an emphatic flick of his left wrist, playing in his mother's fantasy the role of her bitchy brunch bestie.[45]

This collective fantasy structure that imagines Gene as daughter, sister, and gal pal might stem from a familial forgetting of Gene's "actual" gender, as if such a thing existed to forget in the first place. Additionally, this fantasy could arise from Gene's repeated gender failures. Returning to "Spaghetti Western and Meatballs," Gene spends much of the episode failing at masculinity alongside his more successful forays into feminine confidence-building using Louisa's pink Little Princess guitar. When Gene first dons Louise's guitar, he cannot replicate Banjo's icy stare, causing Bob to tell Gene that his face is wrong. Then, in a flashback to Bob and Gene trying and failing to bond over music, fishing, and sports, Gene gets distracted while Bob tries and fails to teach Gene how to throw a football, opting instead to run inside and satisfy his desire for peanut butter. Not only can Bob not throw a football, he falls asleep while trying to teach Gene how to fish, and the two have no chemistry as a band. The *Banjo* film series, ultimately, is the only masculine thing Gene and Bob share together, and while it leads to Gene to develop self-confidence in the face of his bully, the two nearly share an uglier father-son bonding moment at the fists of Choo Choo and his father.

This episode, much as it sets the standard for Gene's future gender play, opens him up to a litany of gender failures. In the second-season premiere, "The Belchies," Gene observes Zeke and Jimmy, Jr., wrestling, while commenting to his sisters, "This is why I'm only friends with women."[46] Like fishing, football, and fighting in "Spaghetti Western and Meatballs," Gene opts out of the violent morass of adolescent masculinity. Gene also, echoing his concern that his face might be wrong, announces to everyone,

"Mine's a nightmare if anyone's wondering," after overhearing Linda ask Bob about Bob's penis.[47] Gene focuses his body dysmorphia solely on his genitals, highlighting the fear, consternation, and horror he apparently experiences at possessing a penis. Or, taken less seriously, Gene's flippant attitude to his nightmarish genitals could be heard in the same tone one might discuss a haircut, potentially meaning that, for Gene, a penis is just another style accessory or choice and not a determinant of gender.

"What if I never grow up to have those instincts?"[48] *Technologies of Heterosexuality*

In "Li'l Hard Dad," Gene asks Bob the above question, concerned that he will never develop the quick reflexes required to save someone from falling objects hitting them on the head. In this particular case, the "instincts" are the paternal ones Bob claims kicked in when a squirrel untied a pair of sneakers from a power line and sent them plummeting towards Tina's head. Gene can only ask this question because he does not take for granted the "natural" development of boys into men, men into husbands, and husbands into fathers. Instead, Gene's future lies ahead of him largely, perhaps terrifyingly, unknowable, and, this unknowability allows us to re-phrase Gene's question for him in more open terms: How can Gene develop filial and affective interconnectivity and intuition if he does not want to or never becomes a father, Or, perhaps more directly: how can he be a hero if he will never be a man?

There is something sweetly plaintive in Gene's question, a tentative testing of how Bob might react to Gene never becoming a father or a man. In this tone, we might hear Gene ask Bob, "Will you still love me if I fail to become you (a father, a man)?" These are serious questions being asked by a seriously silly character, and the rest of the episode responds to Gene in ways that return us to Halberstam's insistence on non-traditional sources of knowledge. Bob's obsession with collecting a refund for a faulty toy helicopter leaves him, via multiple escalations of his feud with the seller of the toy helicopter, dangling from the ledge of a roof with an army of other toy helicopters aiming darts at his ass. The tense scene comes to a peaceful end as Gene argues quite compellingly for Bob to "just let it the freak go."

Obviously, Gene means the petty feud with Sheldon the helicopter dealer—not the ledge from which Bob dangles—and his injunction connects with both Bob and Sheldon as the two begin another feud over who will forgive who first. Later, as Gene and Bob drive back home, Bob finally acknowledges that he learned his lesson from Gene. As a child, Gene is presumably too young to have the requisite life experience to teach two adults lessons in humility, forgiveness, and letting go (forgetting)—a presumption that leads Bob to the ledge in the first place—but, clearly, Gene has already learned enough to save the day. An "undisciplined zone of knowledge production," Gene forgoes the heteronormatively prescribed steps to heroism (man, husband, father) and rescues Bob, providing a simple response to his initial question: yes, Gene, you can be a hero without being a man.

As an animated sitcom that does not advance temporally, even if nearly every season of the show features holiday episodes, *Bob's Burgers* simply lacks the linearity that would allow Gene to grow into a man, couple heterosexually, and produce a Tina of his own to save from falling shoes, regardless of whether these are Gene's goals or not. As with holidays, birthdays occur on the show, too, but the characters never really age. This does not mean, however, that Gene is not repeatedly beset by technologies of heterosexuality. These technologies are a myriad of discursive attempts to produce him as a legible, heterosexual subject and to legislate his reproduction of future legible, heterosexual subjects. While the lack of the temporal logics of linear straight time frees Gene from the strictures of chrononormative developmental modes, the repeating and looping temporal logic of the show *does* frequently play out as repeated and loopy attempts to straighten him out. This temporal logic finds its proponents at Wagstaff Elementary[49] and among his friends and family, but Gene—in his insistence on play and delight in failure—repeatedly frustrates and resists such logic.

In "O.T. The Outside Toilet,"[50] Gene and his classmates are assigned life partners and sacks of flour to simulate and train for heterosexual parenthood. Not only does Gene claim to be pregnant upon first being given a flour sack ("Anyone notice anything new about me? I'm pregnant!"), he immediately drops three different flour sacks, spilling their contents on an ever-growing pile on the classroom floor and killing these flour babies. Gene fails at paternity while courting maternity, and, in doing so, "[destroys] the Child and with it the vitalizing fantasy of bridging, in time, the gap of signification."[51] For Lee Edelman, the Child "marks the fetishistic fixation of heteronormativity: an erotically charged investment in the rigid sameness of identity that is central to the compulsory narrative of reproductive futurism."[52]

The Child *is* the figuration of the temporal logic dictated by the technologies of heterosexuality that convince educators of the naturalness of heterosexual reproduction, precluding an even cursory examination of the grotesquery of forcing eleven-year-old children into pretending to raise children of their own in the classroom. Such grotesquery, though, is at the heart of both Edelman's reproductive futurism and Freeman's chrononormativity; schools, like Wagstaff, only exist as producers and artifices of straight time. No wonder, then, that Gene kills his flour children but succeeds in tending to and protecting a talking toilet he finds in the woods.

"O.T. The Outside Toilet" again finds Gene forging his own path and repudiating his school's insistence on heteronormative gender and sexual development. Gene's home life, while often accommodating of his gender play and sideways growth, also has its moments of heteronormative discursive instruction. In "Slumber Party,"[53] an episode structured around Linda forcing a sleepover (and thus particular normative forms of friendship and relation) onto Louise, Gene hopes to participate in the various sleepover activities with Louise and her "friends." Linda, however, re-directs Gene's desire from tie-dying shirts with the rest of the girls ("I'm gonna make the psychedelic crop-top of my dreams!") to being the "pesky little brother." Obeying his mother, Gene pulls on Abby's braids, adding apologetically, "Sorry, I don't even want to do this. It's my job. I'm making this fun." Gene, who would rather be one of the girls, is tasked with being the boy, and he understands this task as business (as usual). Understanding his role as undesired employment, Gene tries to separate himself from the task at hand, disidentifying from the "pesky little brother" Linda demands he be. Abby, the little girl whose hair gets pulled, enjoys Gene's job as much as he does and adds another dissenting voice to the enforcement of gender roles on a previously sanguine scene. Abby's distress registers the physical violence accompanying the psychical violence Gene undergoes, demonstrating the inveterate link between particular forms of masculinity and misogyny. That Gene must qualify the now-painful party for Abby as "fun" further implicates gender role enforcement in the dictation of imbalanced gender power dynamics constituted by violence and the immediate dismissal of that violence.

The atmosphere created by schools and parents leads to Gene's peers learning their own forms of gender and sexuality enforcement. In "The Unbearable Like-Likeness of Gene,"[54] an episode title in which we can hear the echoes of the "unbearable heaviness of the gender binary" from Freeman's *Time Binds*, Gene is hounded by three schoolmates, Courtney Wheeler and her friends Julie and Rupa, into falsely admitting that he like-likes Courtney, "the most annoying girl in the whole school." Courtney, Julie, and Rupa's coercion of Gene ultimately leads to Gene (out of frustration) publicly humiliating Courtney at her own birthday party, an event that triggers her congenital heart issue and lands Courtney in the hospital. In the hospital, Courtney pretends to die (with the help of her dad and doctor) when Gene *finally* breaks up with her, scaring the hell out of Gene. The episode ends with Gene and Courtney on friendly terms with some sense of understanding or empathy between the two of them, but the placidity of the episode's conclusion does not undo either's trauma.

These two traumatic moments are the unavoidable accumulation of unfeeling demands made of Gene's supposed heterosexuality and the rewards offered to him for his now-assured heterosexuality.[55] While Louise and Tina oppose the relationship from the beginning, dating Courtney comes with material and emotional benefits for Gene, and these benefits keep him coupled to Courtney until their messy break-up. When Bob and Linda discover Gene's relationship, both respond enthusiastically: Linda declares, "I hear dating bells!" while Bob congratulates Gene for getting "on the board." Linda and Bob's mutual enthusiasm captures the chrononormativity of the event, as "dating bells" prefigure "wedding bells" (the future) and Bob's sports metaphor "the board" represents an already-awaiting scoreboard (the past) to register Gene's sexual accomplishments as points in a game. For Gene, dating Courtney is thus the presumptive present in an always already heterosexual temporality. Courtney's dad, a jingle artist named Doug, invites Gene into "Gear Heaven" (his name for his home recording studio and plethora of musical instruments) and offers Gene an "all-access pass" so long as Gene remains committed to Courtney. As a budding musician, this all-access pass to Gear Heaven sends Gene immediately into a fantasy that features a cherubic Gene adorned with keytar wings floating amongst clouds, endless instruments, and a deified six-armed Moby. It is the only moment, in an episode supposedly dealing with desire, when Gene freely experiences his desire and gleefully cathects to the objects of his desire. Gene knows he should break up with Courtney, but the adults involved barter material and emotional rewards for his public avowal of heterosexual desire and identification.

"That's how I wanna go out—dehydrated and covered in tinsel."[56] Gene and the Ghost of the Gay Child

As Gene and Courtney continue to interact in later episodes, their relationship takes the shape of a confusing matrix of material rewards, artistic expression, mutual attraction, and collaboration.[57] In Courtney's second appearance as a major character,[58] the two begin the episode as rival producers of separate school plays before joining together their stage adaptations of *Die Hard* and *Working Girl*[59] into one big-haired musical theater hybridization entitled *Work Hard or Die Trying*. This successful collaboration, done expressly without the help of any adults, leads to a future collaboration: "The Gene and Courtney Show."[60] In this episode, the two challenge Ms. LaBonz for control of the morning announcements, uniting to become a successful musical duo, but wind up, by episode's end, having to break up again. This time, however, the two share multiple kisses, and it is Gene who finds himself saddened by the relationship's end. Their romantic interest in one another has its foundation in the success the two find as artistic collaborators, and this leads the two to confuse a shared desire to succeed artistically with a shared desire to succeed heterosexually. As in the fantasy of Gear Heaven, music and romance again commingle for Gene, producing a complicated nexus of desires.

I am by no means discounting the pleasure Gene takes in kissing Courtney, or the heartbreak he suffers when the two decide to privilege their art over their relationship, but the story of Gene's desire does not end with a kiss. "Desire," Mari Ruti tells us, "is highly nomadic in nature, unfettered by any aim or organizational principle, devoid of lasting allegiances, and wholly divorced from structures of meaning or representation, modes of socialization, or the inculcation of ideas and ideologies."[61] Desire lacks telos and any ontological certainty or finitude, and Gene's relationship with Courtney stages the slipperiness of desire and its various movements and multiple attachments. To read Gene and Courtney's kiss as the culmination of desire towards a socially codified end is to misunderstand how desire remains resistant to discursive control. It also means misreading Gene and Courtney's kiss as irrefutable evidence of Gene's straightness. Misreading Gene as ineluctably straight erases his queerness and conscripts his childhood into the heterosexual matrix. It provides an answer to a question this chapter has avoided asking and will avoid answering: Is Gene gay?

"Kids like Gene, ya know, they get beat up," Teddy reminds Bob in "Spaghetti Western and Meatballs," an episode this chapter cannot seem to forget. Who or what does Teddy mean by "Kids like Gene"? Creative kids? Artistic kids? Unique kids? Effeminate kids? Queer kids? Gay kids? For Teddy, each of these adjectives might suffice, and each of them might mean something of the same thing. They all add up, regardless of their applicability to Gene or kids like him, to violence, so that, again, regardless of Gene's identity, Teddy can only assure Bob that Gene will become a victim of violence. Teddy's parenthetical "ya know" points weightily at some undefined but readily (in)comprehensible signifier, a conferral with Bob that Gene's likenesses are, well, *you know*. This "ya know" encodes a telos into Gene's predicament with Choo Choo as well as Gene's sexuality. Teddy, of course, does not want Gene to be beaten up, but he rationalizes such an outcome anyways, naturalizing homophobic violence as the *only* event that could follow from Gene's presumed (homo)sexuality. Though

Teddy disavows Gene's (homo)sexuality in his parenthetical elision of it, we know *his* answer to the question "Is Gene gay?"

The show repeatedly provides "answers" to the question of Gene's (homo)sexuality, delighting in queerly tinged wordplay that might lead viewers to make similar presumptions about Gene. In "The Unnatural," an episode that's title hauntingly refers to the "unnaturalness" of homosexuality, Gene calls his baseball jersey a "top" and his baseball pants "capris."[62] When Louise responds with "Sounds like a Gay Pride Parade" to Gene's stated desire to go out "dehydrated and covered in tinsel," Gene in turn responds with a spunky "Mmhmm." In the Halloween episode of the eighth season, Gene struts out of his room dressed as a bunch of grapes announcing to his family, "Here comes your favorite fruity boy!"[63] After becoming a cheerleader, an activity he agrees to undertake strictly for the silk cheer shorts, Gene announces to Todd, the self-proclaimed cheer king of the squad, "I'm here, to cheer, get used to it!"[64] He only gets excited for his first sleepover after Tina tells him that, at sleepovers, after the parents go to sleep, you get to stay up late talking about boys (an activity that Gene laments when it fails to come to fruition).[65] He even yells at Mr. Frond, in a story he writes for a school project based on *Rock and Roll High School*, "I'm not coming out, but this is!" before playing a song about farts so radical they explode the school.[66]

Non-hetero sexuality infuses the rest of *Bob's Burgers* as well, engendering a robust queer atmosphere. Bob, while working as a cabby, befriends a group of trans sex workers in the first season, and they provide the episode "Sheesh! Cab, Bob?"[67] with its moral and comedic resolution (teaching Tina what it means to be a woman) as well as Mort the Mortician with his first non-hetero kiss. Marshmallow, one of the trans people Bob befriends in this episode, too, becomes a recurring character in the series. Bob tells a gay butcher propositioning him that he is "straight, well, mostly straight" in an attempt to rebuff him.[68] (Bob also finds out from the gay butcher that he would be a "sloppy bear" in the town's gay scene.) In the episode that features Gene yelling, "Tell that to my vagina!" at Mickey the bank robber, Bob's Burger of the Day is the "We're here! We're gruyere! Get used to it!" burger, a cheesy echo of Gene's chant to Todd in "Gene It On." Speaking of Todd, he tells Gene as the squad prepares to form a human pyramid to win a cheerleading contest, "You deserve the top, *I'll* be the bottom."

"The Bleakening,"[69] season eight's two-part Christmas episode, begins with the news that the town's local gay night club has closed and prominently features Marshmallow and their gay friend Art the Artist. The episode also features a brief appearance by Dalton Crespin, aka Dame Judi Brunch, from "Brunsquatch," showcases a performance by drag queen

Miss Triple X-Mas (voiced by real-life drag performer Todrick Hall), and ends with Bob (dressed as the Bleaken) distracting the cops so they do not find and shut down the makeshift underground gay dance club where hundreds of (queer) people have gathered on Christmas Eve. Nat Kinkle, introduced in season eight's "V for Valentine-detta"[70] and the show's favorite new recurring character, takes the family on an adventure to return a pet snake to her ex-girlfriend in season ten's "Just the Trip."[71]

Clearly, queerness abounds in *Bob's Burgers*, but we cannot forget that Gene tells us, quite emphatically, that he is not coming out. We should not, however, take this declaration as Gene's decision to remain closeted. Instead, we should consider how Gene's staying-in, so to speak (which, in "The Frond Files," leads to a spectacular rainbow- and fart-drenched demolition of the same school that once made him simulate paternity with a flour sack) offers Gene the freedom to express and follow his desires, however fantastical and destructive. Or, perhaps more generatively, we should ditch the metaphor of the closet all together and resist our own impulses to make legible Gene's sexual identity. "Identity," writes Madhavi Menon, "is the demand made by power—tell us who you are so we can tell you what you can do. And by complying with that demand, by parsing endlessly the particulars that make our identity different from one another's, we are slotting into a power structure, not dismantling it."[72] We might desire an affirmative answer to the question "Is Gene gay?" so as to celebrate and support Gene's (homo)sexuality, but that desire, as Menon makes clear, coincides uncomfortably with a desire to make Gene comprehensible in such a way that delimits what Gene might do or who he might be.

What makes *Bob's Burgers* so remarkable is its commitment to Gene's childhood as a space of gender play and failure—as a space of unfettered queerness. "Childhood is an essentially queer experience,"[73] and the show allows Gene to have this queer experience without slotting him into the kind of power structure that will inevitably attempt to, whatever Gene's sexuality, produce him as a legible and reproductive neoliberal subject. In its non-linearity, *Bob's Burgers* makes for a palimpsest of childhood delay, a process of horizontal growth that spreads meaning wide and hangs it in suspense.[74] In this layering of delay, Gene remains limitlessly in the realm of queerness without having any of his actions, desires, or drives concretize into the identity position of the ghostly gay child. "The phrase 'gay child' is a gravestone marker for where or when one's straight life died,"[75] writes Stockton. "And yet,"—and perhaps this is the most salient point regarding Gene, *Bob's Burgers*, and queerness—"by the time the tombstone is raised ('I was a gay child'), the 'child' by linguistic definition has expired."[76] In *Bob's Burgers*, Gene's childhood never expires and thus the raising of the tombstone is perpetually delayed. As long as Gene remains a child, his gender play and his gender failure, coterminous expressions of whimsical, fantastical desires that the show allows him to chase, the question "Is Gene gay?" remains provocatively, fabulously, queerly unanswered.

"The World is full of mystery and magic!"[77] Stand by, Gene

To bring our journey to an end, I want to turn to one more journey led by Gene. In "Stand by Gene," Gene, Tina, and Louise are granted a day off by their parents and head over to Mr. Fischoeder's Wonder Wharf. Once there, they follow the "tried and true" path of looking for loose change under the pier in order to buy fudge and ride the Zany Planes. While looking for change, Gene overhears two teenagers discussing a two-butted goat on a farm out by Route 6. Enthused by such a possibility, Gene runs to tell his sisters, but both Louise and Tina dismiss the idea that any such goat could exist, and Louise attempts to re-direct her siblings' attention back to their originally scheduled plans. In line for the Zany Planes, the Belcher siblings run into a cadre of friends, and Gene turns his focus to convincing the group *en masse* to follow him to find the two-butted goat. Along with support from Zeke, another anally focused child,[78] Gene successfully persuades the group to set out in search of the goat with a stirring speech: "So I ask you: Would you rather have a lifetime of regret or an afternoon of mild disappointment?" In search of something more meaningful than the tried and true, Gene suspends meaning for the time being, opting instead for delay. Asking his friends and siblings to stand by him laterally, Gene also asks them to stand by temporally, giving up the immediate gratification of amusement parks for the risk of a wasted day following Gene's desires. Gene invites his fellow children to grow sideways with him, and, at least on this occasion, they consent.[79]

While indulging Gene is a fraught exercise for the rest of the kids,[80] they do ultimately find the two-butted goat, but not before Gene returns us to both Halberstam and Stockton. When the kids reach the rumored farm and can only find a regular, one-butted goat, Gene laments, "I failed you all!" before resigning himself to adulthood ("It's time for me to grow up, I guess"). When the two-butted goat, nicknamed Li'l Double Butt, finally appears, Gene returns to his initial insistence that "the world is full of mystery and magic!" But even after finding Li'l Double Butt, Gene has still failed, just not in the way he thinks. "Queerness offers the promise of failure as a way of life," and Gene's failure to adhere to the tried and true path towards enjoyment and pleasure has made good on a promise to make "a detour around the usual markers of accomplishment and satisfaction."[81]

By leading his sisters and friends down fire roads, over electric fences, and through fields of poison ivy, Gene cuts an unusual path towards success and fulfilment that privileges the nonsensical and reaffirms the queerness of childhood. As the promise Gene offers and makes good on, Li'l Double Butt, with its heart-shaped ass and accompanying two tails and two anuses, is an immensely silly but indispensable injunction against growing up too quickly. Gene keeps himself and the other children from leaving childhood too early, instead offering a form of relational and developmental delay that, I believe, mirrors our journey through this chapter. Reading Gene's gender play and following Gene to find a two-butted goat are two paths that embrace the "absurd, the silly, and the hopelessly goofy"[82] in hopes to remind us that taking ourselves—and our work—a little less seriously might lead to more enriching, more encompassing, and more rewarding forms of knowledge production.

NOTES

1. Wesley Archer, dir. "Beefsquatch." *Bob's Burgers*, season 2, episode 9, Fox, 2012.
2. Elizabeth Freeman, *Time Binds: Queer Temporalities, Queer Histories* (Durham: Duke University Press, 2010), 3. Freeman coins this concept to explain "the use of time to organize individual human bodies toward maximum productivity."
3. Judith Halberstam, *The Queer Art of Failure* (Durham: Duke University Press, 2011), 6.
4. *Ibid.*
5. *Ibid.*, 11–15. In the Introduction to *The Queer Art of Failure*, Halberstam proposes three new theses to add to Fred Moten and Stefano Harney's "Seven Theses." The first thesis, "Resist mastery," involves "investing in counterintuitive modes of knowing such as failure and stupidity" (11). The second thesis, "Privilege the naïve or nonsensical (stupidity)," is an argument "for the nonsensible or nonconceptual over sense- making structures that are often embedded in a common notion of ethics" (12). Finally, Halberstam's third thesis, "Suspect memorialization," advocates "for certain forms of erasure over memory precisely because memorialization has a tendency to tidy up disorderly histories (of slavery, the Holocaust, wars, etc.)" (15).
6. *Ibid.*, 2–3.
7. Kathryn Bond Stockton, *The Queer Child* (Durham: Duke University Press, 2009), 6.
8. *Ibid.*
9. Halberstam, *Failure*, 18.
10. Boohwan Lim and Kyounghee Lim, dir. "Tina and the Real Ghost." *Bob's Burgers*, season 5, episode 2, FOX, 2014.
11. Halberstam, *Failure*, 59.
12. Winner of Primetime Emmy Award for Outstanding Animated Program in 2014 for "Mazel-Tina" and 2016 for "Bob Actually."
13. Like Springfield in *The Simpsons*, the show never reveals the city's corresponding state, though all signs point to Bob's restaurant being in New Jersey.
14. Part of what makes childhood queer for Stockton is the dramatic change in children's economic roles in the twentieth century (38). Stockton asks about children who, because of labor laws, "cease to work for wages," "How, then, are children made unique and strange by money?" That Gene and his sisters *do* work but not for direct pay leads us to think about the imbalanced but more lateral relation between the Belcher kids and their

parents. To be sure, the kids barely work at all, except for maybe Tina, but they do labor, potentially illegally, making Gene and his sisters doubly unique and strange.

15. Kyounghee Lim, dir. "Crawl Space." *Bob's Burgers*, season 1, episode 2, FOX, 2011.

16. In "Wharf Horse" (2014, written by Nora Smith), we learn that Bob's arm hair reminds Mr. Fischoeder of his father's arm hair, prompting unsolicited advice from Mr. Fischoeder on which side Bob should part his arm hair.

17. Lauren Berlant, *Cruel Optimism* (Durham: Duke University Press, 2011). Lauren Berlant defines the "relation of cruel optimism" as "when something you desire is actually an obstacle to your flourishing" (1).

18. Anthony Chun, dir. "Human Flesh." *Bob's Burgers*, season 1, episode 1, FOX, 2011.

19. Madhavi Menon, *Indifference to Difference* (Minneapolis: University of Minnesota Press, 2015), 14.

20. Halberstam, *Failure*, 3.

21. *Ibid.*

22. Wes Archer, dir. "Spaghetti Western and Meatballs." *Bob's Burgers*, season 1, episode 9, FOX, 2011.

23. Halberstam, *Failure*, 27.

24. *Ibid.*, 73.

25. *Ibid.*

26. Stockton, *The Queer Child*, 11.

27. Anthony Chun. "Synchronized Swimming." *Bob's Burgers*, season 2, episode 3, FOX, 2012.

28. Consider Stockton's reading of the protagonist of *The Hanging Garden*: "Fat, we find, is a thick figuration and referent for a child (a sexual child) we cannot fully see. Fat is the visible effect, in this instance, of a child unable to grow up in his family as his preferred self. So he grows sideways—literally, metaphorically" (20). Though Gene is frequently accommodated and supported by his family, this sideways growth—both literal and metaphorical—finds its expression in both Gene's weight and his non-normative approach to gender expression.

29. Later in season two, Gene will proclaim, "In the meantime, enjoy the show!" as he shows his nipples to the Moody Foodie ("Moody Foodie," 2012, written by Jon Schroeder). Here, Gene plays on the sexist double-standard of whose breasts can be bared, and he takes pleasure both in showing off his own breasts and in performing the lewd indecency of women's nudity.

30. Instead of just throwing a chocolate bar in the pool, as is done in the film *Caddyshack*, Louise actually does what *Caddyshack* only implies.

31. Freeman, *Time Binds*, 3.

32. *Ibid.*, 5.

33. *Ibid.*, 11.

34. According to José Esteban Muñoz, straight time is a linear and "self-naturalizing temporality" that "needs to be phenomenologically questioned" (*Cruising Utopia* 25).

35. Halberstam, *Failure*, 15.

36. Boohwan Lim and Kyounghee Lim, dir. "Bob Fires the Kids." *Bob's Burgers*, season 3, episode 3, FOX, 2012.

37. John Rice, dir. "Mutiny on the Windbreaker." *Bob's Burgers*, season 3, episode 4, FOX, 2012.

38. Boohwan Lim and Kyounghee Lim, dir. "The Kids Run the Restaurant." *Bob's Burgers*, season 3, episode 20, FOX, 2013.

39. Dillihay, Tyree, dir. "Carpe Museum." *Bob's Burgers*, season 3, episode 22, FOX, 2013. Throughout this episode, Gene impatiently waits to stick his hands into the "Sands from the Exotic Lands" exhibit that ends the tour of the museum.

40. In "Carpe Museum," Gene's partner for the day Zeke makes the two go on a "boob hunt" across the museum, resulting in Gene admitting, "I never heard of anyone havin' a boob fetish."

41. Wes Archer, dir. "Bob Day Afternoon." *Bob's Burgers*, season 2, episode 2, FOX, 2012.

42. Jennifer Coyle, dir. "Bad Tina." *Bob's Burgers*, season 2, episode 8, FOX, 2012.

43. Ian Hamilton, dir. "The Gayle Tales." *Bob's Burgers*, season 5, episode 13, FOX, 2015.

44. Ian Hamilton, dir. "Brunchsquatch." *Bob's Burgers*, season 8, episode 1, FOX, 2017. The episode was nominated for the WGA Award for Best Animation and runs as an exquisite-corpse pastiche of over 60 fan artists' renderings of the Belcher family. The whole Belcher clan, as well as their friends (the Fischoeders) and rivals (Jimmy Pesto), perform forgetting, erasure, and spectrality to dizzying levels across the 60 different versions of themselves, making the viewer hyper-aware of the show's slipperiness, inscrutability, anti-teleology, and play.

45. Gene, with his low-cut top and pithy retort, is clearly the Samantha Jones to his mother's Carrie Bradshaw. (Tina is Charlotte York and Louise is Miranda Hobbes, to round out Linda's *Sex and the City* fantasy.)

46. Boohwan Lim and Kyounghee Lim, dir. "The Belchies." *Bob's Burgers*, season 2, episode 2, FOX, 2012. Beginning in the eighth season, this will change as Gene becomes friend with a boy named Alex.

47. Linda has slipped Bob a Viagra for their now-interrupted scheduled sex night, a penis she fears he has damaged after falling down a shaft—of all things—in the abandoned taffy factory.

48. Chris Song, dir. "Li'l Hard Dad." *Bob's Burgers*, season 5, episode 14, FOX, 2015.

49. A possible reference to the character Prof. Quincy Adams Wagstaff in the Marx Brothers' film *Horse Feathers*. It also occurs to me that "wag" and "staff" are loose synonyms for "shake" and "spear." In this case, the Belcher's very school is a (literary) penis joke.

50. Anthony Chun, dir. "O.T. The Outside Toilet." *Bob's Burgers*, season 3, episode 15, FOX, 2013.

51. Lee Edelman, *No Future* (Durham: Duke University Press, 2004), 16.

52. *Ibid.*, 21.

53. Jennifer Coyle, dir. "Slumber Party." *Bob's Burgers*, season 4, episode 9, FOX, 2014.

54. Don Mackinnon, dir. "The Unbearable Like-Likeness of Gene." *Bob's Burgers*, season 3, episode 8, FOX, 2012.

55. As Stockton points out, U.S. culture assumes all children are straight, though they are stuck as "not-yet-straight" since children are "not allowed to be sexual" (7).

56. Jennifer Coyle and Bernard Derriman, dir. "Christmas in the Car." *Bob's Burgers*, season 4, episode 8, FOX, 2013.

57. "We used to date. Now we just collaborate," sings the duo ("The Gene and Courtney Show," written by Rich Rinaldi).

58. Jennifer Coyle, dir. "Work Hard or Die Trying, Girl." *Bob's Burgers*, season 5, episode 1, FOX, 2014.

59. Bob claims that *Working Girl* is the movie that made him want to be a chef.

60. Chris Song and Bernard Derriman, dir. "The Gene and Courtney Show." *Bob's Burgers*, season 6, episode 7, FOX, 2016.

61. Mari Ruti, *Reinventing the Soul* (New York: Other Press, 2006), 147.

62. Wes Archer, dir. "The Unnatural." *Bob's Burgers*, season 3, episode 23, FOX, 2013.

63. Mauricio Pardo and Bernard Derriman, dir. "The Wolf of Wharf Street." *Bob's Burgers*, season 8, episode 3, FOX, 2017.

64. Chris Song, dir. "Gene It On." *Bob's Burgers*, season 4, episode 20, FOX, 2014.

65. Bernard Derriman and Tyree Hillihay, dir. "Cheer Up, Sleepy Gene." *Bob's Burgers*, season 8, episode 13, FOX, 2018.

66. Jennifer Coyle, dir. "The Frond Files." *Bob's Burgers*, season 4, episode 12, FOX, 2014.

67. Jennifer Coyle, dir. "Sheesh! Cab, Bob?" *Bob's Burgers*, season 1, episode 6, FOX, 2011.

68. Boohwan Lim and Kyounghee Lim, dir. "Turkey in a Can." *Bob's Burgers*, season 4, episode 5, FOX, 2013.

69. Brian Loschiavo, dir. "The Bleakening Parts I and II." *Bob's Burgers*, season 8, episodes 6 & 7, FOX, 2017.

70. Bernard Derriman and Ian Hamilton, dir. "V for Valentine-detta." *Bob's Burgers*, season 8, episode 8, FOX, 2018.

71. Chris Song, Bernard Derriman, and Tony Gennaro, dir. "Just the Trip." *Bob's Burgers*, season 10, episode 17, FOX, 2020.

72. Menon, *Indifference*, 2.

73. Halberstam, *Failure*, 27.

74. Stockton, *The Queer Child*, 4.

75. *Ibid.*, 7.

76. *Ibid.*

77. Tyree Dillihay, dir. "Stand by Gene." *Bob's* Burgers, season 6, episode 12, FOX, 2016.

78. Jennifer Coyle, dir. "Broadcast Wagstaff School News." *Bob's Burgers*, season 3, episode 12, FOX, 2013. In this episode, Zeke assists Tina's dreams in being a news anchor for the school by going on a pooping rampage, earning himself the moniker "The Mad Pooper." Gene spends much of this episode dressed as and imitating Bob, a costume he ditches over the impossible-to-control excitement of watching Zeke poop in front of the whole school in the auditorium.

79. "We never do anything I wanna do!" complains Gene earlier in the episode.

80. Tina attempts to map onto Gene's journey her desire to have her "destined true love" revealed to her, but, after eliminating all four potential true loves (Regular-Sized Rudy, Zeke, Daryl, and Jimmy, Jr.), she winds up standing in goat shit once the kids reach their destination. Jimmy, Jr., his plans to spend the day with his best friend Zeke spoiled by Gene's journey, instead spends the day jealous over the attention Zeke lavishes on Gene. Jocelyn and Tammy, two of their travel companions, repeatedly frame Jimmy, Jr.'s foul mood as (homoerotic) jealousy. They first identify that Jimmy, Jr., is jealous of Gene ("You're a Gene jelly donut!") and then advise him on how "to get Zeke back." Later, when Zeke grabs ahold of Gene while touching an electric fence, Jocelyn proclaims, "Electricity was literally running through them," much to Jimmy, Jr.'s chagrin. After the group navigates the electric fence, Jocelyn and Tammy, along with Daryl, abandon the adventure when confronted with a seemingly impassable field of poison ivy, a field the group only passes because Gene offers to carry the remaining adventurers across the field individually. Zeke, as eager as Gene to find the two-butted goat, hops on Gene's back enthusiastically, spanking him (like a rider whipping a horse) as Gene ferries him across.

81. Halberstam, *Failure*, 186.

82. *Ibid,* 187.

Giving Cinderella a Girlfriend

Queerness and Subversion in Non/Disney Fan Videos

Danielle Hart

Mainstream animated films aimed at young audiences have, until recently, adhered to a heteronormative romantic plot that involves a man and a woman meeting and falling in love. Although recent animated films such as *Brave*, *Frozen*, and *Moana* have begun to prioritize female agency and independence, neither Disney nor other prominent animation studios have included a queer heroine. Since mainstream animated films have yet to give a princess a girlfriend or stage a wedding between two princes, amateur video editors on YouTube do it themselves. Mash-up videos of animated films, known by fans as "Non/Disney AMVs" (animated music videos), often depict well-known animated characters as queer, revealing the power of fanworks to subvert the heteronormativity prevalent in animated children's media. As an indication of their popularity and appeal, some of these videos on YouTube have views in the millions. Non/Disney fan videos provide queer-friendly alternatives to mainstream animated films for children while paying homage to the source material.

Non/Disney Videos as Fanworks

First, a clarification: "Non/Disney" does *not* mean "non–Disney" or "anti–Disney." "Non/Disney" refers to videos that incorporate animation from *both* Disney animated films *and* films from other studios that are animated in a similar style to Disney films. The latter films make up the "non" portion of the term. Non/Disney fan editors use animation from already-existing cartoons in two distinct ways. The first is to tell a new story about the characters that already exist in the canonical films (Rapunzel and Elsa meeting, perhaps). The second is to tell a new story unrelated to any of the canonical films, with the original characters serving as actors or "puppets," virtual stands-ins that have the same appearance as canonical characters but exist outside the canon. (In these videos, two women who *look* like Rapunzel and Elsa may meet, but they are not connected to the original Rapunzel or Elsa aside from appearance and occasionally name.) This second type of video allows editors who may not have the time, ability, or finances to animate their own shorts from scratch to share their original stories.

The practice of "vidding" is not a new phenomenon in fan communities; however, typical fan-made videos, or "fanvids," usually edit together entire clips from one television show or movie (or occasionally, more than one) and set these clips to music. Francesca Coppa writes that "in vidding, the fans are fans of the visual source, and music is used as an interpretive lens to help the viewer to see the source text differently."[1] For example, these videos are often used to "ship" characters, i.e., support a romantic and/or sexual relationship between them. A fanvid shipping two TV characters may show a series of clips from the show set to romantic music to propose a potential relationship or suggest that such a relationship already exists.

Many Non-Disney videos are similarly focused on shipping, but they can differ from more traditional fanvids because they often tell new stories unrelated to the source materials rather than support a relationship between two canonical characters. Non/Disney videos frequently move characters into new settings and ship characters from different sources (e.g., Rapunzel from *Tangled* and Elsa from *Frozen* could have a date in the castle from *Shrek*). Because of the differences between typical fanvids and Non/Disney fanvids, I want to be clear why I am using a fan studies approach to study Non/Disney videos, as they fall into the category of fan texts for several reasons:

1. Just like other forms of fanworks, Non/Disney video creators draw from elements of already-existing texts (in this case, animated characters and backgrounds) to create their own stories.

2. Like fanfiction, Non/Disney videos are protected by Fair Use laws, which allow the creators to publish their work on platforms like YouTube, but prevent the creators from profiting from such work. Websites like Patreon do allow fans to give money to creators, but not in direct exchange for any creative product that infringes on another's copyright.[2]

3. Non/Disney communities—which include both the editors and those who watch and comment on the videos—function similarly to other types of online fan communities. Social media platforms like Tumblr allow for communication between members of the Non/Disney community, and these members share knowledge of the genre

and a common vocabulary. In addition, fannish activities like writing fanfiction or drawing pictures (either about the Non/Disney videos or the canonical films) are prevalent in Non/Disney communities.

4. Non/Disney editors often describe themselves as "fan editors," clearly situating themselves as part of a fan community.

Due to the similarities between Non/Disney videos and communities to other forms of fan texts and communities, fan studies scholarship is a productive place to better understand the functions of these videos.

Fan studies is a growing intersectional field with a focus on communities (fandoms) centered on appreciation for a piece of popular media, as well as the creative products that these communities produce. One point of entry into fan studies is the notion of resistance and subversion in fanworks. I want to acknowledge that the subversive power of YouTube content in particular has been explored extensively outside of fan studies; for example, Robin J. Phelps-Ward and Crystal T. Laura discuss how YouTube communities can function as sources of counternarratives to the sexist and racist narratives which constantly bombard young Black women.[3] Others have discussed how online videos have the potential to cross physical boundaries; at a time when "students of color and their families live and are being educated in the most segregated settings since the 1970's," the Internet can help to bridge these gaps by bringing together people with common interests.[4] What fan studies can add to the conversation on resistance and community in online spaces is an analysis of a fanwork's complicated relationship to its source material.

In terms of Non/Disney videos, fan studies can help to explain this genre's potential for subversion. In fan studies scholarship, fanworks are often discussed as subversive forces that work against the narrative of the original texts. Lev Grossman, for example, proclaims that fanfiction is "subversive and perverse and boundary-breaking, and it *always has been*."[5] Many scholars have demonstrated how the subversiveness of fanworks often extends beyond the works themselves and directly inspires social action. For example, in a study of the effects of slash fiction[6] on the LGBTQ+ community in Russia, Sudha Rajagopalan writes that Russian "slashers" were able to apply the conversations about sexuality that occur in slash fiction spaces and extended such conversations to reach other audiences, "cut[ting] across fannish and nonfannish spaces, shaping political rhetoric and everyday conversations about sexual choice and cultural norms in contemporary Russia."[7] In situations such as the one Rajagopalan describes, it becomes clear that social attitudes promoted through the creation and consumption of certain fanworks can be powerful forces that can lead to social change.

Without disregarding the real changes that have come about through fan activity, I want to be clear that I am not arguing that fanworks are *inherently* forces for social justice. Henry Jenkins writes that "resistance has always been a somewhat odd point of entry into studying fans. After all, fans also act out of a strong attraction to the source material content, even if they read it in terms which are not fully authorized by the media producers."[8] Fans can have myriad reasons for creating fanworks, and these desires can stem from wanting "more of" the source material, or more of the same, or "more from" the source material, which usually involves challenging the norms of the canon.[9] What this dichotomy tells us is that fanfiction can be both a progressive and a normalizing, even reactionary force. Kyra Hunting, Berit Åström, and Monica Flegel and Jenny Roth have argued that fanworks can support normative conceptions of gender and sexuality, and Rebecca Wanzo and Dominique Dierdre Johnson have discussed the racism present in fandom and fanworks, especially against Black characters and fans.[10]

Rather than assume a fanwork is more progressive than its source material, we must investigate a fanwork's relationship to the source to determine how it engages with the canon's norms, values, and messages. Non/Disney videos, like other forms of fanworks, are always in conversation with the source material. A fan editor, in crafting their videos, is making conscious choices in music, characters, backgrounds, and plot. Whether the editor decides to go along with the canon of the source material or deviate from it, the connection to the previous iteration will always exist in some form. I wish to reiterate that the intimate connection between fanworks and their source texts does not mean that the fanworks are inferior or mere copies of the original. Rather, like any other form of media, Non/Disney videos carry with them connections and allusions that shape the way we interpret these texts.

"Someday my prince will come": The History of Gender Roles and Romantic Relationships in Animated Children's Films

To understand the narratives of romance, sexuality, and gender that Non/Disney videos work with and against, it is important to understand the source material these editors use and its resonance in popular culture. For the purposes of this piece, the historical background of gender and sexuality in animated children's films is key to understanding the work of many Non/Disney videos. I will focus on animated Disney movies in particular in my discussion, not only because animated Disney films make up the vast majority of fodder for Non/Disney crossover videos, but also because of Disney's enormous cultural influence, especially on youth, and the fact that Disney films tend to exemplify historical trends in children's media and because. Disney as a company and as a body of work, writes Henry A. Giroux, "functions as an expansive teaching machine in which it appropriates media and popular culture to rewrite public memory and offer students an almost entirely privatized and commercialized notion of citizenship."[11] Disney's influence cannot be understated here; Disney "texts hold deep cultural recognizability and popularity," and the films shape the way their audiences see the world.[12]

I am paying special attention on the Disney films focused on human characters, most specifically the "princess" films (a label applied to Disney films with a female lead, even if they are not technically "royalty"), because non-human characters feature less frequently than humans in Non/Disney videos. Although there is much to be said about gender roles and depictions of sexuality in the source material for animated Disney films—most commonly fairy tales and folktales—I will limit my analysis to the realm of animation. However, the fact that most Disney princess films are adaptations themselves hopefully reminds us of the value of adaptation, including fan adaptation.

The Original Princesses:
The 1930s Through the 1950s

The three earliest animated Disney princesses, Snow White (*Snow White and the Seven Dwarfs*, 1937), Cinderella (*Cinderella*, 1950), and Aurora (*Sleeping Beauty*, 1959), frequently demonstrate stereotypical gendered behavior and female precarity, and these tales are all centered on heterosexual romance. As England et al. write, the first three Disney princesses displayed stereotypically feminine traits; Snow White, Cinderella, and Aurora are "affectionate, helpful, troublesome, fearful, tentative, and described as pretty."[13] These early Disney princesses are often shown engaged in domestic housework and other traditionally female pursuits. Consider Snow White's display of domesticity and mothering instincts when she stumbles upon the dwarfs' grimy home, assumes it belongs to children, and cleans it from top to bottom.[14]

The oft-critiqued "damsel in distress" trope is present in all three films; both Snow White and Aurora are rescued from magical spells by the kiss of their respective princes, and Cinderella spends a large part of the film's third act trapped in her bedroom. Elizabeth Marshall and Leigh Gilmore write that girls in visual media have often been depicted as vulnerable and in need of rescue; their precarity and "vulnerability permits the heroism of others," like the princes in Disney films, "while [the girls] remain stubbornly stuck in material conditions of danger as well as visual and narrative practices that habituate audiences to see this as their inevitable fate."[15]

Updating or adapting a fairy tale as the Disney films do does not necessarily critique the misogyny of the source material and, in fact, "habituates audiences to seeing girls' endangerment as typical."[16] The early Disney princess films depict—but do not critique—the precarity of girlhood, which includes violence at the hands of those more powerful and an inability to rescue one's self.

In addition to relying on the helplessness of women as a plot point, all three of the early princess films culminate in marriage between the heroine and a prince, although there is little exploration of any of the relationships and, even more concerningly, little interaction between the heroes and heroines in general. Both *Sleeping Beauty*'s Prince Philip and *Cinderella*'s Prince Charming want to marry their respective love interests after knowing them for only one day, and *Snow White*'s prince barely talks to Snow White before kissing her when she is unconscious, an act that would be shocking today in the era of the #MeToo movement.[17] Developing a complex and realistic relationship is less important in the narratives of the early Disney princess films than forcing a marriage upon the hero and heroine.

Renaissance-Era Disney Princesses: The 1980s and the 1990s

During the sixties and seventies, Disney movies made some changes in the way gender and sexuality were depicted, yet the studio produced few memorable animated films with human leads, entering into "a creative and, subsequently, financial slump for nearly two decades."[18] Disney's highly successful film *The Little Mermaid* (1989) began a resurgence era known as the "Disney Renaissance" which lasted roughly from 1989 to the new millennium and produced some of the most memorable princesses: the mermaid Ariel, *Beauty and the Beast*'s Belle (1991), and *Aladdin*'s Jasmine (1992), among others.[19] Maja Rudloff writes that Disney intended that these princesses to be a departure from the "passive, submissive female characters" of the earliest Disney films "and to reflect more modern, contemporary, agentic and realistic role models for young viewers."[20] In some ways, Disney was successful in presenting young audiences with updated female role models; characters like Belle and Jasmine certainly have more initiative and personality when compared to their earlier counterparts. Jasmine, for instance, at first resists her father's attempts to find a suitor for her, and Belle does not meekly obey the Beast while trapped in his castle. The titular heroine in *Mulan* (1998) is particularly noteworthy in her bending of gender roles; she disguises herself as a man throughout most of the movie in order to fight in the Chinese army. Compared to the behavior of the first three Disney princesses, the Renaissance princesses do indeed demonstrate more agency and indicate an attempt to correct previous representations of princesses as weak and helpless women.

However, despite some progress, often these films still buy into "conservative, patriarchal, sexist and even racist representations of gender and ethnicity, featuring love-hungry princesses with no real control over their destinies."[21] Just as with the early-era films, there are no overtly queer Disney women, and the princesses of the Disney Renaissance era inevitably enter into a romance or marriage with a male character; this holds true even in the animal-centered *The Lion King* (1994) and the gender-bending *Mulan*. Many have also questioned *Beauty and the Beast*'s seeming acceptance of the Beast's imprisonment of Belle and their subsequent romance while she is in his captivity; Kathryn M. Olson writes that "Disney's rhetorical choices make concrete acts of romantic violence both realistic and familiar, yet position them as not causes for concern or sympathy for the victim or as a reason to end a relationship; instead, it signals an opportunity for the lover to reform the violent with the result that the efforts end in happily-ever-after love."[22] In addition, although there is more racial diversity among the Renaissance princesses than in the past era of Disney films, all of them are still drawn as conventionally attractive, denying young audiences a variety of body types in their animated role models. For these reasons, the changes to animated film narratives in the Renaissance era do indicate some progress in the depiction of women and relationships, but these depictions are still far from ideal.

"I'll be shooting for my own hand": The Current State of Gender, Relationships, and Sexuality in Animated Children's Films

In *The Queer Art of Failure*, Jack Halberstam cites Kathryn Bond Stockton's idea that "heterosexuality is something not born but made," and that popular media is often the tool through which to "deliver us our common destinies of marriage, child rearing, and hetero-reproduction."[23] We can see popular media functioning in this way with the Disney films of the past and their reliance on marriage and heterosexual romance as tropes. Halberstam lauds animated films like Pixar's *Monsters, Inc.* (2001) and Aardman Animation's *Chicken Run* (2000) for providing alternatives to this narrative: "the allegory and the formula [of these films] do not simply line up with the conventional generic schemes of Hollywood cinema."[24]

Although I agree that the films Halberstam mentions are quite radical in their themes of revolt and the twisting and turning of conventional movie plots, this overt radicalness has not quite extended to the subgenre of animated princess films, despite the fact that the most recent animated princess films have presented us with something different from the past.

Recent animated films targeted at young audiences, including princess-centric Disney films, have more frequently broken away from the "girl meets boy and falls in love" formula predominant in both early and Renaissance-era Disney films. A prime example of the changing attitudes toward depicting relationships in animated films is the 2012 Disney/Pixar film *Brave*, notably the first Pixar film with a woman, Brenda Chapman, as one of the directors. In *Brave*, the Scottish princess Merida is forced to marry the winner of an archery competition between neighboring princes. However, during the competition, Merida stands and declares that she will "be shooting for [her] own hand," asserting her independence and unwillingness to get married.[25] Rather than dwell on any aspect of Merida's romantic life, the rest of the movie is concerned with the relationship between Merida and her mother Elinor, who is magically transformed into a bear. By the end of the film, Merida convinces the neighboring clans to end the tradition of forcing their young princes and princesses to marry against their will. There is a clear contrast between *Brave* and films like *Cinderella* and *The Little Mermaid*, which inevitably end in the marriage of the heroine and her prince.

Similarly, in Disney's 2016 computer animated feature *Moana*, the topic of marriage or romance does not appear at all. The titular character, the only child of a chief, would seem a likely candidate for an arranged marriage plot. However, not only does the film focus instead on Moana's quest to restore the heart of the goddess Te Fiti but also the village assumes that Moana will take up the position of chief after her father's death whether or not she is married. *Moana* is shown to be smart, capable, and independent, and, like Mulan, Moana is one of the only Disney princesses to be shown excelling at physical activities. The characterization of Moana is a far cry from the helpless early princesses and the love-obsessed women of the Disney Renaissance era.

Frozen (2013), another Disney film, is also notable in its treatment of romantic relationships. Early in the film, Princess Anna meets and gets engaged to Prince Hans after they have just met each other. Anna's sister Elsa declares, "you can't marry a man you just met," a humorous nod back to the hasty marriages in earlier Disney films that suggests *Frozen* rejects that kind of rushed romance plot.[26] Although Anna does find a real love interest in Kristoff by the end of the film, the couple do not marry right away, and Elsa does not end up with a partner at all. The true love that saves Anna from a curse is the sisterly love between her and Elsa; the women do not need a prince to save them. The 2019 sequel, *Frozen 2*, emphasizes similar themes of family and still does not introduce a romantic interest for Elsa.[27]

The prioritization of women's agency in films like *Brave, Moana*, and *Frozen* has led many to declare them "feminist" children's films that have, at last, broken away from Disney's problematic relationship with female agency and sexuality.[28] Admittedly, these films have indeed distanced themselves from the "damsel in distress" stereotype and the obligatory heterosexual romance plot. Although this is laudable, neither the absence nor the presence of romance inherently makes a film fall into the nebulous categories "feminist" or "anti-feminist." Feminism is not a monolithic belief system, and what is often described as "feminism" in popular culture is often a narrow, non-intersectional form of feminism that disregards the important work and lived experiences of queer and trans women and women of color.[29] As Rudloff discusses in an analysis of *Frozen*, even the most independent of Disney heroines still conform to idealized and sexualized Western and Eurocentric notions of beauty: "In Elsa, the feminist ideals of empowerment, self-realisation and liberation are confused with her outward appearance and sexualization, which equates her inner sense of self with a femininity that is located in her body."[30] Although both Merida and Moana do depart somewhat from the traditional Disney ideal of female beauty, they are both still conventionally attractive and, in that sense, "wear" a normative female form. The character design in even the most recent animated princess movies insists on the oversexualization of young female protagonists and a dedication to Eurocentric ideals of beauty.

In addition, although Merida, Moana, and Elsa remain single at the end of their respective films and seem overall uninterested in romance, this only presents one form of resistance against the heteronormative script upon which many Disney movies rely. Recent animated princess films have failed to present audiences with alternative versions of romance and sexuality. For example, none of the Disney princesses are canonically lesbian or bisexual. Rather than offer alternatives to heterosexual relationships, there are no overt depictions of relationships in these films whatsoever. Although an asexual or aromantic Disney princess would also be positive representation for a community often rendered invisible in popular culture, the romantic and sexual orientations of princesses like Merida are not overt enough for the characters to function as explicit ace representation. This is not to say that there must be a romantic subplot in every animated children's film, but rather that the absence of queer identities in *every* film of this kind indicates discomfort on the part of both studios and adult audiences to allow young audiences to be exposed to LGBTQ+ representation in media. This discomfort has been made clear when any hint of queerness in children's films is presented to mainstream audiences. Several niche/indie animated films targeted at children in recent years have presented queer relationships positively, like the 2017 critically-acclaimed short *In a Heartbeat*, but no mainstream full-length children's animated films have done so.[31] This is likely in part to the hypersexualization of gay and lesbian relationships in media that have contributed to the notion that depictions of said relationships are inherently unsuitable for young audiences.[32]

The Finding Dory *Trailer, #GiveElsaAGirlfriend, and Lefou*

As I have established, gay and lesbian relationships in media targeted at children, especially animation, is rare. It is not uncommon that even hints of LGBTQ+ characters in children's animated films are met with a backlash. One instance of this occurred in 2016 after the release of a trailer for the Disney/Pixar film *Finding Dory*, an animated family film about a fish (voiced by Ellen DeGeneres) who is trying to find her family. At one point in the trailer, two female characters appear together outside of an aquarium. One woman tries to return a knocked over cup to a child, only for the women to realize there is an octopus in the stroller, and both draw back in shock.[33] Other than the proximity of the women, nothing in the trailer indicates whether or not these characters are in a relationship, or even if they know each other. The whole scene in the trailer only lasts for a few seconds.

Upon the release of the trailer in the spring of 2016, social media sites were abuzz with speculation about the relationship between the two women.[34] The fact that the voice actor for Dory is Ellen DeGeneres, who is a lesbian, further fed the speculation that the women were intentionally meant to be in a relationship. On Twitter, many gushed about their excitement that Disney was finally representing lesbian characters in their films.[35] As a counter to these supportive comments, other people on social media disapproved of even the merest hint of a lesbian couple in the trailer.[36] A third group supported the representation of queer characters in animated family films, yet felt that the brief glance of the women in the *Finding Dory* trailer was not sufficient, and perhaps was an example of queerbaiting. Queerbaiting refers to a piece of media dropping hints or alluding to queerness (usually in an attempt to appeal to fans), but never explicitly stating or depicting said queerness.[37] The full scene in *Finding Dory* is just as short and unclear about the women's relationship as the trailer, leaving many fans disappointed.

A similar discussion emerged with the popular hashtag #GiveElsaAGirlfriend, which circulated on social media in 2016 amid rumors of a sequel to *Frozen*, as well as news that Walt Disney Studios failed GLAAD's[38] most recent "Studio Responsibility Index," which evaluates the depiction of LGBTQ+ individuals in films.[39] Because Elsa did not have a relationship in the first *Frozen* film, she seemed to many to be an ideal candidate for the first lesbian Disney princess. However, *Frozen 2* did not end up giving Elsa a romantic relationship, although many shipped her with a new female character, Honeymaren.[40]

In addition, the release of the 2017 live action version of Disney's *Beauty and the Beast* hinted that the character Lefou was gay, and featured him dancing with another man at the end of the film.[41] Both of these instances were also met with backlash on social media, with many citing concerns that Elsa having a girlfriend or Lefou having a boyfriend would be inappropriate for a children's film, while others believed that Lefou's queerness was not overt enough. In all of these cases, social media exploded with different opinions on the portrayal of possibly queer characters in animated media. These online discussions reinforce not only how far-reaching this conversation is, but also how popular media companies like Disney inform our conversations on gender and sexuality.

"Illuminating" Queerness in Non/Disney Videos

I delved into the history of animated princess films in order to explain the context of Non/Disney videos and demonstrate how Non/Disney videos function as an alternative to mainstream animated films. I first became aware of Non/Disney crossover videos when I stumbled upon a *Huffington Post* article a few years ago that discussed the work of an editor that went by the title "TheNamelessDoll" on YouTube and Tumblr.[42] I followed a link to her YouTube page and soon learned that she was not the only animator participating in this kind of work, although she is still one of the most prolific today. Many of TheNamelessDoll's videos, and Non/Disney videos more generally, explore queer relationships between characters originally found in children's animated films. Non/Disney videos are born in the midst of mainstream animation's portrayals of gender and sexuality, as well as the heated discussions surrounding these topics in children's media.

Non/Disney videos can fulfill several functions for the editors and viewers. Like other forms of fanworks, Non/Disney videos can function as safe spaces to form and articulate non-normative/queer identities, especially for young people. Catherine Tosenberger writes, "fandom is more than a space to simply acquire technical expertise at writing," or, in the case of Non/Disney videos, editing and animation; Tosenberger explores the way adolescents entering into fan communities may have the "potential to encounter and experiment with alternative modes of sexual discourse, particularly queer discourse."[43] Non/Disney videos that depict queer relationships can provide a counternarrative to heteronormative animated films. Although not all Non/Disney films do this type of work, it is no exaggeration to say that the number of queer relationships in Non/Disney videos far outnumbers those in mainstream animated media aimed at young audiences.

In this section, I will examine two popular Non/Disney videos by two different editors that nonetheless have similar themes and plotlines, most notably the emphasis on a romantic relationship between two female characters. The first Non/Disney video, "ILLUMINATED" by TheNamelessDoll, tells the story of a romance between two women in a steampunk/outer space setting.[44] "ILLUMINATED" is one of the most popular videos of TheNamelessDoll's; it was uploaded in 2013 and had more than 800,000 views as of August 2020. The editor used the characters of Jane Porter from Disney's 1999 film *Tarzan* and Captain Amelia, a catlike alien woman, from Disney's 2002 film *Treasure Planet*. The second video, "Kamikaze" by TheNight130, focuses on the relationship between two women depicted by the Disney version of *Cinderella* and *The Hunchback of Notre Dame*'s Esmeralda.[45] The video takes place vaguely in *Hunchback*'s setting of Renaissance Paris, borrowing from many of the film's backgrounds and settings. Like "ILLUMINATED," "Kamikaze" is another of the most popular Non/Disney videos on YouTube, having attracted more than one million views between October 2017 and August 2020.

As is typical with Non/Disney films, there are no subtitles or sound effects throughout the entirety of either video. The only audio in "ILLUMINATED" is the song "Illuminated" by the band Hurts, which is the source of the video's title; in "Kamikaze," the background song is the song "Kamikaze" by Night Argent. Naming Non/Disney videos after a song is common in the Disney AMV community. As Coppa states, while music is almost never the focal point of fanvids, it is still important, as it helps to set the tone of the video and allows the editor to comment on not only the source material but also how the song adds to the fan video's message.[46] In this case, the song "Illuminated" lends the video drama and subtle sexual undertones, with lyrics like "Just take my hand, I'll make it feel so much better tonight."[47] The song "Kamikaze" by Night Argent tells the story of a torrid romance, the lyric "Should I let you go? / Or watch this love explode?" reflecting the dramatic ending of "Kamikaze."[48]

TheNamelessDoll's "ILLUMINATED" and TheNight130's "Kamikaze" both present the viewer with a multiplicity of sexual orientations and identities that sets them apart from similar animated Disney fare. In "ILLUMINATED," Jane is depicted as bisexual or pansexual, as it is established she previously was in a relationship with the male Thrax (the villain from Warner Bros' 2001 *Osmosis Jones*), and, throughout the video, she falls in love with Amelia (and Amelia with her). Similarly, Cinderella and Esmeralda fall in love with each other in "Kamikaze" and eventually try to get married, marking their relationship as overtly romantic. Although both "ILLUMINATED" and "Kamikaze" use the Disney characters as puppets in a new story, divorcing the princesses from their original films and treating the women as new characters, the audience is still reminded of the characters the women were in the source material. Because all four of these female characters are depicted as heterosexual in their original films, entering into romantic relationships with male characters, "ILLUMINATED" and "Kamikaze" disrupt the expectations of those familiar with the characters as they appeared in the canonical movies.

"ILLUMINATED" and "Kamikaze" both make use of overt images of romance without being sexually explicit. In "ILLUMINATED," Jane boards Amelia's spaceship to flee Thrax's domestic abuse (shown in flashbacks), and the two women slowly form a romantic relationship during their travels in space. The relationship between Jane and Amelia is not merely hinted at—there are numerous scenes of the two cuddling in bed or staring longingly at each other—but it is no more sexual than what you might find in a Disney film. Cinderella and Esmeralda in "Kamikaze" similarly kiss and hold hands, and later in the video, Esmeralda proposes to Cinderella.[49] Making the romantic aspects of Jane and Amelia's and Cinderella and Esmeralda's respective relationships overt (while making the videos suitable for younger audiences) helps to dispel the notion that same-gender relationships are inherently more sexual or inappropriate for general audiences than heterosexual relationships. Although there are several scenes of violence in "ILLUMINATED" and "Kamikaze" that place them more on par with the grittier *Hunchback of Notre Dame* than some of Disney's tamer films, neither is unsuitable for older children and teenagers.

Having said this, I would like to note that Non/Disney videos are not homogenous, and there are many that depict sexual content (which are usually labeled 13+ for alert viewers). The depiction of sexual content does not make these Non/Disney videos more or less subversive than any other; rather, the work that "ILLUMINATED" and "Kamikaze" is doing is a different sort of project from that of a more sexually explicit Non/Disney video. Both types of Non/Disney videos have their place in disrupting expectations of what an animated video using Disney characters can be. In the case of "ILLUMINATED" and "Kamikaze," they serve to normalize the depiction of queer relationships in a very specific genre of animation geared toward younger audiences.

Both "ILLUMINATED" and "Kamikaze" include depictions of violence against queer women that both disrupts and upholds negative tropes about queer couples that are common in mainstream media, as well as complicates the videos' relationships with their source material. Near the end of "ILLUMINATED," Thrax murders Amelia in an act of revenge, and Jane blows up the ship to kill Thrax, also dying in the explosion. "Kamikaze" features Esmeralda being burnt at the stake by Claude Frollo (as he attempts to do in *Hunchback*) and Cinderella leaping in to join her, leading to both their deaths. The final scene of both videos shows the lovers' ghostly forms happily reuniting in the afterlife. Although Disney cartoons are no stranger to major character death, the deaths of the main characters so late in the fan videos signals a departure from mainstream animated children's films. The deaths of Jane and Amelia in "ILLUMINATED" and Cinderella and Esmeralda in "Kamikaze" both uphold and subvert the pop culture trope called "Bury Your Gays," which refers to the disproportionately high number of deaths of LGBTQ+ characters in popular media.[50] "Bury Your Gays" is a potentially dangerous message to send to audiences because it shows non-heterosexual characters as primarily victims and creates a dearth of happy endings for these characters.

However, although "ILLUMINATED" and "Kamikaze" do perpetuate the "Bury Your Gays" trope in some ways, they are also able to subvert it by giving the couples a happy ending of a sort. The ending sequences of the women's spirits living on in heaven demonstrates a continuation of their stories in a way that most instances of this trope denies their gay characters. In addition, the relationships between Jane and Amelia and Cinderella and Esmeralda respectfully are the main focus of the stories rather than token gay or bisexual characters included to please a diverse audience. I also want to emphasize that a great many fan artists, including Non/Disney editors, identify as LGBTQ+ themselves.[51] Identifying as part of the LGBTQ+ community means that these writers and editors often engage with the personal in fanworks exploring queer relationships, and they are typically quite aware of mainstream depictions of queer couples.

Ultimately, both "ILLUMINATED" and "Kamikaze" serve an important function in providing an alternative to the depictions of sexuality and gender in the Disney and non–Disney source materials. Katie Kapurch discusses the subversive power of fanfiction that focuses on a relationship between the princesses of *Tangled* (2010) and *Brave*: "In the case of Meripunzel [the shipping portmanteau of the characters' names], femslash does not exist in order to oversexualize hyper-feminine bodies, but to suggest lesbian romance has a place alongside the Disney studio's representation of princes and princesses."[52] "ILLUMINATED" and "Kamikaze" function in a similar way to Meripunzel slash fiction, refusing to oversexualize the couples in the videos and offering an alternative vision of sexuality that normalizes queerness in animated fare. In short, these videos make a place for queer princesses that did not exist before.

Limitations of Non/Disney Videos

Although Non/Disney videos do have the potential to disrupt the heteronormative narratives common in western animation, and likely have a wider range than written fanfiction that is mostly confined to fan sites, they are not without limitations. One limitation of Non/Disney videos is their potential lack of accessibility. As Phelps-Ward and Laura write, people "from poor and working class families … may not have the resources (e.g., technology, permission/support/quiet space/time/skills to record, edit, upload, and respond to inquiries about the videos)"; this can be true for potential Non/Disney editors.[53] Some types of editing software are expensive, Photoshop in particular, and some people do not own computers due to their cost. Young people, too, may find that these kinds of tools are inaccessible if, for example, they have to share a computer with others at home. This can limit those who are able to create and/or enjoy Non/Disney videos.

I am also considering accessibility in terms of disability. Non/Disney videos' meaning-making relies primarily on visuals, without which the storyline could be lost. Although there is often background music and a title that could be read aloud by screen readers, characters are not usually given audible dialogue, and often not even subtitles. Although not including speech or text in Non/Disney videos allows them to cross language barriers, it also means they are mostly inaccessible to anyone who is blind or vision-impaired.

Another limitation exists in the range of characters that fan editors can use, especially in terms of race and gendered physical appearance. In Non/Disney videos, the character forms are placed into stories that are often a departure from Disney fare, but still rooted in the embodiedness of the original character models. Because Non/Disney animators are drawing exclusively from already-existing media, they can only use the types of bodies that exist in the original films. This makes it more difficult for fan animators to portray characters who are gender nonconforming, or who do not represent an idealized body type. This can also limit the number of characters of color in a Non/Disney video.

However, some editors have been attempting to push the boundaries on character body types and skin colors by editing clips of the source material to "racebend" or "genderbend" canonical characters. TheNamelessDoll has several videos of these types of "manips" (image manipulations). One video features a plus-sized Belle, a Black Cinderella, and a female Naveen from *The Princess and the Frog* (2009).[54] In an interview with *The Huffington Post*, TheNamelessDoll is quick to point out that many of her manips are an exercise in editing rather than a political statement[55]; however, in the comments to this video, when a YouTube user argues that the genderbend of Naveen is still too masculine, TheNamelessDoll replies, "He/she did go [through] a big change, but the end result is still pretty 'butch,' something that I wanted to maintain because I wanted to show a 'different kind of beautiful,'" a comment which again exposes the limited depictions of beauty in the original Disney films.[56] Although edits to characters' bodies are often too time consuming for an entire AMV, these short clips and still images do expose audiences to different body types, and, no matter the stated intentions of the editors, help to work against the monolithic "princess" (thin, beautiful, Eurocentric) body type that dominates in mainstream animated films.

The limitations of Non/Disney videos do not necessarily bar them from doing productive work in subverting traditional narratives in animated media, nor should the editors be condemned for not making the videos accessible to everyone. Rather, Non/Disney videos are only one avenue in providing counternarratives to heteronormative tropes in animated media for children, and other possibilities could be explored. In addition, based on my personal experience, people in online fan communities seem highly willing to make fanworks accessible to all. Visual art on social media sites like Tumblr (a favorite of fan communities) often features descriptive text-based captions legible to text-to-voice programs, and podfics (audio versions of fanfiction) are very common. I could easily envision Non/Disney videos receiving a similar treatment if there is demand to make them more accessible. In terms of diversity of source material, that is something that mainstream animation studios will have to grapple with in the future. Based on the popularity of Non/Disney edits, there is a desire among fans for more representation and diversity in animated films.[57]

Conclusion

Non/Disney videos are a rich place to begin work on fans' subversive takes on mainstream animated films. Although I want to emphasize again that fanworks do not inherently resist the narratives of their source materials, Non/Disney short films like TheNamelessDoll's "ILLU-MINATED" and TheNight130's "Kamikaze" help to work against the heteronormative storytelling of canonical children's films provided by companies like Disney, which have massive cultural influence. Understanding how and why fanworks operate both differently and similarly to the source material allows us to not only better understand fan communities, but also to understand how different genres respond to heteronormativity in the twenty-first century. Although often-denigrated, genres like children's animation and fanworks shape our worldviews and negotiate with cultural norms, especially in conjunction with each other.

Further work could be done on different types of Non/Disney fan videos, including the large number of those concerning transgender characters or coming out narratives. Another area of inquiry could be how fan-edited visual media like Non/Disney videos affects viewers outside of fan spaces; are these videos promoting social justice in the same way that slash fiction has in Russia? As children's animated films continue to be hugely popular and influential among both young and older audiences, it will be interesting to see, once queerness begins to be depicted more overtly in mainstream children's media (and I do believe we are on this path), how Non/Disney videos change accordingly.

NOTES

1. Francesca Coppa, "Women, Star Trek, and the Early Development of Fannish Vidding" In *Transformative Works and Cultures 1, no. 1* (2008).

2. "Patreon Community Guidelines," *Patreon.* Last modified 2018, https://www.patreon.com/guidelines#authenticity.

3. Robin J. Phelps-Ward and Crystal T. Laura, "Talking Back in Cyberspace: Self-Love, Hair Care, and Counter Narratives in Black Adolescent Girls' YouTube Vlogs," *Gender and Education* 28, no. 6 (2016): 807–820.

4. David I. Hernández-Saca, Laurie Gutmann Kahn, and Mercedes A. Cannon, "Intersectionality Dis/Ability Research: How Dis/Ability Research in Education Engages Intersectionality to Uncover the Multidimensional Construction of Dis/Abled Experiences," *Review of Research in Education* 42, no. 1 (March 2018): 288.

5. Sujin Kim and Alina Salpac, "Culturally Responsive, Transformative Pedagogy in the Transnational Era: Critical Perspectives," *Educational Studies* 5, no. 1 (2015): 17.

6. Lev Grossman, "Foreword," in *Fic: Why Fanfiction is Taking Over the World*, ed. Anne Jamison (Dallas: Smart Pop, 2013), xii.

7. Slash fanfiction is known for its depiction of queer relationships.

8. Sudha Rajagopalan, "Slash Fandom, Sociability, and Sexual Politics in Putin's Russia," *Transformative Works and Cultures* 19 (2014).

9. Henry Jenkins, *Textual Poachers* (New York: Routledge, 1992), xxi, Sheenagh Pugh, *The Democratic Genre* (Bridgend: Seren, 2005), 19.

10. Kyra Hunting, "Queer as Folk and the Trouble with Slash," *Transformative Works and Cultures* 11 (April 11, 2012); Monica Flegel and Jenny Roth, "Annihilating Love and Heterosexuality without Women: Romance, Generic Difference, and Queer Politics in

Supernatural Fan Fiction." *Transformative Works and Cultures* 4 (July 2010); Berit Åström, "'Let's Get Those Winchesters Pregnant': Male Pregnancy in *Supernatural* Fan Fiction," *Transformative Works and Cultures* 4 (January 7, 2010); Dominique Dierdre Johnson, "Misogynoir and Antiblack Racism: What *The Walking Dead* Teaches Us About the Limits of Speculative Fiction Fandom." *The Journal of Fandom Studies* 3, no. 3 (September 2015): 259–75; Rebecca Wanzo, "African American Acafandom and Other Strangers: New Genealogies of Fan Studies." *Transformative Works and Cultures* 20 (September 15, 2015).

11. Henry Giroux, "Cultural Studies and Public Pedagogy," in *Encyclopedia of Educational Philosophy and Theory*, ed. Michael A. Peters (Singapore: Springer, 2016), 3.

12. Maria Patrice Amon, "Performances of Innocence and Deviance in Disney Cosplaying," *Transformative Works and Cultures* 17 (2014).

13. Dawn Elizabeth England, Lara Descartes, and Melissa A. Collier-Meek, "Gender Role Portrayal and the Disney Princesses," *Sex Roles* 64, no. 7–8 (October 2011): 562.

14. David Hand, dir. *Snow White*. Walt Disney Pictures, 1937.

15. Elizabeth Marshall and Leigh Gilmore, "Girlhood in the Gutter: Feminist Graphic Knowledge and the Visualization of Sexual Precarity," *Women's Studies Quarterly 43, no. 1/2* (2015): 95.

16. Marshall and Gilmore, "Girlhood," 95–96.

17. *Cinderella*, directed by Clyde Geronimi, Hamilton Luske, and Wilfred Jackson, Walt Disney Pictures, 1950; *Snow White*; *Sleeping Beauty*, directed by Clyde Geronimi, Walt Disney Pictures, 1950.

18. Elizabeth Balboa, "From Zero to Hero: A Look Back at the Disney Renaissance," *Benzinga*, March 20, 2017. https://www.benzinga.com/general/education/17/03/9193277/-from-zero-to-hero-a-look-back-at-the-disney-renaissance-period.

19. Balboa, "Zero to Hero."

20. Maja Rudloff, "(Post)feminist Paradoxes: The Sensibilities of Gender Representation in Disney's *Frozen*," *Outskirts: Feminisms Along the Edge 35* (2016): 2.

21. Rudloff, "(Post) Feminist," 2.

22. Kathryn M. Olson, "An Epideictic Dimension of Symbolic Violence in Disney's *Beauty and the Beast*: Inter-Generational Lessons in Romanticizing and Tolerating Intimate Partner Violence," *Quarterly Journal of Speech* 99, no. 4 (2013): 465.

23. Judith Halberstam, *The Queer Art of Failure* (Durham: Duke University Press, 2011), 27.

24. Halberstam, *Queer Art*, 29.

25. *Brave*, directed by Mark Andrews, Brenda Chapman, and Steve Purcell, Walt Disney Pictures, 2012.

26. *Frozen*, directed by Chris Buck and Jennifer Lee, Walt Disney Pictures, 2013.

27. *Frozen 2*, directed by Chris Buck and Jennifer Lee, Walt Disney Pictures, 2019.

28. Rudloff, "(Post) Feminist," 1.

29. Kimberle Crenshaw, "Mapping the Margins: Intersectionality, Identity Politics, and Violence against Women of Color," *Stanford Law Review 43*, no. 6 (1991): 1241–99. doi:10.2307/1229039.

30. Rudloff, "(Post) Feminist," 17.

31. *In a Heartbeat*, directed by Beth David and Esteban Bravo, Ringling College of Art and Design, 2017.

32. Ana-Isabel Nölke. "Making Diversity Conform? An Intersectional, Longitudinal Analysis of LGBT Specific Mainstream Media Advertisements," *Journal of Homosexuality* 65, no. 2 (February 2018): 226.

33. *The Ellen Show*, "You've Found the Latest 'Finding Dory' Trailer," YouTube, May 24, 2016, https://www.youtube.com/watch?v=MKJA-VLpiCo.

34. Bryan Alexander, "Does 'Finding Dory' Show a Gay Couple? We Asked the Filmmakers," *USA Today*, June 9, 2016, https://www.usatoday.com/story/life/movies/2016/06/09/does-finding-dory-show-gay-couple-filmmakers-discuss/85635846/; Bonnie Malkin, "Finding Dory Trailer Raises Hopes Film Could Include Lesbian Couple," *The Guardian*, May 28, 2016, https://www.theguardian.com/film/2016/may/28/new-finding-dory-trailer-hopes-lesbian-couple-disney-pixar.

35. Alexander, "Gay Couple."

36. I will not directly cite these tweets in an effort to avoid perpetuating the harmful language in many of them, including slurs referring to lesbians.

37. Eve Ng, "Between Text, Paratext, and Context: Queerbaiting and the Contemporary Media Landscape," *Transformative Works and Cultures 24* (2017).

38. Gay & Lesbian Alliance Against Defamation.

39. "2016 GLAAD Studio Responsibility Index," GLAAD, last modified 2016, https://www.glaad.org/sri/2016.

40. Emily St. James, "Why Elsa from Frozen is a Queer Icon—and Why Disney Won't Embrace That Idea," *Vox*, November 22, 2019, https://www.vox.com/culture/2019/11/22/20975178/frozen-2-elsa-girlfriend-lesbian-queer-review.

41. *Beauty and the Beast*, directed by Bill Condon, Walt Disney Pictures, 2017.

42. Taylor Pittman, "What Disney Princesses Would Look Like with Realistic Faces," *The Huffington Post*, December 7, 2017, https://www.huffingtonpost.com/2015/06/03/the-nameless-doll-realistic-disney-princess-faces_n_7493774.html.

43. Catherine Tosenberger, "Homosexuality at the Online Hogwarts: Harry Potter Slash Fanfiction," *Children's Literature*, 36, no. 1 (2008): 186, doi:10.1353/chl.0.0017.

44. TheNamelessDoll, "ILLUMINATED," YouTube, May 16, 2013, https://www.youtube.com/watch?v=JwksqGjidhc&index=4&list=PL339_yyCHKFSoDvRQ3nG-k3zkX6GHgGXm.

45. TheNight130, "'Kamikaze' Esmeralda x Cinderella," YouTube, October 20, 2017, https://www.youtube.com/watch?v=_bq_0ygFysw.

46. Coppa, "Fannish Vidding."

47. Hurts, "Hurts—Illuminated (Live Version)," YouTube, April 8, 2011, https://www.youtube.com/watch?v=6CvuyaKmLnw.

48. Night Argent, "Night Argent // Kamikaze (Audio)," YouTube. March 5, 2016, https://www.youtube.com/watch?v=5e51krtQfqA.

49. TheNamelessDoll, "ILLUMINATED"; TheNight130, "Kamikaze."

50. Erin. B. Waggoner, "Bury Your Gays and Social Media Fan Response: Television, LGBTQ Representation, and Communitarian Ethics," *Journal of Homosexuality* (October 2017): 1–15.

51. Random Nameless Channel, "Watch Me Edit—Creating Myself," YouTube, May 26, 2018, https://www.youtube.com/watch?v=42E8Q-LrGH4&index=12&t=0's&list=PL339_yyCHKFTWQcKUCINKPgfWKZnls-ev; Raven Davies, "The Slash Fanfiction Connection to Bi Men," *Journal of Bisexuality* 5, no. 2–3 (2005): 195–202.

52. Katie Kapurch, "Rapunzel Loves Merida: Melodramatic Expressions of Lesbian Girlhood and Teen Romance in *Tangled, Brave*, and Femslash," *Journal of Lesbian Studies* 19, no. 4 (November 2015): 450.

53. Phelps-Ward and Laura, "Talking Back," 818.

54. Random Nameless Channel, "Random Manips I," YouTube, March 29, 2015, https://www.youtube.com/watch?v=JwksqGjidhc&index=4&list=PL339_yyCHKFSoDvRQ3nG-k3zkX6GHgGXm.

55. Pittman, "Realistic Faces."

56. Random Nameless Channel, "Manips."

57. *Ibid.*

"Who are you? Who am I!?"

The Raunchy Identity Moratorium in Netflix's Big Mouth

Marcus Mallard

The formative years of early adolescence, as we all may recall, are awkward, and really, there is no truer statement. It is a time when we are learning to interpret a much wider variety of signals as we become more self-aware of not only ourselves, but the world and our interactions with it. Accompanying this trying time, of course, is biological evolution as young children begin to develop into their adult selves—experiencing internal changes as well as more obvious, external ones. The development of acne is already bad enough, but hormonal changes that affect our understanding of identity and sexuality throw more gasoline on the proverbial fire of the adolescent stage. Popular media representation of young adolescence tends to focus on the more nostalgic moments, focusing a great deal on the inter-personal relationships between young characters and their peers or young characters and parents, authority figures, or the complexities of the world. Coming of age movies, without much argumentation, would contain such entries as *The Goonies* (1985), *Stand by Me* (1986), and *Sisterhood of the Traveling Pants* (2005) as quick-fire examples.

By no means are these selections meant to establish an over-arching generic category because, even thematically, these films are drastically different, yet they are more intended to demonstrate that audiences are going to look back on a "feel-good" movie when it comes to dealing with our own issues experienced during adolescence. Since the new millennium, though, Young Adult literature has become a financial goldmine of stories that challenge social norms and other complicated social issues, typically with adolescents taking center stage in fighting a corrupt system, one that is localized and familiar or distant and systematic. Rarely, though, such media look into the struggles of dealing with the intra-personal changes that come through developing from a young person into adulthood, at least in terms of physical or hormonal changes; furthermore, it is rarely been done with the unabashed grotesquery of Netflix's *Big Mouth*.

An avenue that has opened up for exploring the complications of adolescence, surprisingly enough, has been the streaming service progenitor Netflix. The service's slew of young adult fare has already pushed boundaries of social norms by bringing in stories about the adolescent years that are concerned with, what modern audiences would call, non-traditional stories about growing up. Television series such as *13 Reasons Why* (2017) or *Sex Education* (2019) tackle complex issues as suicide and sexual development, respectively, in a way that is direct and blunt, forcing audiences to potentially come to terms with their own experienced traumas let alone those of the characters. But these shows are not aimed at the formative years of early adolescence, dealing with character in their late teens where such issues have become more commonplace in media over the years. Also, it is noted that even such depictions of adolescence are not marketed and meant to be viewed by audiences going through the developmental stages. It's quite the opposite—adult viewership is the primary target audience. It is no surprise, then, that Netflix would also provide a platform for a series that pushes the boundaries for appropriateness and decency when it comes to the issues of identity and sexual development, specifically in a medium that is still typically seen as more marketable to children—animation.

Netflix's *Big Mouth* blew its way onto the streaming giant's radar in September 2017 with critical acclaim as well as severe criticism for its unfiltered take on sexual and identity development in characters that are pre-teens growing into adolescence. This series separates itself from other animated giants such as *Family Guy, American Dad!*, or *BoJack Horseman* with its very direct (rather than tongue-in-cheek) approach to the complicated issues confronted during early adolescence. These shows typically use characters that suffer from some type of arrested development, displaying façades for comedic purposes rather than succinct introspection into the complications of puberty. *Big Mouth* does not shy away from the grotesque and awkward phases that come along with growing up, and often, the show finds itself showing sentimentality and sincerity with these very real experiences.

Within the show, characters are seen acting on their primal (sexual and non-sexual) urges as they begin to develop a sense of who they are as individuals. The series follows the stories of five pre-teens growing into early adolescence and puberty—Nick Birch (Nick Kroll), Andrew Glouberman (John Mulaney), Jessi Glaser (Jessi Klein), Jay Blizerian (Jason Mantzoukas), and Missy Foreman-Greenwald (Ayo Edebiri)[1]—and their interactions with peers, authority figures, and the world's expectations. It is not uncommon within the show to be privy to some of what we would have considered to be the most private, intimate moments that we experienced as a sexually-developing teenager: a young man's first erection, a young girl's first experience with her menstrual cycle, dry-humping a pillow, masturbation, and "jizzing" in your pants as you rub against your crush during a school dance, just to name a few. Each of these moments, and the many others within the show, allow us to relive some of our own experiences through a lens of uncomfortable nostalgia. We all realize that we are awkward, and many of us shared similar experiences while growing up. There are other adults, like this author, that work with teenagers and see many of the parallels between how current teenagers react to situations, the scenes on *Big Mouth*, and our own previous horror stories of those awkward years.

Each of these harrowing experiences during adolescence shaped who we have all become as adults. We have gone through the same developmental stages as these characters that are experiencing them for the first time. But the role animation plays in this exchange allows the examination to be more humorous as well as pretty much the only manner in which a show like this could be made. It would be morally devoid, and borderline criminal, to place—let alone film—teenagers in these scenarios with the detail and unadulterated manner that *Big Mouth* is allowed. It is, then, a wonderful opportunity for us, the media consumers, to look at and understand our own development and maybe, for those out there that have children around this age, what things current adolescents may be going through. Unlike other adult-oriented animated series, *Big Mouth* uses adolescence as the narrative driving force as we see characters struggle with issues including, but not limited to, sexual development, sexual identity, identity of self, and group acceptance. But to understand the necessity of the gratuitous nature of the content of the show, we need to first grasp the psychology behind the development of such identities.

Theories of the Developing Adolescent

Adolescence is a time for searching for inclusion and understanding of our own person, and developmental psychologists such as Erik Erikson—who coined the phrase "identity crisis"—and his contemporary James Marcia provide a framework for the creation of social and personal identities that does not rear away from the difficulties of adolescence. Both theorists indicate that a child that experiences some type of trauma will attempt to make changes to their ego-identity and experience identity diffusion to accommodate to their external stimuli. Marcia, however, expands on Erikson's work where "ego-identity and identity diffusion refer to polar outcomes of the hypothesized psychosocial crisis occurring in late adolescence."[2] However, it can be argued that such traumas can be experienced in the early years of adolescence, and a modification of what is termed "Identity Moratorium" will show that certain identities are fickle and vaguely defined; this allows for other identities to be more fluid and subsumed by the adolescent. Furthermore, Marcia identifies a crisis as "the adolescent's period of engagement in choosing among meaningful alternatives."[3] Hence, a crisis or trauma is not so much an earth-shattering experience as it is an unwillingness to make a commitment.

Such developmental theories can be used to explore how *Big Mouth* treats adolescence. Many of the characters attempt to come to terms with developing LBGTQ+ or cisgender identities as they are controlled by their id's primal urges through the representation of each child's Hormone Monster that is assigned to them as puberty begins. The Hormone Monsters do not hold back from influencing each teenager's sexual exploration of self or others and often within the spectrum of individual, socio-cultural, or gender identities. Within the series, characters change identities rapidly, as they each experience new traumas that signal the necessity for change. The Hormone Monsters control not only psychological responses to external stimuli but also, to a much greater degree, the physical responses of the children's bodies. Audiences, however, come to learn that there is a vast array of Hormone Monsters and others that exist in this unseen webwork of controlling the oncoming of puberty.[4] Within the show, Hormone Monsters simply act as the oncoming of the physical and sexual changes that are experienced during adolescence, and the psychological aspect that is explored in the following analysis looks to add to the overall understanding of these creatures' operation not only within the show but also in terms of understanding development. Therefore, viewing *Big Mouth* through the lens of developmental psychology, we can understand how adolescent development of sexuality and identity can be uncomfortable and controversial but still completely human.

Developmental psychology starts with the work of Sigmund Freud. The delicate balance of the natural urges of the id and attempts at control from the ego are central tenets to understanding the phases that are explicated by the work of Erik Erikson and James Marcia. In his work *Identity: Youth and Crisis*, Erikson challenges the work of Freud by addressing its limitations through the boundaries established by the understanding and "general state of psychoanalytical theory at the time and on the sociological formulation of this era."[5] This claim should appear to be obvious, but Freud sets his limits for psycho-sexual development at the onset of puberty. His work, detrimentally so, focuses on stages that occur in childhood rather than within the adolescent years in which the characters from *Big Mouth* must come to terms with during puberty. Erikson differs greatly because his studies focus on how a child is growing into an adult that will take part in the greater society. This study would argue that the developing child—in terms of sexuality and identity, as well as their function within the society—is interrelated and must be taken into consideration. It is within the reality of the environment of the adolescent that identity formation becomes so prevalent, and in this regard, Erikson may be agreeing with some of his own criticisms of Freud.

Most undergraduate institutions tend to explicate and cover the developmental stages that Erikson's work outlines in order to qualify the life-cycle changes within our human lives, of which there are eight in total. Of primary significance is the fifth developmental stage identified as "Identity vs. Confusion," which begins during adolescence. Within this stage, the adolescent[6] is faced with experiences where individual response and decisions affect the way in which the child codifies their identity, personality, or persona in both inter- and intrapersonal levels, to a point where their identity is related to their parents and into their own perceptions. Erikson indicates that "the child's original state of naïve self-love is said to be compromised. He looks for models by which to measure himself, [sic] and seeks happiness in trying to resemble them."[7] Even at this point in development, the adolescent will look toward the outward stimuli in order to inform their own identities, and in the case of *Big Mouth*— as it is with many children growing up—the influential stimuli are that of their peers and popular trends. Erikson's theories could have never imagined the influence of social media, but as he criticizes Freud's limitations, his may also be criticized.

Big Mouth, of course, tackles the idea of social media, peer influences, and peer pressure head on. It is these moments within developing adolescents—as well as with the characters of *Big Mouth*—that become the points in time in which a crisis culminates, forcing the individual to rethink their approach and interactions within a group or within society. The studies of Erikson show us that even over sixty years ago, the way in which identity forms has altered. He explicates on the role of a group would play on an individual child's role was fairly-well defined within an existing system:

> In a primitive plan, men have a direct relation to the sources and means of production. Their tools are extensions of the human body. Children in these groups participate in technical and in magic pursuits; to them, body and environment, childhood and culture may be full of dangers, but they are all one world. The inventory of social prototypes is small and static. In our world, machines, far from remaining an extension of the body, destine whole human organization to be extensions of machinery; magic serves intermediate links

only; and childhood becomes a separate segment of life with its own folklore. The expansiveness of civilizations, together with its stratification and specialization, demanded that children base their ego models on shifting, sectional, and contradictory prototypes.[8]

As we've moved away from primitive models, the expectations are not nearly as clear as they once were for the growing child. Identity formation, as Erikson and James Marcia examine it, tends to rely heavily on the occupational or economical role that the child will play within society, and this is where a modification of their theories must be understood.

Erikson popularized the idea of the identity crisis experienced within this developmental stage, and a crisis is triggered by an event in which the adolescent must reinterpret their interactions with their surroundings. In an article for *The Guardian*, Zoe Williams points out that children are beginning to develop sexually and going through puberty earlier than ever before, citing a study from the American Academy of Pediatrics that indicates a prevalence of puberty beginning in some children as young as the age of six,[9] or what pediatrician Dr. Robert Scott-Jupp refers to as the physical changes experienced, as opposed to the psycho-social changes of adolescence.[10] William's also cites Philp Hodson, a fellow of the British Association for Counseling and Psychotherapy, who maintains that anxiety can ultimately create the very scenarios that necessitate the existence of an identity crisis. Hodson states, "the mercilessness of children is well known [and] difficulties are compounded in the age of social media, and the way in which people can be instantly, broadly vilified. But the anxieties of those with early puberty are dwarfed, to a degree, by the anxieties of those children who get left behind."[11] The psycho-social elements, it is argued, take precedence over the sexual development of the child.

Shows like *Big Mouth* allow viewers to recognize similar situations in regards to our own mystery and peel back the curtain on how we view our sexuality; however, most memories, at least for this author, are relegated to how we interacted with our peers—discovering likes and dislikes as well as similarities and dissimilarities. And, it is because of this that even the overt emphasis on sexual development within a serialized animated series should take a back seat to understanding how children interact within their group as they attempt to find their own identities with a complex social system. It is a combination of the psycho-social development compounded with sexual development that relegates the most significant changes within the adolescent years, especially considering our current historical moment.

Erikson's theories, born out of Freudian psychology, emphasize the idea of a crisis event to the point in which an individual begins to question their own status. This is furthered by James Marcia, who performed various studies over the past sixty years that explore the formation of what is termed "ego-identity," even though his studies also focused on individuals in later adolescence. In a 1966 study of eighty-six male college students, Marcia notes that previous studies in identity formation "have not dealt explicitly with the psychosocial criteria for determining degree of ego-identity, nor with testing hypotheses regarding direction behavioral consequences of ego-identity."[12] He also clearly indicates within this same study that "formulation of the identity crisis as a *psychosocial* task."[13] Looking at *Big Mouth*, many of the decisions the children make in order to accommodate their changing bodies and psyche are clearly made to either fit within existing group formations or be part of a new group within these codified structures. The research of Marcia again points to individuals finding their place within their given environment:

> The identity-diffuse individuals to which Erikson refers and identity-diffusion subjects in this study may be rather different with respect to extent of psychopathology. A "playboy" type of identity diffusion may exist at one end of a continuum and a schizoid personality type at the other end. The former would more often be found functioning reasonably well on a college campus.[14]

The diffusion state is a phase during this time period where a person is trying on different identities in order to fulfill their pursuit of a final ego-identity, but as Marcia points out with his (more-simplified) categories, an attempt to find oneself is full of indecisions, altered commitments toward being a member of a specific group, and the struggle to maintain that identity within it.

The "Identity vs. Confusion" stage that encompasses adolescence, according to Erikson's eight developmental stages, is split by Marcia's work into four categories, first outlined in his 1973 article "Ego-Identity Status: Relationship to Change in Self-Esteem, General Maladjustment, and Authoritarianism," where the level of commitment the child places on a new identity influences how much crisis exists at any given moment. Of course, a child can shift between the phases, but the ultimate goal would be attaining Identity Achievement, where the "status has experienced a crisis period and is committed to an occupation and ideology."[15] This is opposite Identity Diffusion, where there are no commitments to a specific identity but also no indication of the presence of a crisis. Identity Foreclosure is similar to Erikson's observation of primitive cultures in that individuals "seem to have experienced no crisis, yet have firm, often parentally determined commitments."[16] (Identity Foreclosure can be placed in many different cultural texts, but one that stands out as an example of this is in the film *Varsity Blues* [1999]. James Van Der Beek's character, high school football phenom Mox, reminds his father that "I don't want your life!" indicating a resistance to expectations of family and his community.) Most important to understanding *Big Mouth*, however, would be Identity Moratorium.

Often, a moratorium of identity is seen, especially by parents of teenagers of all ages, as just going through a *phase* (i.e., the Goth phase, the jock phase, the preppy phase, etc.), conscious or otherwise, where our actions challenge authority. In adolescence, we are in a constant state of flux, experiencing crises at every turn. Marcia states, "the bases for these states of growth lies in body changes, social expectations concerning these changes, and social/cultural institutions [and] the individual is undergoing significant physiological, sexual, and cognitive changes."[17] And with some children showing signs of adolescence and puberty earlier and earlier in the life cycle, the opportunity for crisis to be experienced becomes more apparent as well as more significant in these formative years.

It should be noted that the changes in social interaction since the advent of the Internet and further development of social media have grossly affected the way in which a person can interact with external stimuli, creating an atmosphere that is more likely to develop a crisis scenario, as perceived by the individual. We may also never know what is going to be the catalyst for a crisis to occur and an adolescent to begin re-aligning commitments and expectations in order to form a new identity. Marcia also explains that "it is not external events that impact individual growth and development, but built-in conflicts [and] each developmental stage is a crisis wherein the individual may move forward, backward, or remain stuck,"[18] indicating that this flux is seemingly endless until identity achievement has been obtained where there is no longer a conflict or a crisis to respond to.

An adolescent within the identity moratorium is testing the waters of social awareness and appropriateness based on the given criteria of external stimuli. Do we identify ourselves at these ages based on our occupational interests, as a child may express a desire to want to be an officer of the law for example? Are we sexually attracted to a gender opposite, similar, or different than our own? Are we going to wear pink on Wednesdays, as Regina George demands of her cohorts in *Mean Girls* (2004)? Each of these questions—even at the base level—forces an individual to make a decision (or choose not to) in order to react to each scenario, and we see many of these same decisions occur with the characters in *Big Mouth*. For example, in the episode "Am I Gay?," Andrew begins asking himself some of these very questions based on his body's reaction to a trailer for a new movie starring Dwayne "The Rock" Johnson. This question, even though comical, shows how something that seems trivial could set off a series of internal crises. It becomes then more about how each individual adapts to the rapidly changing environment and expectations:

> Psychotherapists informed by Erikson tend to look more to issues of adaptation [...] than to repetition of early conflicts. The past is important, but of equal importance is the current level and style of coping with predominant life cycle challenges as well as the pursuit of future goals. Conflict is still important, as it is within any psychodynamic approach, but the stage on which the conflicts are played out is much expanded.[19]

Conflicts can also change immediately and without notice further complicating the moratorium. It is, then, up to the individual to navigate the social mores and adjust accordingly as they deem fit. An adolescent is going to make their best guess in how to interpret the scenario and respond, and it is through the system of choices, social successes, and social failures that will cause a person to end up with some type of identity achievement. Their guesses are what they have to go by because, systematically speaking, the world drastically changes.

The entrance into this age range of adolescence is in and of itself traumatic. In his 2010 article "Life Transitions and Stress in the Context of Psychosocial Development" Marcia claims:

> The beginning of childhood's end in early adolescence sees the young person hopefully having accrued all of the psychosocial raw material needed for achieving Freud's vision of optimum development: the ability to love (basic trust, autonomy) and to work (initiative, industry). Identity formation becomes paramount during this life-cycle era because the individual is required to make a transition both physically and socially from child to adult, from receiver to provider.[20]

Adults like to see children become more and more independent, and with the advent of the Internet and social media, in particular, the move to independence has become more prevalent, making this already awkward time in the life-cycle even more difficult. It makes it appear as though that the shifting, changing, and altering identities never ends. We see children that would not normally get into trouble at school start getting into trouble, or we may see a child more comfortable with their sexuality and being open amongst their peers and family members (or, in some cases, afraid to be open with themselves). An A-student may have slipping grades, a teenager may become sexually active, and another may feel like they were born to be a farmer, having never been on—let alone even seen—a farm. This jockeying for position is necessary for the child to understand who they are not only to themselves but also to those that are in their worlds. The end game is to settle on an identity. According to Marcia, "the achievement of ego-identity requires the individual to relinquish his claims to infantile sources of gratification and to renounce lingering infantile fantasies of omnipotence. In short, he must choose among alternatives and make a subsequent commitment to the alternative chosen."[21] The exploration of alternatives and the lack of commitment to personal beliefs, ideas, or *definitions* demonstrate the complexity of adolescence.

The Moratoriums of Big Mouth

Most animation, especially serialized animation, targets children as their primary audience, but creators such as Matt Groening and Seth Mac-Farlane—creators of *The Simpsons* and *Family Guy*, respectively—brought (and continue to bring) more adult fare to the medium on the small screen. Of course, the latter tends to push the boundaries of appropriate humor for even its Sunday night timeslot on the Fox Network. Hyperbolic and somewhat sophomoric humor characterizes the show's narrative and its characters. This trend was followed with MacFarlane's two follow up series, *American Dad!* and *The Cleveland Show* (a *Family Guy* spinoff). Other serialized animations following this brand of comedy permeate much of popular culture and social media, fighting for their place in the current socio-cultural moment: *Bob's Burgers*, *Rick and Morty*, *BoJack Horseman*, and *Paradise PD* are some highlights of an ever-growing list. *Big Mouth*, however, takes the style of humor inherent within these similar programs into uncharted territory through its exploration of adolescent sexuality, doing so in such a brazen nature that we, the audience, feel just as uncomfortable as the characters.

The series is the brainchild of comedians Nick Kroll and Andrew Goldberg, and encapsulates a group of pre-teens and early adolescents entering the early stages of sexual development. Both creators have been vocal about the reality of their animated series, as each Kroll and Goldberg—who are childhood friends—admit that many of the grotesque stories are based on of their own experiences or those of some of their closest friends. And, they are risqué for a reason. The absolute trauma of such experiences is essential to going through this process of identity formation that is pivotal to understanding this series, such as Andrew (based on Goldberg) ejaculating in his pants while dancing with his crush, or Jessi experiencing her first menstruation while on a class trip to the Statue of Liberty.[22] Each character suffers their own experiences, both enlightening and traumatic, that dictates how each interprets and interacts with the world surrounding them. Sexuality, however, complicates not only how the characters act but leads to viewers being more cautious in how to approach the show.

Personified through what the show calls "the Hormone Monster," these imaginary guides help dictate and navigate this complicated time in human development. Not only do the Hormone Monsters control sexual urges, but they also influence each child's fluctuating emotions. The Hormone Monsters are also a great way to remove sexuality from the children themselves, though, for many of the jokes are taken through these filters. This allows some of the more grotesque moments to appear less transgressive because these ancient Hormone Monsters are the "face" of puberty, controlling the adolescents' actions. Hence, each kid may not be fully responsible for any deplorable action they enact as a result of their hormones or Hormone Monster. We see Maury, Andrew's Hormone Monster through the series (also voiced by Kroll), help put Andrew in moments of pure machismo when his character would otherwise by reserved. And Connie, Jessi's Hormone Monstress (voiced by comedienne Maya Rudolph), guides her through the up and down rollercoaster of becoming a woman, where one minute Connie leads Jessie through a rage-filled tirade aimed at her mother and the next consoles Jessi through a sob-fest in a bubble bath. In an article for online entertainment magazine *Vox*, Caroline Famke speaks to how Maury influences Andrew as "Murray [sic] in particular is a walking, talking id who takes gleeful advantage of Netflix's lack of censors"[23] through his countless jokes about dicks, genitals, and so many other sexual comments. Of course, these jokes are degrading, but they embrace all natural urges. For example, when Maury is attempting to help Andrew discover if he is gay through an eye test similar to a vision test at the optometrist ("Am I Gay?"), Maury writes down the results and Andrew asks, "Are you filling out a form?" Maury responds, "No, I'm just drawing a picture of a unicorn [...] butt-fucking Mr. Clean!" to reveal to Andrew the very drawing he described.

Big Mouth does not shy away from raunchy, unfiltered portrayal of adolescence. And for some, this is truly uncomfortable, uncouth, and downright immoral. Parenting advocacy groups, such as Protect Young Minds, warns about the show on their website, addressing not only the sexual situations that the children are going through but also the fact that adults are watching the show where children are put in sexual situations—and potential sexualized by adults. The website calls *Big Mouth* an "animated disaster" that is "downright obscene," and they warn of its explicit content for parents to determine if the show is appropriate: "If you would like to get a (bitter) taste of what kids are being exposed to in this show, you could search for clips on YouTube. We found it so disturbing that we didn't want to share it [on our website]."[24] But others, like Hank Stuever of *The Washington Post*, find the humor to be heartfelt and with the best of intentions:

> There's a frankness and honesty beneath the show's raunchiness that sometimes echo the best work of Judy Blume and other great chroniclers of adolescent angst, especially where the fraught and seldom discussed feelings of boys are involved. It's charming and repulsive all at once.[25]

Much of the charm rests on the young characters; the raunchiness is often delivered through the Hormone Monsters and Monstresses. In the online periodical *IndieWire*, Ben Travers details the importance and value of these characters:

> These two creations are not only two of the funniest characters, but they may be the key to keeping 'Big Mouth' on the right side of the obscene. By disembodying Andrew, Nick, and Jessi's most depraved thoughts, the show creates an obvious disconnect between who the kids are and what their bodies are doing to them. The theme is emphasized again and again, from the opening credits to the fine line between reality and imagination, but it's never more effective than with the Hormone Monster and Monstress.[26]

By showing the influences of the Hormone Monsters, or the child's id, then we cannot blame the child for the actions they take; the audience can then connect with the struggles, trials, and traumas these adolescents experience, sympathizing with the characters through our own adult knowledge of this shared, difficult time in our lives.

Even without the overtly sexual implications of *Big Mouth*, the heart of the story is each of the children trying to discover their identity that will guide them not only through adolescence but also into the next of Erikson's phases. Many responses to the show (the first season in particular) tends to bring this juxtaposition to light where "[*Big Mouth*] honestly captures the horrors of adolescence with the sagacious perspective of an adult [...] moreover, it treats each child's predicament as an incredibly awkward problem,"[27] or by pointing out that "what makes Big Mouth [sic] more than the sum of its many, many dick jokes is the fact that beneath its raging hormones and truly gross humor lies an enormously sympathetic heart."[28] Again, the children's growth as they navigate the intricacies of inter- and intrapersonal relationships is the primary focus of the show.

Character Analysis

Each of the five main characters—Nick, Andrew, Jessi, Jay, and Missy—bring their own identity moratoriums as they try to adapt to each other and those around them. By looking at each character's evolution, as well as some of the secondary character's story arcs, we can see the gross, yet highly accurate, portrayal of adolescence and the process of discovering their identities. It is worth noting that for a moratorium to exist, as described by Marcia's theories, that an adolescent must be within a time where there are low commitments but high engagements in exploring new opportunities. The following analysis, then, is not to demonstrate which phases or identities the teenagers don and shed but to acknowledge that experiences signify a change in the way characters interpret their world or themselves.

Andrew and Nick take the majority of the narrative for much of the first season. Their friendship, along with its ups and downs, traces the roles that Nick and Andrew take upon themselves in identity formation. Their friendship is called into question multiple times, indicating that what was once known is beginning to alter and adapt to the world around them. Erikson points this out as well:

> A child has many opportunities to identify himself, more or less experimentally, with real or fictitious people of either sex and with habits, traits, occupations, and ideas. Certain crises force him to make radical selections. However, the historical era in which he lives offers only a limited number of socially meaningful models for workable combinations of identification fragments.[29]

As the boys are now moving from childhood into adolescence, they interpret the world around them differently, and at drastically different rates.

In the first episode of the series, aptly titled "Ejaculation," we discover that Nick is somewhat of a late bloomer, and Andrew is fully within the confusing throes of puberty. Much of the first season of *Big Mouth*, actually, follows Andrew's relationship with his body—always pushed to the brink by his Hormone Monster, Maury. Andrew is a 12-year old Jewish boy that is very much the definition of awkward and nerdy, but he appears to be experiencing puberty much earlier than his male counterparts. His body is pear-shaped, and he displays the beginnings of a mustache on his upper lip. As the episode unfolds, Nick and Andrew are in school watching a Sex Ed video explaining the uterus. Maury pops up and convinces Andrew, much to his chagrin, to get to the bathroom to "finish the job." As Andrew's Hormone Monster, many of the sexual explorations are seen as happening to Andrew, and these episodes of sex-driven trauma force Andrew to find and shift his identity in order to fit within the always-altering parameters. It is Andrew's ego combatting Maury, his id, that places him within this identity moratorium, as Andrew and Nick come to confrontation because of the differences in sexual development between the boys.

Later in the episode, Andrew comes to Nick's house for a sleepover to discuss their plans for the upcoming school dance. The boys are trying to interpret what their friend Jay said about "getting fingered" at the dance, which neither boy truly understands, and Nick informs us that he does not want to go to the dance for fear of being rejected if he asked someone. Before bed, Andrew uses the restroom, and as he walks out of the bathroom, Nick unintentionally sees Andrew's more developed and slightly hairy penis—as does the audience—which causes Nick to question his own physical maturity, and the friendship that we believe is going to be the main part of the show is challenged. Nick, throughout most of the first season, battles with this lack of identity based on his sexual development—an issue that continues to have an effect on his character through the duration of the series. The intended adult audience knows that he will get there eventually, but his progression into his identity is curious, as he has not yet met his Hormone Monster. The audience, in a way, is growing up alongside him. Before the end of the sequence, though, Andrew is visited by his own Monster, Maury, who convinces Andrew to pleasure himself in bed next to his friend, while Andrew envisions his father's secretary metamorphosized from the cat clock on the wall.

Nick's anxiety about seeing Andrew's penis, however, controls how he interacts with his family and those at school the next day. His previous identity as a young boy, like that of his friend, is in crisis—the rules have changed. Nick, however, attempts to move into a more masculine identity after receiving advice from his parents, who are very open about their own sexual exploits (arguably, this is more gut-wrenching than the interactions between the kids), and the ghost of Duke Ellington (Jordan Peele), who lives in Nick's attic. The advice inspires Nick to go against what he had planned earlier. Here we see Nick switch in his identity, unsure of who he is and what he is doing, and not five minutes prior in the show, Nick was certain of his identity. Battling his own insecurities, Nick goes against his previous identity and asks the popular Olivia to the dance, shattering not only his individual identity but also that of his group, who had planned to attend the dance together. This enrages Andrew who, prodded along by Maury, lets Nick have it with a simple statement: "Just ... fuck you, man."

The dynamic of Andrew and Nick dealing with their masculine identities further demonstrates the idea of an Identity Moratorium, as recognized by James Marcia. The hormonal and physical changes in Andrew cause him to give in to his passions and anger toward the changing identity, as he and Nick were once identified as a group. Nick's move, therefore, also forces Andrew's identity to change as well. Marcia states "the changes that are attendant upon puberty and subsequent adolescence have two effects: they disequilibrate the fairly structured live of the latency-aged child; and they require an accommodation in the form of a new integration of physique, sexuality, ideology, abilities, personal needs, and perceived social demands."[30] In response to Nick's bold move, Andrew then asks his crush, Missy, to the dance. Once the dance begins, the characters' decisions play out: Nick is stood up by Olivia, and he ends up kissing Jessi—exiting and entering multiple crises; and Andrew *comes to fruition* while dancing close to Missy, which results in Nick and Andrew mending their friendship, albeit slightly, while cleaning Andrew's pants in the bathroom. "Ejaculation" sets the precedent for the series in terms of how problems arise for teens to adjust to as well as extremely uncomfortable sexual situations.

Each of the children go through many experiences where they change their identities to fit new parameters, and the continuation of this process will continue as the show moves into its later seasons.[31] The third episode, entitled "Am I Gay?," Andrew explores the possibility of his own homosexuality based on his reaction to Dwayne "The Rock" Johnson, which only adds to the confusion arising from the incident at the school dance, and this ends with Andrew dressed as Freddy Mercury hanging out with Duke Ellington's ghost in Nick's attic. In the following episode, "Sleepover: A Harrowing Ordeal of Emotional Brutality," Andrew and Nick get suckered into a fight club of sorts while at a sleepover at Jay's house. It is here when we see Andrew's more masculine side come out, unintentionally fighting Nick to gain a peak at his first porno—*Italian Stallion* starring Sylvester Stallone. Andrew, unlike Nick, will put his own identity into question for his own sexual exploration, which is his driving force throughout much of the first season.

Andrew spends a great deal of time in an on and off relationship with Missy, as both are trying to struggle with their own sexuality. (It is later revealed that Missy is also dealing with her own Hormone Monstress.) Andrew attempts to change, such as joining the jazz club and donning a fedora-like hat in the episode "Pillow Talk." This happens as Nick takes on an identity of a "cool kid" by skipping school to go the New York City to meet a girl. But Andrew's uncontrollable urges, through Maury, tend to drive the decisions he makes within his group of friends, and self-gratification through masturbation wins out. But the boys' relationship through this journey of identities is heartfelt, and "when Andrew's not caught up in his lustful reveries (not to mention Maury's encouragement to indulge every last deranged one of them), his friendship with Nick is genuinely touching, and a real portrayal of how hard it can be for teens to navigate relationships when they're growing at different rates."[32]

Nick, on the opposite end of the spectrum, uses his social interactions to guide his moratorium. Through the first season, Nick has not yet entered puberty, and many of the feelings and actions that we see coming from Andrew, Nick finds to be confusing. He does, however, recognize the differences that exist, as "conflicts are not just internal, but between alternative ways of being in the world, of being with oneself, and being with others."[33] Nick uses his relationships with his parents, his siblings (older brother Judd and older sister Leah), the ghost of Duke Ellington, and his friends to interpret the world around him and find alternatives to try out. After the school dance, Nick traverses the dangerous territory of being identified as one half of a couple along with Jessi who unfortunately experiences her first menstrual period while visiting the Statue of Liberty during a school trip in season one's second episode, "Everybody Bleeds." After the relationship fails, Nick also attempts to get in touch with his feminine side and learns that women think about sex just about as much as men do via a conversation with his older sister. This, again, is done indirectly. Girls at school are interested in a book, *The Rock of Gibraltar*, that details the forbidden love between a girl and a man who is transformed into a horse, a lá *50 Shades of Gray*. Leah becomes Nick's guide to understanding how women think about sex, and Nick is convinced to read the book for a report to give in school. When he gives the report, his teacher incorrectly calls him Gustavo, the man-horse love interest from the novel, reacting to Nick's dramatic reading of a monologue from the book, which emphasizes the importance of all the nuances that surround sex rather than the act itself. And this draws attention to the way in which women are supposed to respond to sex and "the little things" as opposed to the male-hormone-driven focus on copulation.

Nick's interaction with his feminine side is a common theme throughout the series as well. He displays mannerisms that are often stereotypically applied to females: overly sensitive reactions and being open about feelings, for example. Show creator Kroll points out that boys are not often cast in that light in an interview with NPR's Cory Turner and Anya Kamentz:

> [B]oys don't want to talk, and so we don't talk to them. We don't talk to them about what they're physically going through. And we don't talk to them about what they're emotionally going through. And it's a real disservice to the boys that we don't.[34]

But even then, Nick can't escape masculine urges, as it becomes apparent that he wants to experience receiving a blowjob from a high school girl at one of his sister's parties in "The Head Push."

Nick, under the influence of alcohol, is brought to a party by Jay and begins to pursue Tallulah, who has a reputation giving blow jobs (as indicated by Nick's brother Judd). Again, Nick finds himself looking for social acceptance in an attempt to find who he is and do what he thinks kids are supposed to do in these types of situations. Yet because he is not guided in the same way as Andrew (i.e., sexually) he does not yet have a Hormone Monster. That changes at the beginning of the second season, when he is assigned Ricky—a decrepit monster that is much older than Maury and a former monster to Coach Steve, a teacher at the school that is highly inappropriate and arrested developmentally. The appearance of Ricky and his ineptitudes as a Hormone Monster lead Nick to believe that something is wrong with him developmentally. This leads Nick through a slew of Hormone Monsters before being reassigned Connie, the former monster for both Jessi and Missy. Each reassignment causes Nick to rethink his inter-actions because of the effects on his actual hormones.

Jessi's journey through the first season is much more significant than Missy's; however, we discover in "The Head Push" that Missy is a sexual explorer in much the same way as Andrew is, pressing her *mons pubis* into Andrew's groin during a make-out session in the closet. But Jessi goes through a more intense emotional roller coaster, experiencing her first menstrual period, first relationship, first kiss, masturbation, trying to fit in with the popular girls, discovering her mother is a lesbian, realizing her father is a burned-out stoner, and preparing for her bat mitzvah. Alone, any of what Jessi goes through would be traumatic, but taken together they provide a wonderful exposé of female adolescence. Ben Travers for *IndieWire* points out "Jessi (voiced by Jessi Klein) is the third member of the trio, and her arc is her own: it's about becoming a woman. The char-acter's perspective not only comes as a great relief given the onslaught of raunchy male-centric movies, but her journey often provides the rich-est, freshest narratives."[35] With Connie as her Hormone Monstress guid-ing her, Jessi is taken down a path of emotions, strong independence, and moments of absolute stress.

Jessi's path is much more individual than Nick's and significantly less sexually driven than that of Andrew's path, even though Connie does convince Jessi to get to *know* herself; Jessi uses a hand mirror to view her anthropomorphized genitalia (voiced by comedienne Kristen Wiig). Jessi's vagina provides a tour of her anatomy and physiology before convincing Jessi to have some fun, to which Jessi obliges. This sequence is Jessi's most overtly sexual; however, she is not immune from trying on new identities. In the first episode, Jessi is portrayed as a smart, young girl that is inde-pendent. Before Connie arrives (along with Jessi's first menstrual cycle) she experiences her first kiss while consoling Nick at the dance. The two of them, then, explore the uncharted territory of coupledom in the sub-sequent episode, resulting in Connie entering Jessi's life. In "Sleepover: A Harrowing Ordeal of Emotional Brutality" though, Jessi attempts to break from her former group identification with Nick, Andrew, and Jay, and throw her own sleepover party.

Jessi admits that she does not have many girlfriends, and that becomes more apparent as the sleepover festivities go on. It begins inno-cently enough with Jessi receiving a makeover from Devon and Lola, and some quips are exchanged that are okay because, according to Lola, "What? We're all joking." A sugar-emboldened Missy goes out of con-trol, and Jessi is forced to choose between protecting the nerdy girl or fit-ting in with the popular girls, adjusting to her environment as both Nick and Andrew had to do—a marquee of an Identity Moratorium with "the presence of struggle and attempts to make commitments."[36] But after this experience, Jessi returns to a more recognizable version of herself, devoid of the influence of the popular girls.

The rest of the first season pits Jessi up against her mother, whom is revealed to be having an affair with Cantor Dina. At the end of her bat mitzvah Jessi kisses Jay, and they begin a relationship that ends up with them both running away at the very end of the first season, only to return in the season two premiere "Am I Normal?" Jessi's identity continues to be influenced, by her relationship with each of the boys, by her mother's revealed lover, and by her father being kicked out of the house. How Jessi deals with her social issues is important because girls are often overlooked in how their development is treated. Caroline Framke is correct to explain that *Big Mouth* "is careful to not only differentiate Jessi and Missy's experiences from those of their male classmates, but to point out how messed up people's reactions to them going through similar stages are by comparison."[37] Too often, boys are just boys, and girls are seen as emotional wrecking balls that no one knows how to deal with, and *Big Mouth* is careful in attempting to construct a relatable experience for female viewers and more-than-likely an educational one for its male audience.

Another interesting take on childhood development comes in the form of Jay Blizerian, the group's resident hothead/magician/misogynist. Jay's identity is very much decided for him based on his home life; this attitude carries over in how he reacts not only to his friends but complex situations as well. However, as the show progresses into season two and three, Jay develops a dynamic character arc that places him in firm opposition to where he originally started. Jay emulates his father, a mostly-absent slime-bag divorce lawyer that openly discusses his frivolous affairs with various women with his children that we meet through various commercials for his sleazy law firm. Jay and his two older brothers take on this persona, and because of this they grossly misinterpret the complex feelings of those around them. James Marcia discusses this form of identity formation in reference to a child following in the footsteps of his parents "with little or no though in the matter, certainly cannot be said to have 'achieved' an identity, in spite of his commitment."[38]

For example, Jay's response to some of the more heartfelt moments is to perform a magic trick as a diversion or to make an extremely rude or vulgar comment. The darkness of his reality comes to fruition in the "Sleepover" episode, set antithetical to Jessi's story of discovery through trauma. We discover Jay is tormented by his brothers, and the two attempt to convince Jay, Andrew, and Nick to participate in a fight club in order to watch porn and, after that does not satiate their twisted needs, get the boys to play a game of "cum on a cracker"—a perverted sex game intended to degrade the younger of the boys. While this is happening, Jay's mother is absent, despite being in the house. Nick and Andrew meet her in their hasty attempt to escape, and Jay's mom calls out to her eldest children that there are some runners. As disturbing as this is, Jay's deep-seated social and emotional problems are put on display before his brothers interrupt. Jay introduces an extremely violent game in which you go around Vatican City killing prostitutes and steal their souls for points. Andrew is taken aback by this: "Oh, they die in real time!"

Jay's expression shows us how he has accepted this misogynist identity, but he does not find solace in this skewed way of thinking. In the episode "Pillow Talk," Jay must come to terms with potentially becoming a father himself because he impregnated the pillow that he uses to masturbate (it is truly one of the most harrowing episodes). Jay verbalizes whether or not the pillow should keep his baby or if he is going to be a good father or not. All the while, the anthropomorphized pillow and Jay continue to fornicate multiple times throughout. Eventually, the pillow gives birth, and Jay names his new baby pillow Scorpion (who Jay comments looks like his brother), and by the end of the episode, the pillow and Scorpion leave Jay to find happiness without him. Out of all of the instances in the show, it could be argued that this is the most adult-oriented content of the show up to this point. Its humor lies in its hyperbolic nature, but the message is dark and real. Jay's pillow metamorphosizes after he runs away with Jessi and begins to explore his own sexuality, as he returns to pillow humping in the second season. This time he sleeps with an array—female and male—of comfy couch cushions, and we follow his journey into identifying as bisexual. He, more so than Andrew does in "Am I Gay?," commits to this new found identity, but he also explores other options including homosexuality and pansexuality.

The topic of pansexuality, in particular, has been judged for its misrepresentation on the show from the pansexual community from the third season episode "Rankings," but were quick to admit their wrongdoings. Entertainment website *AV Club* reported co-creator Andrew Goldberg states:

> He and the writers "missed the mark" in a sincere apology, capping it with a thank-you to "the trans, pan, and bi communities for further opening eyes to these important and complicated issues of representation. We are listening and we look forward to delving into all of this in future seasons."[39]

This comes about because Jay asks the new student Ali (Ali Wong) what it means to be pansexual, and she makes a comparison to Mexican food saying:

> But I'm saying I like tacos and burritos, and I could be into a taco that was born a burrito, sure, 'kay, or a burrito that is transitioning into a taco. *Comprende?* And honey, anything else on the fucking menu.

For a show that takes on real issues, you cannot fault them for trying, and the writers and creators of the show appear to want to make sure that they get as much right as they can, especially because many of these stories are their own.

Conclusion

Entertainment is often an avenue to mask our attempt to interpret and understand the world around us, and a show about horny little teenagers is no different. For all the grotesqueness that *Big Mouth* tackles, it is an apt, albeit animated, exploration of the complexities and hardships of the adolescent years. Even though adults can view this with a nostalgic sense, the issues are very real for current adolescents on their very own journey through puberty and identity formation, not to mention the show's adult audience. By placing the show's narrative within the context of developmental psychology, the raunchiness of the show's content may be seen as an earnest attempt to better understand a time in our lives where we all thought we understood the world around us, but in all actuality, did not. Looking at shows that make us, the audience, uncomfortable makes us feel this way, allowing for a fruitful discussion of issues that we may not know how to articulate.

NOTES

1. For the upcoming fourth season of the show, Ayo Edebiri has been cast to provide the voice of Missy, as previous voice actor Jenny Slate stepped down in light of the Black Lives Matter movement to show solidarity and support that BIPOC (black, indigenous, and people of color) characters should be portrayed by BIPOC actors.

2. James E Marcia, "Development and Validation of Ego-identity Status," *Journal of Personality and Social Psychology 3, no.5* (1966), 551.

3. *Ibid.*

4. In season two, the characters of the Shame Wizard and Depression Kitty also begin to influence the characters and act as a foil to the id that is represented by the Hormone Monster.

5. Erik Erikson, *Identity: Youth and Crisis* (New York: Norton, 1968), 45.

6. The term *adolescent* seems to be the most appropriate term to use for the study; however, other terms such as *pre-teen* and the colloquial *tween* could be substituted here, as these terms tend to refer to children within the same age range as the characters depicted in *Big Mouth*.

7. Erikson, *Identity: Youth and Crisis*, 46–47.

8. *Ibid.*, 48–49.

9. Zoe Williams, "Early Puberty: Why are Kids Growing Up Faster?" *The Guardian*, October 25, 2012. https://www.theguardian.com/society/2012/oct/25/early-puberty-growing-up-faster: Within the article, Williams cites the study from the American Academy of Pediatrics that white and Hispanic boys are beginning puberty, on the average, around the age of ten, and Afro-American boys can begin to show signs at the age of nine.

There is also a small prevalence of children showing signs of puberty as early as the age of six: one in ten in white males and one in five black males.

10. *Ibid.*

11. *Ibid.*

12. Marcia, "Development and Validation of Ego-Identity Status," 551.

13. *Ibid.*, 5: italics Marcia's.

14. *Ibid.*, 558.

15. James E. Marcia, "Ego-Identity Status: Relationship to Change in Self-Esteem, General Maladjustment, and Authoritarianism," *Social Encounters: Contributions to Social Interaction*, ed. Michael Argyle (Chicago: Aldine Publishing Co., 1973). 341.: For this purpose, as indicated above, focuses more so on ideology rather than the emphasis of occupational influences on identity formation.

16. *Ibid.*, 341.

17. James E. Marcia, "Transitions and Stress in Context of Psychosocial Development," *Handbook of Stressful Transitions Across the Lifespan* (New York: Springer, 2010), 20.

18. *Ibid.*, 20.

19. *Ibid.*, 30.

20. *Ibid.*, 21.

21. Marcia, "Ego-Identity Status," 340.

22. Carrie Witmer, "The Creator of Netflix's 'Big Mouth' Shares which Embarrassing Puberty Stories Happened in Real Life," *Business Insider*, October 15, 2017, businessinsider.com/netflix-big-mouth-creator-shares-which-puberty-stories-were-real-2017–10?utm_source=feedburner&=&utm_medium=referral.

23. Caroline Framke, "Netflix's Big Mouth Takes a Sharp, Surprisingly Joyful Look at the Gross Time that is Puberty," *Vox*, September 30, 2017, vox.com/fall-tv/2017/9/29/16382984/big-mouth-netflix-review-kroll-mulaney.

24. Stacey Dittman, "Parent Alert! Watch out for Netflix's Shocking 'Big Mouth' (and More!)." *Protect Young Minds*, November 20, 2018, protectyoungminds.org/2018/11/20/parent-alert-netflix-big-mouth-ebsco-kids-screen-time/.

25. Hank Stuever, "Netflix's 'Big Mouth' Finds a Smart Way to Wrestle with the Monster Called Puberty." *The Washington Post*, September 29, 2017, washingtonpost.com/entertainment/tv/netflixs-big-mouth-finds-a-smart-way-to-wrestle-with-the-monster-called-puberty/2017/09/28/df72e252-a3be-11e7–8cfe-d5b912fabc99_story.html.

26. Ben Travers, "'Big Mouth' Review: Nick Kroll's Exemplary Netflix Comedy is a Horrifying and Hilarious Portrait of Childhood," *IndieWire*, September 29, 2017, indiewire.com/2017/09/big-mouth-netflix-review-best-animated-series-spoilers-1201881766/.

27. *Ibid.*

28. Framke, "Netflix's Big Mouth Takes a Sharp, Surprisingly Joyful Look."

29. Erikson, *Identity: Youth and Crisis*, 53.

30. Marcia, "Transitions and Stress in Context of Psychosocial Development," 21.

31. There are currently three seasons of the show, but the production company has penned a deal with Netflix for at least three more seasons. The fourth season is set to be released in October 2020, but was not examined for this study.

32. Framke, "Netflix's Big Mouth Takes a Sharp, Surprisingly Joyful Look."

33. Marcia, "Life Transitions," 30.

34. Cory Turner and Anya Kamentz, "'Big Mouth' Creators on Embracing the Awkwardness of Puberty," *NPR*, March 12, 2020, npr.org/2020/03/11/814559208/big-mouth-creators-on-embracing-the-awkwardness-of-puberty.

35. Travers, "'Big Mouth' Review."

36. Marcia, "Ego-Identity Status," 340.

37. Framke, "Netflix's Big Mouth Takes a Sharp, Surprisingly Joyful Look."

38. Marcia, "Ego-Identity Status," 340.

39. Randall Colburn, "Nick Kroll on Making Comedy in a 'Woke Culture': 'You Can Still Do and Say Some Pretty Crazy, Wild Shit.'" AV Club, October 22, 2019, news.avclub.com/nick-kroll-on-making-comedy-in-a-woke-culture-you-c-1839265725.

Daria

Still Standing on Our Necks, Then and Now

DAVID S. SILVERMAN

At 10:30 p.m. Eastern time on March 3, 1997, *Daria* debuted on MTV as the highest-rated animated premiere on the network to date.[1] The show follows the high school experiences of millennial Daria Morgendorffer (a character originally created by Mike Judge[2] for *Beavis and Butt-Head*) after her family moves to Lawndale. Any comparison to her origin ends there. Where Beavis & Butt-head are unintelligent losers, Daria "has the attitude about parents, school, siblings that is common to our audience.... She is a good spokesperson for MTV...intelligent, but subversive," according to then MTV Network manager Van Toffler.[3] She has been described her as "a blend of Dorothy Parker, Fran Lebowitz and Janeane Garafolo, wearing Carrie Donovan's glasses."[4] Another perspective was that MTV wanted to broaden its demographic with female viewers. According to co-creator Glenn Eichler, "MTV had no female viewers.... I wouldn't *not* use the word 'desperate.'"[5] While reaching out for a female demographic was MTV's intent, the show's depicting Daria and Jane as "just two misfits trying to survive relatively unscathed. It's everyone's story,"[6] similar to the style of disaffected youth that J.D. Salinger encapsulated in *The Catcher in the Rye*'s Holden Caulfield.[7]

Quite unforeseen to its creators at the beginning, *Daria* would run for five seasons (65 episodes) and has been featured in two TV films, both capturing and transcending the late 1990s and early 2000s. According to Eichler, MTV really did not have a programming plan, which allowed the show's creators to both ground *Daria* in realism while also giving it some continuity and a story arc.[8] Through a closer examination of several key episodes, we can see how *Daria* overcame its limited animation to become an example of "student life at the dawn of the new Millennium."[9] *Daria* would go on to become one of the quintessential cartoons of the late 20th

Century as it untypically explored self-esteem, death, relationships, and body image through the growth of its characters in a manner that featured "a handful of arcs as thoughtful as you'd find on a drama."[10]

Introducing Lawndale High, Jane Lane, and Sick, Sad World: "The Esteemsters"[11]

The tone of *Daria* is set from her first day at her new high school where, upon her arrival in Lawndale, she is subjected to a psychological test—in which she uses her sardonic humor to fail on purpose. When the school calls with the predictable results—that Daria will have to take a class for students with low self-esteem—her sister Quinn[12] quips, "*You* flunked a test?" Daria retorts that it's a mistake: "I don't have low self-esteem. I have low esteem for everyone else."[13] Yet, despite her declared distaste for most of her new classmates, Daria begins a series-long friendship with artist Jane Lane, who has also been placed in the self-esteem course.[14]

As their friendship begins to take off, Daria and Jane begin to spend more time with each other, and discover a shared love for the tabloid show "Sick, Sad World."[15] Jane reveals that she knows all of the answers to pass the self-esteem course, knowledge that Daria uses in a scheme to both rid herself of this humiliated course as well as to humiliate her sister, Quinn. After surprising Mr. O'Neill with the prospect of graduating early from the self-esteem class (by parroting Mr. O'Neill's book-based answers word-for-word), unaware that he is, of course, being "played":

MR. O'NEILL: Okay, question one: "Self-esteem is important because...."
DARIA: It's a quality that will stand us in good stead the rest of our lives.
MR. O'NEILL: Very good. Now, "The next time I start to feel bad about myself...."
JANE: Stand before the mirror, look myself in the eye and say, "You are special. No one else is like you."
MR. O'NEILL: You two really have been paying attention!

The duo continues their ruse at the assembly, where Jane eventually feigns being embarrassed about everyone now knowing that she had self-esteem and runs off the stage in mock tears. Mr. O'Neill shows his confused interest in his students by calling after "Daria" (Jane), while the real Daria takes to the lectern to use the opportunity to cause her sister—who stated earlier in the episode "I'm an only child," a little pain:

DARIA: And so, the one person I'd like to thank more than any other is my very own sister, Quinn Morgendorffer. My *sister* Quinn has forgotten more about self-esteem than I'll ever know. Are you out there, *sis*? Stand up and let me thank you.

High School Parties and How to Avoid Them: "The Invitation"[16]

To further show Daria's social isolation, episode two of the series features a rare venture for Daria to a high school party, which she initially dismisses. The titular invitation, from Brittany, is a thank you for Daria's help in art class:

> BRITTANY: I mean, you're not popular, but you're not so unpopular that you couldn't come to my party Saturday night.
> DARIA: Is that an invitation?
> BRITTANY: Yes! Just this once, though.
> DARIA: Gee, Brittany. I'm overcome with emotion.

However, once she learns that Quinn is also invited, Daria decides to attend with Jane in tow. Quinn's outburst at the dinner table over Daria's decision to go to the party results in their mother's ultimatum: that Daria go to keep an eye on Quinn lest she send them with a babysitter.

We also learn that Jane is a bit more adventurous, as she not only talks Daria into going to the party, but convinces her to go in once they get there:

> DARIA: You really want to do this?
> JANE: You know, just because people are cliquey and snotty is no reason not to like them.
> DARIA: Or hate them.

This adventurous streak continues inside, when Jane notices that two guys are looking their way, but Daria isn't "diving in":

> GUY #1: Hey. Partying hard or hardly partying?
> DARIA: Hardly interested.
> GUY #2: So ... where you girls been all our lives?
> DARIA: Waiting here for you. We were born in this room, we grew up in this room, and we thought we would die here ... alone. But now you've arrived, and our lives can truly begin.
> GUY #2: (to Guy #1) She likes you.

Quinn soon catches Daria chatting with her trio of suitors[17] and bribes her to leave, and she catches Jane leaving the "make out room"[18]:

> DARIA: What happened to "Bobby Bighead"?
> JANE: I wasn't really interested.
> DARIA: Too bad. (picks sock off Jane's shoulder) Is this yours?
> JANE: Okay, fine. He thought my head was a lollipop. Ready to go?
> DARIA: I was ready to go before we got here.

It is in this sequence that we learn Jane is a bit more outwardly open to new experiences, a characteristic that grows as the series progressed. We are also given a brief introduction to Daria's unrequited crush, Trent, Jane's older brother.

The episode typifies one of the reasons that *Daria* attracted a wider audience at the time—beyond the female demographic and those in high school—as it spoke to the socially awkward still in high school (and those whose experiences were still quite fresh), according to Eichler, something that he wasn't quite prepared for at the time.

> I've had a lot of people say to me, you know—that show really got me through high school. And for the first 10–15 years they said that to me, I'd be like oh yeah, okay, sure. But now I'm starting to like hearing that.[19]

Death Comes to Lawndale High: "The Misery Chick"[20]

The final episode of the first season features the return of Lawndale High's winning quarterback, Tommy Sherman, who had a habit of running into the goalpost while running touchdowns. In the first few minutes of the episode, Daria is a quiet witness to Sherman's behavior as "Big Man on Campus" as he manages to alienate nearly everyone he comes across. When finally confronted, Sherman thinks that Daria is interested in him:

> TOMMY: You're one of those misery chicks, always moping about what a cruel world it is, making a big deal about it so people won't notice that you're a loser.

As he walks off, Daria and Jane continue their conversation.

And then, on cue, we hear an off-stage crash—the breakaway goal post (that was supposed to be dedicated in honor to Tommy Sherman) falls on the school hero, killing him.

The rest of the episode focuses on how Lawndale students seek out Daria for advice about how to deal with the Tommy's death (the running joke is, "It really makes you think."). First, it's Kevin, who walks away just as confused as he was when he first approached her. Then Brittany approaches:

> BRITTANY: I mean, you're used to being all gloomy and depressed and thinking about bad stuff....
> DARIA: Why does everyone keep saying that?

As the title of the episode (as well as Sherman's last words vocalized), Daria has come to be known as someone thinks "about the dark side all the time."[21] Even her sister Quinn comes to her for advice on how to deal with death; however, as she's complaining about her newfound popularity to Jane, she misses Jane's quiet plea for both restraint and for help coping with the loss:

> JANE: Boy, Daria, nothing gets through to you, does it.
> DARIA: What's that supposed to mean?
> JANE: A guy died, and you're talking about what a jerk he was.

As the conversation ends, Jane turns down an offer to go for pizza—as Daria misses the idea that Jane is avoiding both the subject of death as well as her best friend.

Daria eventually realizes that Jane has been ditching her, and goes over to the Lane residence, where she encounters Trent, who had had a few classes with Tommy when they were in high school. After initially telling her that "Janey went running," he hints that she might have come back and that she should go upstairs to see if he's right.

This episode represents one of the first hints of Daria's overall humanity—in that she doesn't want to be alone, and in this exchange she reveals this because no one has really asked her how she feels about Tommy's sudden death. It also develops Jane's character further, in that while she's an outsider, her coping mechanism is much more introverted.

> JANE: I've been trying *not* to think. About the way we were making jokes about him dying and then, boom, it happened.
> DARIA: We didn't have anything to do with the guy dying. It was a freak accident.
> JANE: Yeah, well, I don't like it when I say people should die and then they do. I don't want that kind of responsibility. At least not until I've got a job in middle management.

In the end, while they agree that Tommy wasn't particularly nice, he didn't deserve to die.

Of High School and Body Image

If there is one consistent theme throughout the series, it is that of the anti-fashion hero, Daria, challenging the conventions of trying to look good and be popular.[22] Outwardly, like many cartoon characters, Daria's wardrobe suggests that she doesn't care about her outward appearance—the oversized green jacket mated with a pleated skirt and black lace-up boots—"a cross between Carrie Donovan and the Spice Girls."[23] This is starkly contrasted by her sister, Quinn, who is vice president of the Fashion Club.

We are led to believe that aside from her self-professed hatred of fashion, we also learn that most fashion isn't quite designed for her 5'2' frame. In "I Don't,"[24] Daria is forced to submit to the humiliation of being a bridesmaid for her cousin's wedding. During the fitting, the sales clerk is both surprised and disappointed by the challenge in front of her:

CLERK: Pity. They're such lovely dresses. Nature didn't see fit to give you much in the way of hips, did she, dearie?

As the fitting goes on, we see that the dress is never going to fit Daria:

Completing the visual of Daria's ill-fitting dress is the running joke for the episode of everyone asking her why she didn't get the same dress as everyone else. At the wedding, she's paired with a young man named Luhrman,[25] who's attitude and appearance seem to be modeled after comic Steven Wright.

Enter Aunt Amy, who arrives in a red Triumph Spitfire and, as the youngest of Helen's sisters. She meets up with Daria in the women's room, where they begin what will probably be a lifelong mentorship/friendship. As Amy is putting on makeup in the mirror, we see a slight resemblance to Daria from "Quinn the Brain."[26] That episode—which aired only a week earlier—showed the audience that Daria's wallflower persona was just that. As Amy's personality is closely aligned to her own, Daria sees that her potential, future self will emerge (eventually) when her aunt puts on a pair of glasses nearly identical to Daria's.

With regards to those glasses, in "Through a Lens Darkly,"[27] Daria's driving instruction reveals a problem with her peripheral vision,[28] and her mother suggest that contact lenses. Out of hand, she dismisses the idea, but while brushing her teeth, Daria removes her glasses (an image first seen in "Quinn the Brain"), and then goes to see Jane about the issue.

JANE: The glasses are you. They're symbolic of the whole Daria thing. "I wear glasses and I'm not going to apologize for it."
DARIA: Yeah … exactly. Of course, *you* don't wear glasses, so from your point of view, it's all theoretical.

Out of desperation, Daria visits Quinn for advice, which (of course) doesn't help:

QUINN: Contacts? Great! But what color were you thinking? Because clear ones don't call attention to themselves so much, which maybe you want. But then, who could resist being able to change their eye color at will.…

And then, as in any (animated) sitcom world, the coincidences pile up: Helen enters with a letter and photo from her sister (Aunt Amy from "I Don't"), featuring Daria's favorite aunt *without* her glasses ("Like she can even see the camera without her glasses"). Confused by this, Daria decides to call Amy, who provides her with following advice:

So, Daria gets contacts, and finds that everyone keeps commenting on her bravery on trying something new:

When Daria explains that she got them for driving, he (and later, Principal Li) asks, "So why are you wearing them now?" Daria doesn't have an answer.

This notion—"knowing that a brain can be worried about her looks"[29]—comes to the forefront, resulting in an existential crisis for Daria (with the requisite nightmare in a funhouse with and without her glasses) and becomes the focus (if you'll pardon the pun) of the rest of the episode. When Daria's eyes are too irritated by her new contacts, she decides to go to school without them, eventually leading her to hide in a bathroom stall, where Jane eventually finds her:

> DARIA: I'm a hypocrite and a phony. *That's* what's the matter.
> JANE: What are you talking about?
> DARIA: You don't have to pretend. You said it yourself. The glasses are me, uncompromising and unconceited. Well, not anymore.

By the end of the episode,[30] Daria has a moment of self-actualization regarding her looks:

> DARIA: I think to myself, "Never mind glasses. You can see things that other people can't. You can see better than other people. So to hell with them and what they think of you and your glasses."

As the show examined body image in other episodes, Jane enlists Daria to help her create a poster depicting "student life in the new Millennium":

> JANE: You know, nobody said the message had to be positive. I'm going to do something that really represents student life.
> DARIA: Yes.
> JANE: And tell the truth about how much it can suck.

As the two begin their collaboration over pizza (to the point of excess), the conversation inspires Daria to consider a new idea: bulimia[31]:

> DARIA: We were talking about hanging a roll of fly paper and calling it, "It's Important to Be Attractive."
> JANE: Oh, yeah. With or without flies?
> DARIA: Did they add another quart of grease to the pizza recipe?
> JANE: One more slice?
> DARIA: No, I already feel like I might throw up. Hey!

Eventually, Jane paints an attract teenage girl sitting at a mirror, gazing into it, while Daria's contribution is the caption: "She knows she's a winner, she couldn't be thinner, now she goes in the bathroom and vomits up dinner."[32] After convincing her art teacher that the "the choice of words was deliberate, to contrast with the beauty of the image and shock the viewer into paying attention," Mr. O'Neill and Ms. Li try to convince Jane and Daria that the image is fantastic, but that the last line of the poem should be changed. They disagree, but Mr. O'Neill and Ms. Li make the change and display it ahead of a state-wide competition:

> She knows she's a winner, she couldn't be thinner, because she's careful about what she eats for breakfast, lunch, and dinner. Good nutrition rules.

Incensed that the school administration has perverted their original message, they set out to sabotage their own work.

The show also took on the then-alarming rise in plastic surgery among high school students.[33] Daria's producers took on this subject in season one's "Too Cute,"[34] in which a Fashion Club wannabe (Brooke) has recently gotten a nose job. Quinn, already obsessed with her looks, worries that she isn't quite cute enough, but their mother (Helen) offers a word of stern caution:

> I just don't like the idea of you girls talking about cosmetic surgery. Maybe when you're older, and you're doing it for yourself, or there's a sound professional reason for it. I mean, you need to be presentable. Yes, it's a double standard, but women in business are judged on their looks, and there's no getting around that. But breast implants? I just don't know.

Despite this motherly advice, Quinn manages to sneak out of class to visit Dr. Shar by faking cramps, and gets Daria out to accompany her because she's "honest." While there, Dr. Shar uses a computer program to morph Quinn into a younger version of herself, as well as morph Daria into a version of Quinn. Daria is not impressed, but Shar continues to try to convince her that she needs work, going so far as to provide her with a boxed set of breast implants.

Meanwhile, back at Lawndale, the rest of the Fashion Club has not only seen Dr. Shar but are sporting bandages from all having rhinoplasty.[35] This only further worries Quinn, who is threatened with "being fired" from the club to provide a space for Brooke, who has had more work done:

> BROOKE: Dr. Shar says it'll only last a few months, but fortunately I still got my butt. No, seriously. Dr. Shar says the average female has enough fat in her butt to keep her lips luscious until she's, like, seventy.

As the day goes on, Quinn tries to collect money from her admirers around the school to come up with six thousand dollars for the proposed work that Dr. Shar recommended, Daria finally tries one last pitch to convince Quinn that she doesn't need plastic surgery:

> DARIA: You don't need surgery, Quinn. (sighs) I was hoping it wouldn't come to this, and I'll deny I ever said it, but there's nothing wrong with you.

Physically. You've got the kind of looks that make other girls mentally ill. So stop it. You don't need any plastic surgery. You're perfect.

Just as this begins to sink in, the Fashion Club shows up to share horrific news: Brooke's nose job collapsed in the middle of class.[36]

Of Lawndale, Relationships, and "The Kiss"

For a show about the foibles of high schoolers, young relationships often took a backseat for other issues for the first three seasons of *Daria*. Daria's fear of intimacy may be due, in part, to watching the difficulties of her parents, but she also carries an unrequited torch for Jane's older brother (bad boy) Trent.[37] Quinn is shown to be a mercenary dater, jumping from boy to boy for dinner dates, gifts, or ski lodges; and the secondary characters Kevin and Brittany (the quarterback and the head cheerleader) are almost always together, as is Mack and Jodie, throughout the entire run of the series. Until the last episode of Season Three, we also see that Jane is open to flirtations with random boys.[38] This situation changes, however, in "Jane's Addition,"[39] when Jane meets Tom Sloane[40] at a Mystic Spiral concert, and Daria's fantasy vision of a life with Trent turns into something unworkable.[41]

At first, Daria is upset with Jane for ditching her at the Mystic Spiral concert, which foreshadows her fear that Tom might begin to monopolize her best friend's time:

JANE: Hey, I thought I would give you and Trent some one-on-one quality time.
DARIA: Yeah. You and *Tom* were thinking of me.
JANE: Well, I *was* back for the second set like I promised.
DARIA: I thought we weren't staying for the second set.

When Daria shows up the next day to see Jane in order to get Trent to write some music for a school project, Tom suddenly appears, and again we see Daria take an immediate distrust of Jane's new love interest:

DARIA: Do you think it's weird that they just met last night and he's already inviting himself over?
TRENT: I guess he likes her.
DARIA: It's just so fast.

Later in the episode, Tom finds Daria walking home and tries to make peace with her:

TOM: [I]t would be really nice if you could try and get along with me a little. At least in front of Jane.

DARIA: Why should I?
TOM: Because she's your best friend, and I really like her and want to get to
   know her.
DARIA: So?
TOM: So you hating me puts her in a very awkward position.
DARIA: I don't hate you. I don't even know you. But I'm not going to sit by
   while you take my friend away.

Tom's insightfulness overwhelms Daria, and she eventually begins to not
only tolerate him, but begins to hang out with the new couple.

   While the eponymously named show is (mostly) about Daria, much
of Season Four is dedicated to Jane and Tom's relationship, and Daria's
place outside of it. However, what began as an icy acquaintance with her
best friend's boyfriend soon begins to thaw and develop into a season long
"love triangle" story. By the time of Lawndale's homecoming parade,[42]
Daria has discovered that she and Tom have some things in common when
they accidently run into each other. By the penultimate episode of the season ("Fire!"),[43] Jane and Tom are having obvious difficulties, and notices
that Tom is spending more time with Daria than with her ("Damn it!
When did I become a third wheel in my own relationship?").

   Meanwhile, due to a kitchen fire, Daria has moved into the Lane residence,[44] and even Trent has picked up on the vibe between Tom and Daria:

TRENT: Hey, I've seen you together. Guys can always tell when other guys are
   into someone. You know, ethereal transference.
DARIA: Trent, even if what you just said made sense, I think I would know if
   Tom were "into" me … and he's not.
TRENT: Okay. I should go. (starts to leave)
DARIA: (sighs) I'm sorry, Trent. It's just that I don't exactly know what's
   going on.
TRENT: Well, whatever it is, no one said you meant for it to happen.

As Daria is driven home, she ponders Trent's comments, wondering if he
had seen what she wanted to be oblivious to.

   In the season finale, "Dye! Dye! My Darling,"[45] Jane is emotionally on
edge, feeling jealous of Daria so much that she forces her to dye her hair
while questioning her about Tom. Neither goes well. And if things couldn't
get worse between our besties, they do. In a moment referred to in the
Daria fandom as "The Kiss,"[46] they do. Twice. Still in shock, Daria tells Jane
about it at school, but Jane runs off to confront Tom, and the two ultimately
realize that they were bound to break up, and without Jane, Daria reluc-
tantly seeks out her mother for advice. By the penultimate scene of the episode, Jane arrives at Daria's house to confront her about kissing Tom:

JANE: Tom and I broke up.
DARIA: What? Not because of me!

JANE: No. Not because of you. So, I don't care if you go out with him. It's fine
with me.
DARIA: Come on, nobody's *that* well-adjusted.

As the conversation continues, the two struggle with whether they are still friends, or will continue to be. This is meant to be ambiguous to the audience as well:

DARIA: Are we still friends? *Are* we?
JANE: Yeah. We're the kind of friends who can't stand the sight of each other.

Just a few weeks after Season Four, and five months before Season Five, MTV aired the first of two *Daria* TV films, "Is It Fall Yet?,"[47] that acted as a summer vacation story arc between the death of "Jane and Tom" and the start of "Daria and Tom." The film also marks a maturity point not only for the series, but for the characters as well.[48]

With summer vacation about to begin, it's obvious that her relationship with Jane is still strained. In a reversal of their normal positions, Jane announces she will be at an art commune for two months, while Daria is unsure of her plans, and she wants to share her thoughts about Tom with Jane, who leaves for the summer with "the Tom thing" unsettled:

JANE: You don't get it, do you? I don't want to talk about it. I don't want
to think about it. I told you, I'm not mad at you about Tom. Now let it
freaking go, okay?

Dejected, Daria prepares to go out with Tom, but she can't bring herself to call him her "boyfriend." When confronted by Kevin and Brittany, they think he's her brother, and Daria can't bring herself to correct them before they leave. As they walk away from the entrance to the Pizza King, we see that Daria is unsure of what she's gotten into, a theme that becomes the subtext for her first dating relationship:

DARIA: I can't do this. I can't spend the evening in there explaining to
people that no, you're not my brother, and no, you're not Jane's boyfriend,
you're actually my, uh....

By the end of the film, Daria (temporarily) breaks off from Tom, Quinn learns that she can move beyond being simply popular,[49] Daria makes up with Jane, and even manages to help a child at the OK To Cry Day Camp being run by Mr. O'Neill. For the Morgendorffers, a watchful Helen sums it up best to her husband, Jake,

Oh, Jakey, do you realize what a momentous summer our girls have had?
Quinn learned she's smarter than she thought, and Daria has her first
boyfriend.

While much of the focus of this chapter has been spent in discussing how *Daria* seems to have transcended its Millennial-focused characters and spoke to "anyone who ever felt like a precocious young misfit (read: every teenager ever),"[50] any show about teenagers in the late 1990s—even an animated one—would be remiss if the subject of sex wasn't addressed. While there were no "very special episodes" as one might have found on a typical network television show, some of the topics presented on Daria came close (eating disorders, body image, alcoholism,[51] bisexualism[52]). But in what was supposed to be the penultimate episode of the series,[53] sex finally (sort of) enters the picture in "My Night at Daria's."[54]

Well, the truth is, sex was always on the peripheral edges of the show—as it's obvious that Kevin and Brittany have been sexually intimate from their exchanges during the series' run, and it's also clear that Jake and Helen are still "happily married."[55] It's also clear that Quinn (and much of the Fashion Club) are still virgins, as are Jane and Daria. What's less clear is how serious the relationship that Mack and Jody have—until this episode (more on this later).

As with Tom's previous relationship with Jane, Tom and Daria have had their share of misunderstandings and difficulties (such as being so comfortable that Tom doesn't make grand romantic gestures as well as forgets their "six-month anniversary").[56] By the time we get to "My Night at Daria's," even their quiet evening of sitting home and reading on a "date night" is boring:

> DARIA: God, this is dull. So much for my silly childhood dream of becoming a supply side economist.
> TOM: At least you're not reading Kant. This guy gives dry, ponderous intellectuals a bad name.

Interrupted by Quinn, who comes home from a notoriously bad date ("Not only did he wear white pants, his car CD-player skipped."), they head to Daria's room to continue their studies. In a plot seemingly lifted from an old Everly Brothers' song,[57] the pair wake up in a panic at 4:07 a.m. and try to sneak Tom out of the house. Unfortunately, he runs into a half-awake Jake (who's raiding the kitchen for a late-night snack). Daria's mother Helen goes ballistic, demanding to speak with Daria that instant. Meanwhile, Quinn overhears their conversation, and immediately calls Stacy from the Fashion Club, setting off a series of rumors around the school.

Later, at the Pizza King, Tom and Daria field a number of unexplained comments from Upchuck as well as Kevin and Brittany, who declares, "Oh Daria! Now we can have womanly talks!" Tom and Daria are confused, but the audience isn't—the word on the street is that not only did they have sex, but that Daria's father caught them in the act, which becomes clear once Daria phones Jane:

> JANE: Well, there's this rumor going around that you and Tom ... slept together.
> DARIA: Huh?!
> JANE: And that your father walked in right ... well, right in the middle of things.

After confronting Quinn over what she told her friends—the obvious leak of the story—she goes to talk to Jodie. Not only has she heard the rumor, she doesn't believe there is any stigma to it at all (to a point):

> JODIE: Hey, it's no big deal, right? This isn't the 50s, when women had to worry about their reputations.[58]

Daria's search for clarity on the issue turns back to Jane, who we learn didn't sleep with Tom, either:
Eventually, Daria fills Tom in on the rumor, and all kidding aside,[59] we learn that at some point in their relationship, they had had the "talk" about physical intimacy.

> TOM: Boy, people will believe anything. Look, you said you weren't ready. So okay.

As the conversation continues, Daria makes a critical decision about her life and her relationship, surprising Tom with the notion that she's ready for the final step in their intimate relationship.

> DARIA: Okay, fine ... in the interest of moving our relationship forward and taking it to a new, deeper level, I've decided I'm ready, too. Damn it.
> TOM: Really? Are you sure?

Like many "wishful" guys who grew up in the HIV-AIDS era, Daria discovers that Tom indeed carries a condom in his wallet. After her shock subsides, they decide that they'll meet the following weekend while Tom's parents would be out of town. She then shares the news of her scheduled deflowering with Jane, who's stunned and concerned that Daria might not be ready:
In the end, she stands Tom up, who we see sitting on his bed with a bouquet of red roses, which he throws in a trash bin after he tries to phone the Morgendorffer home and Daria waves off the call. Helen suspects that something has happened between the two young would-be lovers, as Daria says she believes that she "should try everything once no matter how unmistakably stupid it is. Almost everything." The next day, Tom discovers a breakup letter attached to the morning newspaper. The couple eventually reunite (again), slightly stronger than before for their attempted union.

Parallel to the growth of Daria's relationship with Tom is the one she experiences with her mother, who has quietly guided her throughout Daria's first romantic relationship,[60] to the point that Daria is able to admit to her mother that she and Tom didn't hook up, much to Helen's relief:

> DARIA: Tom and I didn't have sex, and we're not going to any time soon. Unless, of course, a bomb goes off and, as Earth's last two survivors, we must replenish the human race. Although, frankly, that's not motivation enough for me.

Conclusion

It's difficult to gauge the full impact of a program, even if it was MTV's highest rated show. The best estimate of the program's ratings at the time put it between one to two percent of the available audience (in the last gasps of the age of the VCR), or about one to two million viewers each week. It's enduring legacy among those who watched it at the time, or have sought it out, is that while *Daria* was that while aimed at the MTV demographic, it drew others in.[61] One possible reason, according to Tracy Grandstaff (the voice of Daria), is that "Daria is really a 40-year old man living in Bloomfield, New Jersey. She's Glenn Eichler to the core."[62] This was mixed with the show's co-creator, Susie Lewis, who spent much of her time in college watching MTV and felt that she brought a lot of "hipness" to the show.[63] This combination, despite the fact that either had little experience as show runners, went on to see their creation become the longest running animated program in MTV's history,[64] and did so by "undercutting social fairy tales" with a message that it was "OK to be a confused, mercurial, rebellious, disaffected, lonely teen."[65] As Emily Nussbaum concisely summed up the entire run when she said of *Daria*, "Anyone who ever wanted to opt out of adolescence entirely (writer meekly raises her hand...) could relate."

NOTES

1. Steve Brennan. "Terkhule upped to president of MTV Animation." *The Hollywood Reporter*, April 10, 1997.

2. Judge gave his blessing to series creator Glen Eichler and Susan Lewis Lynn, as he was involved with *B&B* as well as *King of the Hill* on Fox.

3. Qtd. in Newman, 2005, 195.

4. Qtd. in Moore, 2000, D04.

5. Qtd. in Saraiya, 2017.

6. Sonya Saraiya. "'Daria' 20 Years Later: Producers Behind MTV's Iconic Cartoon Look Back," *Variety*, March 1, 2017. Last modified January 25, 2021. https://variety.com/2017/tv/features/mtv-daria-cartoon-20-year-anniversary-1202000114/# on January 21, 2021.

7. There is both a certain timelessness to Caulfield, as well as a certain genderlessness, as the book appeals to disaffected youth across the gender spectrum.

8. Saraiya, "20 Years Later," 2017.

9. The name of an art contest, and eventual proposed story title Daria derives from the events in "Arts 'N Crass" (season 2, episode 1).

10. Hillary Bursis. "Misanthropy has a name—and it's Daria Morgendorffer. Take a trip into the psyche of everyone's favorite sarcastic teen with our guide to the classic 90's cartoon." *Entertainment Weekly*, February 27, 2015.

11. Ken Kimmelman & Paul Sparagano, dirs. "The Esteemsters." *Daria*, season 1, episode 1, MTV, 1997.

12. Quinn is a typical second/youngest child, in which she has very little responsibility yet seems to be both instantly popular anywhere she goes—predominantly based on her looks and fashion sense.

13. *Daria*, "The Esteemsters."

14. *Ibid.* On their walk home, Jane reveals that she's taken the course six times, and while she can "pass the test, I like having low self-esteem. It makes me feel special."

15. A fictional "show-within-the-show" that often acts as a bumper between scenes. The characters, and therefore the audience, never get beyond the pun-filled headlines.

16. Karen Disher, dir. "The Invitations." *Daria*, season 1, episode 2, MTV, 1997.

17. Jamie, Joey, and Jeffy, Quinn's perpetual suitors and running gag.

18. Introduced earlier by another secondary character (Up)Chuck Ruttheimer, that nerdy guy who is always on the make with no chance. Despite that outward appearance, he also, eventually, does the right thing. At the end of the episode, he provides a safe ride home to Jane and Daria.

19. Qtd. in Saraiya, "20 Years Later," 2017.

20. Karen Hyden, Paula Sparagano & Machi Tantillo, dirs. "The Misery Chick." *Daria*, season 1, episode 13, MTV.

21. Mr. O'Neill, season 1, episode 13.

22. As is typical of early episodes in animation, this voiceover work for this episode features slightly different takes on many of the secondary characters. Footballer Kevin's voice isn't quite as "Valley," Brittany's vacuous high-pitch squeal isn't quite there (Up)Chuck's voice isn't quite and nerdy, Fashion Club Tiffany's voice isn't slow and drawn out, and even Trent is a bit less laid back. A work in progress.

23. Qtd. in Catherine Curan, "Breaking through—a *Women's Wear Daily* special report. Daria: Fashion character." *Women's Wear Daily*, June 1998. Last modified January 27, 2021. http://web.archive.org/web/20120420000845/http://www.outpost-daria.com/media_art14.html. The article is described as an "off-canon" interview with Daria. The article is described as an "off-canon" interview with Daria.

24. Tony Kluck, dir. "I Don't." *Daria*, season 2, episode 4, MTV, March 9, 1998.

24. When asked if Luhrman is his first name or his last name, he dryly responds, "Does it matter?"

25. Sue Perrotto, dir. "Quinn the Brain." *Daria*, season 2, episode 3, MTV, 1998. At the end of this episode, Daria uncharacteristically removes her glasses, puts on makeup, and dresses "fashionably" in order to trick Quinn.

26. Guy Moore, dir. "Through a Lens Darkly." *Daria*, season 3, episode 2, MTV, February 24, 1999.

27. Daria nearly hits a dog.

29. A rare, insightful comment from cheerleader Brittany.

30. Growing up, we were conditioned by television shows that all of life's problems could be solved in an hour (for a drama) or half hour (for a comedy), no?

31. Curiously enough, this term, nor anorexia, are ever mentioned in the episode.

32. Karen Disher, dir. "Arts 'N Crass." *Daria*, season 2, episode 1, MTV, 1998.

33. By 2003, more than 39,000 surgeries were being performed annually, including breast augmentations. These were later restricted by the FDA to patients 18 and older.

34. Eric Fogle, dir. "Too Cute." *Daria*, season 1, episode 9, MTV, 1997.

35. Earlier, Quinn had asked Daria what rhinoplasty was, and we're led to believe that she thinks that rhinoceros could use it.

36. Somewhere between five to ten percent of nose jobs fail.

37. Daria had a brief flirtation with Ted DeWitt-Clinton, a former home-schooled student who joins the yearbook staff in season 2, episode 7's "The New Kid," but by the time she opened up to the idea, he decided to keep their relationship "professional."

38. Making out with a random dude at Brittany's party in season 1, episode 2's "The Invitation," and briefly 'dating' fellow track teammate Evan in season 2, episode 11's "See Jane Run."

39. Joey Ahlbum, Aaron Augenblick & Tony Kluck, dirs. "Jane's Addition." *Daria*, season 3, episode 13, MTV, 1999.

40. The character of Tom Sloan was created because, according to a web-based interview between Kara Wild and series co-creator Glenn Eichler, it would be unrealistic to feature a high school student who didn't date at all, yet Eichler also noted that the show "was not about Daria's love life."

41. Especially since her flash-forward in season 3, episode 8's "Lane Miserables" had her working while Trent was an unemployed musician.

42. Guy Moore, dir. "I Loathe a Parade." *Daria*, season 4, episode 6, MTV, 2000.

43. Guy Moore, dir. "Fire!" *Daria*, season 4, episode 12, MTV, 2010.

44. In a reversal of Jane and Trent moving in with the Morgendorffers in "Lane Miserables."

45. Karen Disher, dir. "Dye! Dye! My Darling" *Daria*, season 4, episode 13, MTV, 2010.

46. "Tom Sloane." Daria Wiki. Accessed January 29, 2021. https://daria.fandom.com/wiki/Tom_Sloane.

47. Guy Moore, dir. "Is It Fall Yet?" (MTV Studios), 2000.

48. Harry Thomas, dir. "Daria: Is it fall yet?" *Rolling Stone*, August 31, 2000, 79.

49. In one of the many subplots to the film, Quinn decides to try to study so she can get into college.

50. Bursis, "Misanthropy," 20.

51. Lindy, Quinn's restaurant co-worker, in "Is It College Yet?"

52. Alison, an artist that Jane meets at the Ashfield Community for the Arts, reveals that she is bi-sexual in "Is It Fall Yet?"

53. According to series co-creator Eichler, "Boxing Daria" was supposed to be the series' finale. According to an interview with Bill Desowitz in 2002, he was convinced to produce the second TV film, "Is It College Yet?" to wrap up all of the show's story lines.

54. Ted Stern, dir. "My Night at Daria's." *Daria*, season 5, episode 12, MTV, 2001.

55. Most notably in season 4, episode 12's "Fire!" when they share a hotel room for two weeks following a house fire.

56. Guy Moore, dir. "Sappy Anniversary." *Daria,* season 5, episode 2, MTV, 2001.

57. The Everly Brothers, vocalists, "Wake Up Little Susie," by Felice Bryant and Boudleaux Bryant, recorded August 16, 1957, A-side, Cadence Records, 45 rpm. The lyrics follow a high school couple who fall asleep at a drive-in theatre only to fall asleep and wake up at 4 a.m. The song was "Banned in Boston" for the suggestive lyrics at the time of its release.

58. As in the previously mentioned song "Wake Up Little Susie."

59. He wonders if it could get started at his school.

60. Beginning with the advice she provides after "The Kiss" back in season 4, episode 13's "Dye! Dye! My Darling."

61. According to John Garrett Andrews, supervising producer, while Daria tested best among its initial pilot season offerings, it tested strongest with junior high kids. Quoted in Conti, 2017.

62. Qtd. in Allie Conti. "The oral history of 'Daria.'" *VICE*, March 2, 2017. Accessed February 1, 2021. https://www.vice.com/en/article/qkxbvb/the-oral-history-of-daria.

63. One of the features of the original series was the use of contemporary pop music; however, due to the short sidedness of the original production contracts, none of the original broadcast music is included with the series on DVD. The problem of such music

clearances was encountered by other productions, such as *WKRP in Cincinnati* and *The Wonder Years*, in bringing these shows to DVD, with generic music replacing tunes that could not be acquired.

64. Conti, "Oral History," 2017.

65. Nussbaum, Emily. "Requiem for Daria: Daria slips into the Ghost World of great high-school drama," *Slate*, January 21, 2002. Last modified February 1, 2021. https://slate.com/culture/2002/01/requiem-for-daria.html.

Bibliography

Adams, Dale. "Saludos Amigos: Hollywood and FDR's Good Neighbor Policy." *Quarterly Review of Film & Video* 24, no. 3 (2005): 289-290.

AfterBuzz TV. *Charlie Adler, Carlos Alazraqui, & Joe Murray at San Diego Comic-Con.* July 20, 2017. YouTube. https://www.youtube.com/watch?v=3eVdah2hgqY.

Ahlbum, Joey, Aaron Augenblick, and Tony Kluck, dirs. "Jane's Addition." *Daria*, season 3, episode 13, MTV, 1999.

Albrecht-Crane, Christa, and Dennis Ray Cutchins, eds. *Adaptation Studies: New Approach.* Madison: Fairleigh Dickinson University Press, 2010.

Alexander, Bryan. "Does 'Finding Dory' Show a Gay Couple? We Asked the Filmmakers." *USA Today*, June 9, 2016. https://www.usatoday.com/story/life/movies/2016/06/09/does-finding-dory-show-gay-couple-filmmakers-discuss/85635846/.

Amidi, Amid. *Cartoon Modern: Style and Design in Fifties Animation.* San Francisco: Chronicle Books, 2006.

_____. "The End of the Creator-Driven Era in TV Animation." *Cartoon Brew*, October 19, 2010. Accessed August 31, 2018. https://www.cartoonbrew.com/ideas-commentary/the-end-of-the-creator-driven-era-29614.html.

Amon, Maria Patrice. "Performances of Innocence and Deviance in Disney Cosplaying." *Transformative Works and Cultures* 17 (2014).

Andrews, Mark, Brenda Chapman, and Steve Purcell, dirs. *Brave.* Walt Disney Pictures, 2012.

Archer, Wesley, dir. "Beefsquatch." *Bob's Burgers*, season 2, episode 9, Fox, 2012.

_____, dir. "Bob Day Afternoon." *Bob's Burgers*, season 2, episode 2, FOX, 2012.

_____, dir. "Spaghetti Western and Meatballs." *Bob's Burgers*, season 1, episode 9, FOX, 2011.

_____, dir. "The Unnatural." *Bob's Burgers*, season 3, episode 23, FOX, 2013.

Argyle, Michael, ed. *Social Encounters: Contributions to Social Interaction.* Chicago: Aldine Publishing Co., 1973.

Ashby, LeRoy. *With Amusement for All: a History of American Popular Culture Since 1830.* Lexington: The University of Kentucky Press, 2006.

Ashliman, D.L. *Folk and Fairy Tales: A Handbook.* London: Greenwood Publishing Group, 2004.

Åström, Berit. "'Let's Get Those Winchesters Pregnant': Male Pregnancy in *Supernatural* Fan Fiction." *Transformative Works and Cultures* 4 (January 7, 2010).

Bacchilega, Christina. *Fairy Tales Transformed? Twenty-First Century Adaptations & the Politics of Wonder.* Detroit: Wayne State University Press, 2013.

Bakshi, Ralph. Interview by Tasha Robinson. *The AV Club*, December 6, 2000. Accessed August 31, 2018. http://www.avclub.com/article/ralph-bakshi-13690.

Balboa, Elizabeth. "From Zero to Hero: A Look Back at the Disney Renaissance." *Benzinga*, March 20, 2017. https://www.benzinga.com/general/education/17/03/9193277/from-zero-to-hero-a-look-back-at-the-disney-renaissance-period.

Barbera, Joseph. *My Life in 'Toons: From Flatbush to Bedrock in Under a Century.* Nashville, TN: Turner Publishing, 1994.

Barrier, Michael. *Hollywood Cartoons: American Animation in Its Golden Age*. London: Oxford University Press, 1999.

Basset, Delfin Carbonell. "Speedy Gonzales' Relationship with the Hispanic Community." *The Huffington Post* October 10, 2013. http://www.huffingtonpost.com/2013/10/03/speedy-gonzales-hispanic_n_4039787.html.

Beck, Jerry, ed. *Animation Art: From Pencil to Pixel, the History of Cartoon, Anime, and CGI*. New York: Harper Design International, 2004.

_____. *The Flintstones: The Official Guide to the Cartoon Series*. New York: Running Press, 2011.

_____. Review of *Sick Little Monkeys: The Unauthorized Ren & Stimpy Story*, by Thad Komorowski. *Cartoon Brew*, February 1, 2013. Accessed August 31, 2018. https://www.cartoonbrew.com/books/book-review-sick-little-monkeys-the-unauthorized-ren-stimpy-story-77286.html.

_____. *Warner Brothers, Animation Art: The Characters, the Creators, the Limited Editions*.

Beckerman, Howard. *Animation: The Whole Story*. New York: Allworth Press, 2003.

Bell, Elizabeth, Lynda Hass, and Laura Sells, eds. *From Mouse to Mermaid: The Politics of Film, Gender and Culture*. Bloomington: Indiana University Press, 1995.

Berg, Madeline. "'The Simpsons' Signs Renewal Deal For The Record Books." *Forbes*, November 4, 2016. https://www.forbes.com/sites/maddieberg/2016/11/04/the-simpsons-signs-renewal-deal-for-the-record-books/#612cdf9c1b21.

Berlant, Lauren. *Cruel Optimism*. Durham: Duke University Press, 2011.

Berninger, Mark, Jochen Ecke, and Gideon Habercorn, eds. *Comics as the Nexus of Cultures: Essays on the Interplay of Media, Disciplines, and International Perspectives*. Jefferson, NC: McFarland, 2010.

Bernstein, Robin. "Toys Are Good for Us: Why We Should Embrace the Historical Integration of Children's Literature, Material Culture, and Play." *Children's Literature Association Quarterly* 38, no. 4 (Winter 2013): 458–463.

Bettelheim, Bruno. *The Uses of Enchantment: The Meaning and Importance of Fairy Tales*. New York: Vintage Books, 2010.

Booker, M. Keith. *Drawn to Television: Prime Time Animation from the Flintstones to Family Guy*. Santa Barbara: Praeger, 2006.

Borbolla, Manuel Hernández. 2018. "Poder adquisitivo de los mexicanos cae 80% en 30 años, revela la UNAM." *Huffington Post*, January 15, 2018, sec. México. https://www.nvinoticias.com/nota/93279/poder-adquisitivo-de-los-mexicanos-cae-80-en-30-anos-revela-la-unam.

Boxer, Sarah. "The Exemplary Narcissism of Snoopy." *The Atlantic*, November, 2015. http://www.theatlantic.com/magazine/archive/2015/11/the-exemplary-narcissism-of-snoopy/407827/.

Boyer, Peter J. "F.C.C Treated TV as Commerce." *The New York Times*, January 19, 1987. https://www.nytimes.com/1987/01/19/arts/under-fowler-fcc-treated-tv-as-commerce.html.

Breaking the Mold: The Remaking of Mighty Mouse. Directed by Jeffrey Eagle. Los Angeles: Giant Interactive Entertainment, 2010.

Brennan, Jason. "What the Mickey Mouse Club says about Capitalism" *Fortune*, June 19, 2014. http://fortune.com/2014/06/19/what-the-mickey-mouse-club-says-about-capitalism/.

Brennan, Steve. "Terkhule upped to president of MTV Animation." *The Hollywood Reporter*, April 10, 1997.

Bricks in Motion. Philip Heinrich, dir. Cinemation Studios, 2017.

Brill, Marlene Targ. *America in the 1990's*. Minneapolis: Twenty-First Century Books, 2010.

Bryant, J. Alison, ed. *The Children's Television Community*. Mahwah, NJ: Lawrence Erlbaum, 2007.

Bryman, Alan. *The Disneyization of Society*. London: Sage Publishers, 2004.

Buck, Chris, and Jennifer Lee, dirs. *Frozen*. Walt Disney Pictures, 2013.

_____, dirs. *Frozen 2*. Walt Disney Pictures, 2019.

Burke, Timothy, and Kevin Burke. *Saturday Morning Fever: Growing Up with Cartoon Culture*. New York: St. Martin's, 1999.

Burgess, Jean, and Joshua Green. "How YouTube Matters." *YouTube: Online Video and Participatory Culture*. Cambridge: Polity, 2010.

Bursis, Hillary. "Misanthropy has a name—and it's Daria Morgendorffer. Take a trip into the psyche of everyone's favorite sarcastic teen with our guide to the classic 90's cartoon." *Entertainment Weekly*, February 27, 2015.

Burt, Richard. "What Is Called Thinking with ShaXXXspeares and Walter Benjamin?: Managing De/Kon/Struction, Toying with Letters in The Lego Movie." *Journal for Early Modern Cultural Studies* 16, no. 3 (2016): 94–115.

Butler, Judith. *Gender Trouble: Feminism and the Subversion of Femininity*. New York and London: Routledge, 2011.

Carlsson-Paige, Nancy, and Diane Levin. "The Subversion of Healthy Development and Play: Teacher's Reactions to Teenage Mutant Ninja Turtles." *Day Care and Early Education* 19, no. 2 (1991): 14–20.

Cavalier, Stephen. *The World History of Animation*. Berkeley: University of California Press, 2011.

Cawley, John, and Jim Korkis. *"The Encyclopedia of Cartoon Superstars*. Las Vegas: Pioneer Books, 1990.

Cheng, Stephanie. "Radical Democracy Conference at The New School for Social Research in NYC." In *Radical Democracy*, 2018. https://www.radicaldemocracy.org/conference/2018-conference/.

Chun, Anthony, dir. "Human Flesh." *Bob's Burgers*, season 1, episode 1, FOX, 2011.

_____, dir. "O.T. The Outside Toilet." *Bob's Burgers*, season 3, episode 15, FOX, 2013.

_____, dir. "Synchronized Swimming." *Bob's Burgers*, season 2, episode 3, FOX, 2012.

Cicero, Ron and Kimo Easterwood, dirs. *Happy Happy Joy Joy: The Ren & Stimpy Story*. 2020; New York; Kino Lorber, 2020. DVD.

Clyde Geronimi, Hamilton Luske, and Wilfred Jackson, dirs. *Cinderella*. Walt Disney Pictures, 1950.

Cogan, Brian. *Deconstructing South Park: Critical Examinations of Animated Transgression*. Lanham, MD: Lexington Books, 2012.

Cohen, Rich. "Why Generation X might be our last, Best Hope." Last modified August 11, 2017. https://www.vanityfair.com/style/2017/08/why-generation-x-might-be-our-last-best-hope.

Colburn, Randall. "Nick Kroll on Making Comedy in a 'Woke Culture': 'You Can Still Do and Say Some Pretty Crazy, Wild Shit.'" *AV Club*, October 22, 2019. news.avclub.com/nick-kroll-on-making-comedy-in-a-woke-culture-you-c-1839265725.

Comstock, George, and Erica Sharrer. *Media and the American Child*. London: Oxford University Press, 2007.

Condon, Bill, dir. *Beauty and the Beast*. Walt Disney Pictures, 2017.

Conti, Allie. "The oral history of 'Daria.'" *VICE*, March 2, 2017. Accessed February 1, 2021. https://www.vice.com/en/article/qkxbvb/the-oral-history-of-daria.

Coppa, Francesca. "Women, Star Trek, and the Early Development of Fannish Vidding." *Transformative Works and Cultures* 1, no. 1 (2008).

Coyle, Jennifer, dir. "Bad Tina." *Bob's Burgers*, season 2, episode 8, FOX, 2012.

_____, dir. "Broadcast Wagstaff School News." Bob's Burgers, season 3, episode 12, FOX, 2013.

_____, dir. "The Frond Files." *Bob's Burgers*, season 4, episode 12, FOX, 2014.

_____, dir. "Sheesh! Cab, Bob?" *Bob's Burgers*, season 1, episode 6, FOX, 2011.

_____, dir. "Slumber Party." *Bob's Burgers*, season 4, episode 9, FOX, 2014.

_____, dir. "Work Hard or Die Trying, Girl." *Bob's Burgers*, season 5, episode 1, FOX, 2014.

Coyle, Jennifer, and Bernard Derriman, dir. "Christmas in the Car." *Bob's Burgers*, season 4, episode 8, FOX, 2013.

Crenshaw, Kimberle. "Mapping the Margins: Intersectionality, Identity Politics, and Violence against Women of Color." *Stanford Law Review* 43, no. 6 (1991): 1241–99.

Curan, Catherine. "Breaking through—a *Women's Wear Daily* special report. Daria: Fashion character." *Women's Wear Daily*, June 1998. Last modified January 27, 2021. http://web.archive.org/web/20120420000845/http://www.outpost-daria.com/media_art14.html.

Curtin, Michael, and Jane Shattuc. *The American Television Industry*. London: BFI/Palgrave Macmillan, 2009.

David, Beth, and Esteban Bravo, dirs. *In a Heartbeat*. Ringling College of Art and Design, 2017.

Davies, Raven. "The Slash Fanfiction Connection to Bi Men." *Journal of Bisexuality* 5, no. 2–3 (2005): 195–202.

Deneroff, Harvey. "TV Wakes Up." In Beck, *Animation Art*: 272–273.

Derriman, Bernard, and Ian Hamilton, dir. "V for Valentine-detta." *Bob's Burgers*, season 8, episode 8, FOX, 2018.

Derriman, Bernard, and Tyree Hillihay, dir. "Cheer Up, Sleepy Gene." *Bob's Burgers*, season 8, episode 13, FOX, 2018.

Dillihay, Tyree, dir. "Carpe Museum." *Bob's Burgers*, season 3, episode 22, FOX, 2013.

_____, dir. "Stand by Gene." *Bob's Burgers*, season 6, episode 12, FOX, 2016.

Disher, Karen, dir. "Arts 'N Crass." *Daria*, season 2, episode 1, MTV, 1998.

_____, dir. "Dye! Dye! My Darling" *Daria*, season 4, episode 13, MTV, 2010.

_____, dir. "The Invitations." *Daria*, season 1, episode 2, MTV, 1997.

Dittman, Stacey. "Parent Alert! Watch out for Netflix's Shocking 'Big Mouth' (and More!)." *Protect Young Minds*, November 20, 2018. protectyoungminds.org/2018/11/20/parent-alert-netflix-big-mouth-ebsco-kids-screen-time/.

Dixon, Wheeler Winston, and John Kricfalusi. "Interview with John Kricfalusi." *Film Criticism* 17, no.1. (Fall 1992): 45.

Dobson, Nichola. *Historical Dictionary of Animation and Cartoons*. Lanham, MD: Rowman & Littlefield, 2020.

Dougall, Alastair, ed. *The DC Comics Encyclopedia*. New York: Dorling Kindersley, 2008.

Druetta, Delia Crovi. "Televisión por cable en México: una industria en busca de nuevos rumbos." *Comunicación y Sociedad* 35. Universidad de Guadalajara. January-June 1999.

Edelman, Lee. *No Future*. Durham: Duke University Press, 2004.

"85 Years Ago Today, Mickey Mouse's Career Turned a Page." *D23*. https://d23.com/first-mickey-mouse-comic-strip/.

Eiss, Harry, ed. *Images of the Child*. Bowling Green, OH: Popular Press, 1994.

The Ellen Show. "You've Found the Latest 'Finding Dory' Trailer." YouTube, May 24, 2016. https://www.youtube.com/watch?v=MKJA-VLpiCo.

En Picada, Calidad de Los Salarios En México: INEGI. Vanguardia.

England, Dawn Elizabeth, Lara Descartes, and Melissa A. Collier-Meek. "Gender Role Portrayal and the Disney Princesses." *Sex Roles* 64, no. 7–8 (October 2011): 555–567.

Erickson, Hal. *Television Cartoon Shows, An Illustrated Encyclopedia* 1949–1993. Jefferson, NC: McFarland: 1995.

Erikson, Erik. *Identity: Youth and Crisis*. New York: Norton, 1968.

Ezell, Sila Kaine. *Humor and Satire on Contemporary Television: Animation and the American Joke*. New York: Routledge, 2016.

Fairclough, Norman, Giuseppina Cortose, and Patrizia Ardizzone, eds. *Discourse and Contemporary Social Change*. Bern: Peter Lang, 2007.

Fisch, Shalom M., and Rosemarie T. Truglio, eds. *"G" Is for Growing: Thirty Years of Research on Children and Sesame Street*. Mahwah, NJ: Lawrence Erlbaum Associates, 2001.

Flegel, Monica, and Jenny Roth. "Annihilating Love and Heterosexuality without Women: Romance, Generic Difference, and Queer Politics in *Supernatural* Fan Fiction." *Transformative Works and Cultures* 4 (July 2010).

Fogle, Eric, dir. "Too Cute." *Daria*, season 1, episode 9, MTV, 1997.

Framke, Caroline. "Netflix's Big Mouth Takes a Sharp, Surprisingly Joyful Look at the Gross Time that is Puberty." *Vox*, September 30, 2017. vox.com/fall-tv/2017/9/29/16382984/big-mouth-netflix-review-kroll-mulaney.

Freeman, Elizabeth. *Time Binds: Queer Temporalities, Queer Histories*. Durham: Duke University Press, 2010.

Freeman, Hadley. "'People opened up because I'm the Beavis and Butt-Head Guy': Mike Judge on his New Funk Direction." Last modified April 15, 2020. https://www.

theguardian.com/tv-and-radio/2020/apr/15/mike-judge-interview-beavis-butthead-silicon-valley-tales-from-the-tour-bus ion | Television & radio | The Guardian.

Gabler, Neal. *Walt Disney: The Triumph of the American Imagination*. New York: Random House, 2007.

Gauntlett, David, ed. *Making Media Studies: The Creativity Turn in Media and Communications Studies*. New York: Peter Lang, 2015.

Geronimi, Clyde, dir. *Sleeping Beauty*. Walt Disney Pictures, 1950.

Gibson, Jon M., and Chris McDonnell. *Unfiltered: The Complete Ralph Bakshi*. New York: Universe, 2008.

Gimlin, Debra. *Body Work: Beauty and Self-Image in American Culture*. Berkeley: University of California Press, 2002.

Giroux, H.A. "Animating Youth: The Disneyfication of Children's Culture." *Socialist Review* 24 (1995): 23–55.

Gitlin, Todd. *Inside Prime Time*. New York: Pantheon, 1983.

Glimps, Blanche Jackson, and Theron Ford, eds. *Gender and Diversity Issues in Religious-Based Institutions and Organizations*. Hershey, PA: Information Science Reference, 2016.

Gluck, Keith. "The Genesis of Disney Television," *The Walt Disney Family Museum*, July 23, 2014, https://www.waltdisney.org/blog/genesis-disney-television.

Goldmark, Daniel Ira, and Charles Keil. *Funny Pictures: Animation and Comedy in Studio-Era Hollywood*. Berkeley: University of California Press, 2011.

Goldsmith, Elizabeth Edwards. *Life Symbols as Related to Sex Symbolism*. New York: The Knickerbocker Press, 1924.

Goodman, Martin. "Dr. Toon: When Reagan Met Optimus Prime." *Animation World Network*, October 12, 2010. http://www.awn.com/animationworld/dr-toon-when-reagan-met-optimus-prime.

Greenberg, Raz. "The Animated Text: Definition," *Journal of Film and Video* 63, no. 2 (Summer 2011): 3–10.

Greenhill, Pauline, and Sidney Eve Matrix, eds. *Fairy Tale Films: Visions of Ambiguity*. Logan: Utah State University Press, 2010.

Grobovaite, Dalia. "Politics of Bricolage and the Double-sided Message of *The LEGO Movie*." *Canadian Journal of Media Studies* 15, no. 1 (2017).

Grossman, Gary H. *Saturday Morning TV: Thirty Years of the Shows You Waited All Week to Watch*. New York: Dell Publishing, 1981.

Gymnich, Marion, Kathrin Ruhl, and Klaus Scheunemann, eds. *Gendered (Re)Visions: Constructions of Gender in Audiovisual Media*. Gottingen: Vandenhoeck & Ruprecht, 2010.

Haase, Donald, ed. *The Greenwood Encyclopedia of Folk Tales and Fairy Tales, Volumes 1–3*. London: Greenwood Press, 2008.

Halberstam, Judith. *The Queer Art of Failure*. Durham: Duke University Press, 2011.

Hall, Karen J. "A Soldier's Body: GI Joe, Hasbro's Great American Hero, and the Symptoms of Empire. *Journal of Popular Culture* 38, no. 1 (2004), 34–54.

Hamilton, Ian, dir. "Brunchsquatch." *Bob's Burgers*, season 8, episode 1, FOX, 2017.

_____, dir. "The Gayle Tales." *Bob's Burgers*, season 5, episode 13, FOX, 2015.

Hand, David, dir. *Snow White*. Walt Disney Pictures, 1937.

Hanley, Tim. *Wonder Woman Unbound*. Chicago: Chicago Review Press, 2013.

Harrison, Colin. *American Culture in the 1990's*. Edinburgh University Press, 2010.

Henricks, Thomas S. "Play as Self-Realization—Toward a General Theory of Play," *American Journal of Play* 4, no. 2 (Summer 2011): 190–213.

Henry, Matthew A. *The Simpsons, Satire and American Culture*. New York: Palgrave Macmillan, 2012.

Hernández-Saca, David I., Laurie Gutmann Kahn, and Mercedes A. Cannon. "Intersectionality Dis/Ability Research: How Dis/Ability Research in Education Engages Intersectionality to Uncover the Multidimensional Construction of Dis/Abled Experiences." *Review of Research in Education* 42, no. 1 (March 2018): 286–311.

Honeyman, Susan. "Manufactured Agency and the Playthings Who Dream It for Us." *Children's Literature Association Quarterly* 31, no. 2 (Summer 2006): 109–131.

Hoofnagle, Chris. "KidVid in Context." *Technology | Academics | Policy*, June 8, 2018. Accessed August 31, 2018. http://www.techpolicy.com/Hoofnagle_KidVidInContext_TH-0608.aspx.

"How It Works." LEGO IDEAS. Last modified July 31, 2020. https://ideas.LEGO.com/howitworks.

Howe, Sean. *Marvel Comics: The Untold Story.* New York: HarperCollins, 2013.

Hunting, Kyra Hunting. "Queer as Folk and the Trouble with Slash." *Transformative Works and Cultures* 11 (April 11, 2012).

Hurts. "Hurts—Illuminated (Live Version)." YouTube, April 8, 2011. https://www.youtube.com/watch?v=6CvuyaKmLnw.

Hyden, Karen, Paula Sparagano, and Machi Tantillo, dirs. "The Misery Chick." *Daria*, season 1, episode 13, MTV.

Inge, M. Thomas. "Mark Twain, Chuck Jones, and the Art of Imitation." *Studies in American Humor* 10 (2003): 11–17.

Is It Fall Yet? Guy Moore, dir. MTV Studios, 2000.

Itzkoff, Dave. "Beavis and Butt-Head Revived at Comedy Central." Last modified July 1, 2020. https://www.nytimes.com/2020/07/01/arts/television/beavis-and-butt-head-comedy-central.html.

Jamison, Anne, ed. *Fic: Why Fanfiction Is Taking Over the World.* Dallas: Smart Pop, 2013.

Jenkins, Henry. *Textual Poachers.* New York: Routledge, 1992.

Johnson, Dominique Dierdre. "Misogynoir and Antiblack Racism: What *The Walking Dead* Teaches Us About the Limits of Speculative Fiction Fandom." *The Journal of Fandom Studies* 3, no. 3 (September 2015): 259–75.

Jones, Christa, and Claudia Schwabe, eds. *New Approaches to Teaching Folk and Fairy Tales.* Logan: Utah State University Press, 2016.

Jones, Gerard. *Men of Tomorrow: Geeks, Gangsters and the Birth of the Comic Book.* New York: Basic Books, 2004.

Kapurch, Katie. "Rapunzel Loves Merida: Melodramatic Expressions of Lesbian Girlhood and Teen Romance in *Tangled, Brave,* and Femslash." *Journal of Lesbian Studies* 19, no. 4 (November 2015): 436–53.

Kent, Steven L. *The Ultimate History of Video Games: The Story Behind the Craze that Touched Our Lives and Changed the World.* Roseville, CA: Prima Publishing, 2001.

Kim, Sujin, and Alina Salpac. "Culturally Responsive, Transformative Pedagogy in the Transnational Era: Critical Perspectives." *Educational Studies* 5, no. 1 (2015): 17–27.

Kimmelman, Ken, and Paul Sparagano, dirs. "The Esteemsters." *Daria*, season 1, episode 1, MTV, 1997.

Kluck, Tony, dir. "I Don't." *Daria*, season 2, episode 4, MTV, March 9, 1998.

Komorowski, Thad. *Sick Little Monkeys: The Unauthorized* Ren & Stimpy *Story.* Albany, GA: BearManor Media, 2013.

Korkis, Jim. *The Book of Mouse: A Celebration of Walt Disney's Mickey Mouse,* New York: Theme Park Press, 2013.

Kricfalusi, John. "From *The Jetstones* To *Mighty Mouse*." *John K. Stuff.* November 02, 2007. Accessed August 31, 2018. http://johnkstuff.blogspot.com/2007/11/from-jetstones-to-mighty-mouse.html.

_____. "'How Can I Get Life In My Drawings?'—Tell A Story." *John K. Stuff.* February 13, 2010. Accessed August 31, 2018. https://johnkstuff.blogspot.com/2010/02/how-can-i-get-life-in-my-drawings-tell.html.

_____. "John K. Talks Ren & Stimpy, Mighty Mouse, Ralph Bakshi." Interview by Cliff Broadway, *TheOneRing*, August 1, 2012.

_____. "'My Intended Audience Was Everybody': An Interview with *Mighty Mouse: The New Adventures'* John Kricfalusi." Interview by Harry McCracken. *Animato* 16, Spring 1988. https://harrymccracken.com/blog/my-intended-audience-was-everybody/.

_____. "Origins of Wonky." *John K. Stuff* (blog), September 21, 2008. Accessed August 31, 2018. http://johnkstuff.blogspot.com/2008/09/origins-of-wonky.html.

Kuiper, Kathleen, ed. *Merriam Webster's Encyclopedia of Literature.* Springfield, MA: Merriam-Webster, 1995.

Lamarre, Thomas. *The Anime Machine: A Media Theory of Animation*. Minneapolis: University of Minnesota Press, 2009.

Lamerichs, Nicolle. "Post-Object Fandom: Television, Identity and Self-Narrative by Rebecca Williams (Review)." *Cinema Journals* 55, no. 3 (Spring 2016): 171–175.

Lammie, Rob, "The History of G.I. Joe: A Real American Hero." *Mental Floss*, July 4, 2015. http://mentalfloss.com/article/62636/history-gi-joe-real-american-hero.

Landler, Mark. "Turner to Merge into Time Warner, a $7.5 Billion Deal." *The New York Times*, September 23, 1995. http://www.nytimes.com/1995/09/23/us/turner-to-merge-into-time-warner-a-7.5-billion-deal.html?pagewanted=all.

Lange, Ariane. "The Disturbing Secret Behind An Iconic Cartoon." *BuzzFeed News*, March 29, 2018. Accessed August 31, 2018. https://www.buzzfeednews.com/article/arianelange/john-kricfalusi-ren-stimpy-underage-sexual-abuse.

Lashway, Peter. "Ralph Bakshi Panel DragonCon September 2, 2011." YouTube, July 11, 2013. https://www.youtube.com/watch?v=ue2EkHnOwV4.

Latchem, Joe. "Going Retro," *Home Media Magazine*. July 20, 2009, http://www.homemediamagazine.com/tv-dvd/going%E2%80%89retro-16390.

"Lego," *Wikipedia*. Last modified July 30, 2020. https://en.wikipedia.org/wiki/Lego.

The LEGO Batman Movie. Chris McKay, dir. (Warner Bros. Pictures, 2017).

A Lego Brickumentary. Kief Davidson and Daniel Jung, dir. (Global Emerging Markets, HeLo), 2014.

The LEGO Movie. Phil Lord and Christopher Miller, dirs. (Warner Bros. Pictures, 2014).

The LEGO Movie 2: The Second Part. Mike Mitchell and Trisha Gum, dirs. (Warner Bros. Pictures, 2019).

Lepore, Jill. *The Secret History of Wonder Woman*. New York: Alfred A. Knopf, 2014.

Levander, Caroline Field, and Carol Singley. *The American Child: A Cultural Studies Reader*. New Brunswick: Rutgers University Press, 2003.

Lim, Boohwan, and Kyounghee Lim, dir. "Bob Fires the Kids." *Bob's Burgers*, season 3, episode 3, FOX, 2012.

_____, dir. "The Belchies." *Bob's Burgers*, season 2, episode 2, FOX, 2012.

_____, dir. "The Kids Run the Restaurant." *Bob's Burgers*, season 3, episode 20, FOX, 2013.

_____, dir. "Tina and the Real Ghost." *Bob's Burgers*, season 5, episode 2, FOX, 2014.

_____, dir. "Turkey in a Can." *Bob's Burgers*, season 4, episode 5, FOX, 2013.

Lim, Kyounghee, dir. "Crawl Space." *Bob's Burgers*, season 1, episode 2, FOX, 2011.

Loschiavo, Brian, dir. "The Bleakening Parts I and II." *Bob's Burgers*, season 8, episodes 6 & 7, FOX, 2017.

Mackinnon, Don, dir. "The Unbearable Like-Likeness of Gene." *Bob's Burgers*, season 3, episode 8, FOX, 2012.

Malkin, Bonnie. "Finding Dory Trailer Raises Hopes Film Could Include Lesbian Couple," *The Guardian*, May 28, 2016, https://www.theguardian.com/film/2016/may/28/new-finding-dory-trailer-hopes-lesbian-couple-disney-pixar.

Mallory, Michael. *Hanna-Barbera Cartoons*. New York: Hugh Lauter Levin Associates, 1998.

Maltin, Leonard. "Interview with Joseph Barbera." *Archive of American Television*. Studio City, CA. February 26, 1997. Accessed April 29, 2014 from www.emmytvlegends.org/interviews/people/joseph-barbera.

_____. *Of Mice and Magic: A History of American Animated Cartoons*. Rev. ed. New York: Plume Books, 1987.

Marcia, James E. "Development and Validation of Ego-identity Status." *Journal of Personality and Social Psychology* 3, no.5 (1966): 551–8.

Marshall, Elizabeth, and Leigh Gilmore. "Girlhood in the Gutter: Feminist Graphic Knowledge and the Visualization of Sexual Precarity." *Women's Studies Quarterly* 43, no. 1/2 (2015): 95–114.

McDonald, Seth. "UPDATE: A New Teenage Mutant Ninja Turtles Series NOT In Development At CBS All Access." *LRM Online*, June 24, 2020. https://lrmonline.com/news/a-new-teenage-mutant-ninja-turtles-series-is-in-development-at-cbs-all-acess/.

Menegus, Bryan. "The History of Adult Swim's Rise to Greatness." *Sploid*, April 11, 2016. http://sploid.gizmodo.com/an-oral-history-of-adult-swim-1770248730.

Menon, Madhavi. *Indifference to Difference*. Minneapolis: University of Minnesota Press, 2015.

Mey, J. L., ed. *Concise Encyclopedia of Pragmatics*. Oxford: Elsevier, 2009.

Mighty Mouse: The New Adventures. Season 2, episode 4, "Don't Touch That Dial." Directed by Kent Butterworth, and written by Jim Reardon and Tom Minton. Aired October 8, 1988, on CBS. Disc 3. *Mighty Mouse: The New Adventures*. DVD. Hollywood: Paramount Pictures, 2010.

Miller, Bob. "Fine Tooning: After Battling Bart Simpson, Kent Butterworth Helps Raise Bugs Bunny's Heirs." *Comics Scene* 16, 1990.

Miller, Thomas, ed. *Handbook of Stressful Transitions Across the Lifespan*. New York: Springer, 2010.

Miller, Toby, ed. *Television Studies*. London: British Film Institute, 2002.

Minow, Newton. "Television and the Public Interest." Speech to the National Association of Broadcasters, May 9, 1961. Accessed August 31, 2018. http://www.americanrhetoric. com/speeches/newtonminow.htm.

Moore, Guy, dir. "Fire!" *Daria*, season 4, episode 12, MTV, 2010.

_____, dir. "I Loathe a Parade." Daria, season 4, episode 6, MTV, 2000.

_____, dir. "Sappy Anniversary." *Daria*, season 5, episode 2, MTV, 2001.

_____, dir. "Through a Lens Darkly." *Daria*, season 3, episode 2, MTV, February 24, 1999.

Morales, Isidro. "The Mexican Crisis and the Weakness of the NAFTA Consensus." *The Annals of the American Academy of Political and Social Science 550, no. 1* (1997): 130–152.

Morris, Gary. "A Quickie Look at the Life and Career of Tex Avery." *Bright Lights Film Journal*, September 1, 1998. Accessed August 31, 2018. https://brightlightsfilm.com/wp-content/cache/all/quickie-look-life-career-tex-avery/#.W4OGLuhKhhE.

Murray, Joe. *Creating Animated Cartoons with Character: A Guide to Crafting and Producing Your Own Animated Series for TV, Web, and Short Film*. New York: Watson-Guptill, 2010.

Neuwirth, Allan. *Makin' Toons: Inside the Most Popular Animated TV Shows and Movies*. New York: Allworth, 2003.

Ng, Eve. "Between Text, Paratext, and Context: Queerbaiting and the Contemporary Media Landscape." *Transformative Works and Cultures* 24 (2017).

Nick Animation. "Episode 23: Joe Murray." December 2, 2016. *Nick Animation*, YouTube. https://www.youtube.com/watch?v=dGDlufo6CXs.

"Nick Hits (Nickelodeon Latin America Block)." 15 Apr. 2017. *Wikipedia*.

Night Argent. "Night Argent // Kamikaze (Audio)." YouTube. March 5, 2016. https://www.youtube.com/watch?v=5e51krtQfqA.

Ninjago Movie. Charlie Bean, Paul Fischer, and Robert Logan, dirs. *LEGO*. (Warner Bros. Pictures, 2017).

Nölke, Ana-Isabel. "Making Diversity Conform? An Intersectional, Longitudinal Analysis of LGBT Specific Mainstream Media Advertisements," *Journal of Homosexuality* 65, no. 2 (February 2018): 224–255.

Norlund, Christopher. "Imagining Terrorists Before Sept. 11: Marvel's *GI Joe* Comic Books, 1982–1994." *ImageTexT*, vol. 3, no. 1 (2006).

Nussbaum, Emily. "Requiem for Daria: Daria slips into the Ghost World of great high-school drama." *Slate*, January 21, 2002. Last modified February 1, 2021. https://slate.com/culture/2002/01/requiem-for-daria.html.

Olson, Kathryn M. "An Epideictic Dimension of Symbolic Violence in Disney's *Beauty and the Beast*: Inter-Generational Lessons in Romanticizing and Tolerating Intimate Partner Violence." *Quarterly Journal of Speech* 99, no. 4 (2013): 448–480.

Pardo, Mauricio. and Bernard Derriman, dir. "The Wolf of Wharf Street." *Bob's Burgers*, season 8, episode 3, FOX, 2017.

"Patreon Community Guidelines," *Patreon*. Last modified 2018, https://www.patreon.com/guidelines#authenticity.

Perlmutter, David. *American Toons In: A History of Television Animation*. Jefferson, NC: McFarland, 2014.

_____. *The Encyclopedia of American Animated Television Shows*. Lanham, MD: Rowman and Littlefield, 2018.

Perrotto, Sue, dir. "Quinn the Brain." *Daria*, season 2, episode 3, MTV, 1998.

Peters, Michael A., ed. *Encyclopedia of Educational Philosophy and Theory*. New York: Springer, 2016.

Petronille, Marc, and William Audureau. *The History of Sonic the Hedgehog*. Richmond Hill, Ontario, CA: Udon Entertainment, 2013.

Phelps-Ward, Robin J., and Crystal T. Laura. "Talking Back in Cyberspace: Self-Love, Hair Care, and Counter Narratives in Black Adolescent Girls' YouTube Vlogs." *Gender and Education* 28, no. 6 (2016): 807–820.

Phipps, Keith. *"Mighty Mouse: The New Adventures, The Complete Series," The A.V. Club*, January 13, 2010, https://www.avclub.com/mighty-mouse-the-new-adventures-the-complete-series-1798164099.

Piaget, Jean. *The Language and Thought of the Child*, 3rd ed. New York: Routledge, 1959.

Pilling, Jayne, ed. *A Reader in Animation Studies*. London: John Libbey, 1998.

Pittman, Taylor. "What Disney Princesses Would Look Like with Realistic Faces." *The Huffington Post*, December 7, 2017. https://www.huffingtonpost.com/2015/06/03/the-nameless-doll-realistic-disney-princess-faces_n_7493774.html.

Portella, Anna. "Con salarios de pobre y sin seguro social: así viven los jóvenes mexicanos." *Forbes México*. May 4, 2018._ https://www.forbes.com.mx/con-salarios-de-pobre-y-sin-seguro-social-asi-viven-los-jovenes-mexicanos/.

Postigo, Hector. "Video Game Appropriation through Modifications." *Convergence: The International Journal of Research into New Media Technologies*, 14, no. 1 (2008): 59–74.

Postman, Neil. *The Disappearance of Childhood*. New York: Knopf Doubleday Publishing, 2011.

Pritchard, Erin. "The Social and Spatial Experiences of Dwarfs within Public Spaces." PhD diss., Newcastle University, 2014.

Pugh, Sheenagh. *The Democratic Genre*. Bridgend: Seren, 2005.

Rabin, Nathan. "Pixelated Case File #139: *Super Mario Brothers*." *A.V. Club*, June 10, 2009. http://www.avclub.com/article/pixelated-case-file-139-isuper-mario-bros-i-29032.

Rajagopalan, Sudha. "Slash Fandom, Sociability, and Sexual Politics in Putin's Russia." *Transformative Works and Cultures* 19 (2014).

Random Nameless Channel. "Random Manips I." YouTube, March 29, 2015. https://www.youtube.com/watch?v=JwksqGjidhc&index=4&list=PL339_yyCHKFSoDvRQ3n G-k3zkX6GHgGXm.

_____. "Watch Me Edit—Creating Myself." YouTube, May 26, 2018. https://www.youtube.com/watch?v=42E8Q-LrGH4&index=12&t=0's&list=PL339_yyCHKFTWQc KUCINKPgfWKZnls-ev.

Rao, Sonia. "From Peacock to HBO Max, Here's what Every Major Streaming Service Can Offer You" *The Washington Post*, July 15, 2020, https://www.washingtonpost.com/arts-entertainment/2020/07/15/peacock-nbc-hbo-max-streaming-service-guide/.

Raphael, Jordan, and Tom Spurgeon. *Stan Lee and the Rise and Fall of the American Comic Book*. Chicago: Chicago Review Press, 2004.

Rice, John, dir. "Mutiny on the Windbreaker." *Bob's Burgers*, season 3, episode 4, FOX, 2012.

Ro, Ronin. *Tales To Astonish*. New York: Bloomsbury, 2004.

Robbins, Trina. *The Great Women Superheroes*. Northhampton, MA: Kitchen Sink Press, 1996.

Roberts, Lewis. "'It's a Dangerous World out There for a Toy': Identity Crisis and Commodity Culture in the Toy Story Movies." *Children's Literature Association Quarterly* 42, no. 4 (2017): 417–437.

Rudloff, Maja. "(Post)feminist Paradoxes: The Sensibilities of Gender Representation in Disney's *Frozen*," *Outskirts: Feminisms Along the Edge* 35 (2016): 1–20.

Ruti, Mari. *Reinventing the Soul*. New York: Other Press, 2006.

Salmans, Sandra. "Why Saturday Morning Is One Big 'Cartoon Ghetto.'" *The New York Times*, August 25, 1985. https://www.nytimes.com/1985/08/25/arts/why-saturday-morning-is-one-big-cartoon-ghetto.html.

Saraiya, Sonya. "'Daria' 20 Years Later: Producers Behind MTV's Iconic Cartoon Look Back," *Variety*, March 1, 2017. Last modified January 25, 2021. https://variety.com/2017/tv/features/mtv-daria-cartoon-20-year-anniversary-1202000114/#.

Schodt, Frederik L. "Designing a World." *Mechademia* 8 (2013): 228–242.

Schoemer, Karen. "Twisted Humor of Children's Cartoon Gains a Cult." Review of John Kricfalusi, creator. *The Ren & Stimpy Show*. 1991–2; Spumco/Viacom: Nickelodeon. *New York Times*, section C, page 17. March 19, 1992.

Schroeber, Adrian, and Debbie Olsen. *Children, Youth and American Television*. New York: Routledge, 2018.

Shapiro, Mitchell E. *Television Network Weekend Programming, 1959–1990*. Jefferson, NC: McFarland, 1992.

Shayon, Robert Lewis, ed. *The Eighth Art: Twenty Three Views of Television Today*. New York: Holt, Rinehart and Winston, 1962.

Simensky, Linda. "Ed, Edd n Eddy: Three Guys, One 'Toon,'" *Take One* 24 (1999).

Simensky, Linda. "The Revival of the Studio-Era Cartoon in the 1990s." In *Funny Pictures: Animation and Comedy in Studio-Era Hollywood*, edited by Daniel Ira Goldmark and Charles Keil. Berkeley: University of California Press, 2011, 272–291.

Simpson, Janice C. "Show Business: Lean, Green and on the Screen." *Time*, April 2, 1990. http://content.time.com/time/magazine/article/0,9171,969727-2,00.html#ixzz0h91fnBrj.

Sito, Tom. *Drawing the Line: The Untold Story of Animation Unions From Bosko To Bart Simpson*. Lexington: University of Kentucky Press, 2006.

Sommerlad, Joe. "Beavis and Butt-Head at 25: How MTV's original dumbasses stormed America and changed comedy forever." Last modified March 7, 2018. https://www.independent.co.uk/arts-entertainment/tv/features/beavis-and-butthead-25th-anniversary-mike-judge-mtv-tv-comedy-animation-offence-a8243906.html.

"Sonic the Hedgehog enter Book of World Records." *Archie Comics*. July 7, 2007. https://web.archive.org/web/20080912135723/http://archie-blogs.archiecomics.com:80/sonic/2008/07/from_the_cuinness_book_of_worl.html.

Song, Chris, dir. "Li'l Hard Dad." *Bob's Burgers*, season 5, episode 14, FOX, 2015.

_____. "Gene It On." *Bob's Burgers*, season 4, episode 20, FOX, 2014.

Song, Chris, and Bernard Derriman, dir. "The Gene and Courtney Show." *Bob's Burgers*, season 6, episode 7, FOX, 2016.

Song, Chris, Bernard Derriman, and Tony Gennaro, dir. "Just the Trip." *Bob's Burgers*, season 10, episode 17, FOX, 2020.

St. James, Emily. "Why Elsa from Frozen is a Queer Icon—and Why Disney Won't Embrace That Idea." *Vox*, November 22, 2019. https://www.vox.com/culture/2019/11/22/20975178/frozen-2-elsa-girlfriend-lesbian-queer-review.

Stabile, Carol A. and Mark Harrison. *Primetime Animation: Television Animation and American Culture*. New York: Routledge, 2003.

Stern, Ted, dir. "My Night at Daria's." *Daria*, season 5, episode 12, MTV, 2001.

Stockton, Kathryn Bond. *The Queer Child*. Durham: Duke University Press, 2009.

Stoner, Mark, and Sally J. Perkins. *Making Sense of Messages: A Critical Apprenticeship in Rhetorical Criticism*. New York: Routledge, 2015.

Stuever, Hank. "Netflix's 'Big Mouth' Finds a Smart Way to Wrestle with the Monster Called Puberty." *The Washington Post*, September 29, 2017. washingtonpost.com/entertainment/tv/netflixs-big-mouth-finds-a-smart-way-to-wrestle-with-the-monster-called-puberty/2017/09/28/df72e252-a3be-11e7-8cfe-d5b912fabc99_story.html.

Takhvar, Mehri. "Play and theories of play: a review of the literature." *Early Child Development and Care* 39, no. 1 (Oct. 1988): 221–227.

TheNamelessDoll. "ILLUMINATED." YouTube, May 16, 2013. https://www.youtube.com/watch?v=JwksqGjidhc&index=4&list=PL339_yyCHKFSoDvRQ3nG-k3zkX6GHgGXm.

TheNight130. "'Kamikaze' Esmeralda x Cinderella." YouTube, October 20., 2017. https://www.youtube.com/watch?v=_bq_0ygFysw.

Thill, Scott. "How *Mighty Mouse: The New Adventures* Amped Up Animation." *Wired*,

January 5, 2010. Accessed August 31, 2018. https://www.wired.com/2010/01/mighty-mouse-new-adventures/.

Thomas, Harry, dir. "Daria: Is it fall yet?" *Rolling Stone*, August 31, 2000: 79.

"Tom Sloane." Daria Wiki. Accessed January 29, 2021. https://daria.fandom.com/wiki/Tom_Sloane.

Tosenberger, Catherine. "Homosexuality at the Online Hogwarts: Harry Potter Slash Fanfiction." *Children's Literature* 36, no. 1 (2008): 185–207.

"Travel Back To 1990's Cartoon Heaven With 'Rocko's Modern Life' Illustrator Joe Murray." *Huffington Post*, 22 Jan. 2014. https://www.huffpost.com/entry/joe-murray-animator_n_4639041.

Travers, Ben. "'Big Mouth' Review: Nick Kroll's Exemplary Netflix Comedy is a Horrifying and Hilarious Portrait of Childhood," *IndieWire*, September 29, 2017, indiewire.com/2017/09/big-mouth-netflix-review-best-animated-series-spoilers-1201881766/.

Treece, Jordan. "The Double-Sided Message of The Lego Movie: The Effects of Popular Entertainment on Children in Consumer Culture" (2015). *English Seminar Capstone Research Papers* 28.

Trula, Esther Miguel. "La Gráfica Que Resume La Indignación de Los Jóvenes Mexicanos: Estudiar Para Convertirte En Pobre." n.d. *World Economic Forum*. https://es.weforum.org/agenda/2017/06/la-grafica-que-resume-la-indignacion-de-los-jovenes-mexicanos-estudiar-para-convertirte-en-pobre.

Turner, Cory, and Anya Kamentz. "'Big Mouth' Creators on Embracing the Awkwardness of Puberty." *NPR*, March 12, 2020. npr.org/2020/03/11/814559208/big-mouth-creators-on-embracing-the-awkwardness-of-puberty.

Turner, Ted, and Bill Burke. *Call Me Ted*. New York: Grand Central, 2008.

"2016 GLAAD Studio Responsibility Index." GLAAD, last modified 2016, https://www.glaad.org/sri/2016.

Varul, Matthias Zick. "The Cultural Tragedy of Production and the Expropriation of the Brickolariat: The Lego Movie as Consumer-Capitalist Myth." *European Journal of Cultural Studies* 21, no. 6 (December 2018): 724–743.

Waggoner, Erin B. "Bury Your Gays and Social Media Fan Response: Television, LGBTQ Representation, and Communitarian Ethics." *Journal of Homosexuality* (October 2017): 1–15.

Walker, Nancy A. *The Disobedient Writer: Women and Narrative Tradition*. Austin: University of Texas Press, 1995.

Wanzo, Rebecca. "African American Acafandom and Other Strangers: New Genealogies of Fan Studies." *Transformative Works and Cultures* 20 (2015).

Wells, Paul. *Animation and America*. Edinburgh, UK: Edinburgh University Press, 2002.

White, David Manning. and Robert H. Abel, eds. *The Funnies: An American Idiom*. New York: The Free Press, 1963.

Williams, Zoe. "Early Puberty: Why are Kids Growing Up Faster?" *The Guardian*, October 25, 2012. https://www.theguardian.com/society/2012/oct/25/early-puberty-growing-up-faster.

Witmer, Carrie. "The Creator of Netflix's 'Big Mouth' Shares which Embarrassing Puberty Stories Happened in Real Life." *Business Insider*, October 15, 2017. businessinsider.com/netflix-big-mouth-creator-shares-which-puberty-stories-were-real-2017-10?utm_source=feedburner&=&utm_medium=referral.

Wolff, Craig. "Mighty Mouse Flying High On Flowers?" *The New York Times*, July 26, 1988. https://www.nytimes.com/1988/07/26/nyregion/mighty-mouse-flying-high-on-flowers.html.

Wright, Bradford W. *Comic Book Nation: The Transformation of Youth Culture in America*. Baltimore: Johns Hopkins University Press, 2001.

Wu, Quingyun. *Female Rule in Chinese and English Literary Utopias*. Syracuse, NY: Syracuse University Press, 1995.

Wyness, Michael. *Contesting Childhood*. London: Falmer Press, 2000.

Zahed, Ramin. "The Boys are Back in Town." *Animation* 18, no. 9 (2003): 26–27.

_____. "A Double Milestone for Antonucci and the Eds!" 2008. *Animation* 23, no. 1 (2008): 44.

Zipes, Jack. *Breaking the Magic Spell: Radical Theories of Folk and Fairy Tales.* Lexington: The University Press of Kentucky, 2002.
_____. *Fairy Tale as Myth/Myth as Fairy Tale.* Lexington: The University Press of Kentucky, 2013.
_____. *Fairy Tales and the Art of Subversion.* New York and London: Routledge, 2006.
_____. "On re-reading William Steig's book *Shrek!*" Accessed August 15, 2018. https://www.tor.com/2010/02/05/on-re-reading-william-steigs-book-shrek/.
_____, ed. *The Oxford Companion to Fairy Tales.* Oxford: Oxford University Press, 2015.

About the Contributors

Dan **Abitz** is the associate director of the South Atlantic Modern Language Association at Georgia State University. He has been fortunate enough to teach at institutions such as Georgia State, University of Central Arkansas, and Susquehanna University. His scholarly work can be found in *Nineteenth Century Gender Studies*, *The Comparatist*, *Victorians*, *Henry James Review*, *Women's Studies*, the *Palgrave Encyclopedia of Victorian Women Writers*, as well as the edited collection *Utopia and Dystopia in the Age of Trump*.

Chandrama **Basu** is pursuing her doctoral research from the English Department of Presidency University on the reception of Victorian yellowbacks. Her research interests center on Victorian culture, popular culture, and gender studies. She has published research articles in various journals. Her article on "The Shock of Modernity: Travelling the Railways and Reading the First Female Detective(s)" appeared in *The Rail, the Body and the Pen* (Cowlishaw, ed.).

Jane **Batkin** is an employability lead and senior lecturer in the School of Film and Media at the University of Lincoln, UK. She is the author of *Identity in Animation* and has published chapters in several books, including *Aardman Animation: Beyond Stop Motion* (2020) and *Snow White and the Seven Dwarfs: New Perspectives on Production, Reception, Legacy* (2021). She is working on a monograph on childhood in animated film and television.

Jared Bahir **Browsh** is a cultural historian and mass communication scholar whose research examines U.S. media industries, the history of mass communication, and representation in popular culture, focusing on animation, television, and sports. He is a faculty member in the communication program at Thomas Jefferson University.

Lev **Cantoral** is an artist and animator with a BA in studio art from the University of Iowa. He is lead marketing artist at Jackbox Games. His illustrations and animations have been commissioned for Polyvinyl Records, Disney's Hollywood Records, and CLASH Books. His animation has been featured on *The Tonight Show*, and his animated short *Sea Dogs* has screened at several film festivals, including the St. Louis International Film Festival.

Brian N. **Duchaney** holds an MA in editorial studies from Boston University and an MA in English from Bridgewater State University where he serves as director of Military & Veteran Student Services and teaches part-time in both the English and communications departments. His memoir—*The Man I Killed*—was nominated for inclusion in the *Best American Essays of 2014*. He has also held editorial positions with Routledge Academic Press and *The Journal of Popular Culture*.

Adrián **García** holds an MA in visual and critical studies from School of the Art Institute of Chicago. He is a Mexican filmmaker, stop-motion animator, musician and writer. His work ranges from the intersection of art and science to issues about memory and identity. He is an adjunct professor of the School of Humanities and Education at Tecnológico de Monterrey, León Campus.

Danielle **Hart** received her Ph.D. in English literature from Miami University in Oxford, Ohio, in 2021. Her dissertation focused on the intersections of disability studies, video games, and fan studies. In her position of assistant director at Miami's Center for Career Exploration and Success, she works with undergraduate and graduate Arts and Science students.

Sasha Dilan **Krugman** is a Ph.D. candidate at the University of Pennsylvania. With an honors degree in film studies from the University of British Columbia and an MA in film and media studies from Columbia University, she has focused on gendered depictions on-screen, nationalist interventions, and television studies in Turkish cultural productions. She has published an article on the representations of disabled bodies and freakshows in circus-themed television programming.

Marcus **Mallard** is a professor of English, film, and digital media and currently serves as the Program Coordinator of Film Studies and Digital Media at Rose State College. His research focuses on horror films through a historical and sociocultural lens, genre studies, and true crime. He was coeditor for the book *The Walking Dead Live! Essays on the Television Show*.

David **Perlmutter** is a freelance writer based in Winnipeg, Manitoba, Canada. He is the author of two books on animation history: *America Toons In: A History of Television Animation* (McFarland) and *The Encyclopedia of American Animated Television Shows*, as well as essays and works of speculative fiction. He writes online for *Medium* and occasionally appears on social media.

David S. **Silverman** is the academic success coordinator for Kansas State University-Salina. He holds a Ph.D. in communication from the University of Missouri. He is a media historian and has taught communication studies for more than 20 years. His book *"You Can't Air That": Four Cases of Censorship and Controversy in American Television Programming* was an Editor's Pick in *Choice* magazine.

Tyler Solon **Williams** holds a Ph.D. in communication studies from the University of Iowa, and is a faculty lecturer in the Department of Media Studies at the University of Virginia. He is a coeditor (with Kevin Sandler) of *Hanna and Barbera: Conversations* and has presented papers at the annual conferences of the Society for Animation Studies, the International Communication Association, and the Society for Cinema and Media Studies.

Index